SEA KAYAKING

Sea Kayaking

A Manual
for
Long-Distance
Touring

by John Dowd

DOUGLAS & McINTYRE
VANCOUVER
UNIVERSITY OF WASHINGTON PRESS
SEATTLE

Copyright 1981, 1983, 1986, 1988 by John Dowd

93 94 95 96 97 98   10 9 8 7 6 5
Revised edition
Third paperback edition, 1988

Douglas & McIntyre Ltd.
1615 Venables Street
Vancouver, British Columbia

Canadian Cataloguing in Publication Data

Dowd, John, 1945-
Sea Kayaking: a manual for long-distance touring

Bibliography: p.
Includes index.
ISBN 0-88894-598-1

1. Sea Kayaking.   I. Title.
GV788.5.D69 1988   797.1″22   C88-091083-6

Published simultaneously in the United States of America by the University of Washington Press, Seattle

Library of Congress Cataloging-in-Publication Data

John Dowd
Sea kayaking: a manual for long-distance touring

Rev. Ed.
Bibliography: p.
Includes index.

1. Sea kayaking.   2. Sea kayaking--
Safety measures.   I. Title
GV788.5.D68   1988   88-2744
ISBN 0-295-96630-0
(University of Washington Press)

Published simultaneously in Great Britain by
Cordee, Leicester, LE1 7HD
ISBN 0-904405-19-2

Cover photograph by Joel Rogers
Kayakers on the south coast of Crete

Composition: The Typeworks
Printed & bound in Canada by D.W. Friesen & Sons Ltd.

Contents

To Paul Souter
who provided the plans for my first kayak

Acknowledgements

My thanks go to the more than thirty paddlers who contributed to the first edition of this book by answering a lengthy questionnaire about their kayaking habits, and to the many individuals from whose experiences and comments I have benefited from more directly over the past several years: Jim Allan, Greg Blanchette, Matt and Cam Broze, David Burch, Alan Byde, Paul Caffyn, Don Cohen, John Dawson, John Deakins, Tom Derrer, Peter Donnelly, George Dyson, Geoff Evans, Ben Fast, Werner Furrer, Ed Gillet, Bill Guthrie, John Heath, Brian Henry, Creig Hoyt, Evelyn Jones, Alex Lane, Ken Leghorn, Dan Lewis, Hannes Lindemann, Lee Moyer, Duncan Murray, Mike Neckar, Cec and Christine Robinson, Joel Rogers, Mark Rongstad, Doug Simpson, Mercia Sixta, Roy Spicer, Dieter Stiller, Audrey Sutherland, Grant Thompson, Randel Washburne, Glen Williams, David Zimmerly and many others. I am also thankful to the many kayakers whose photographs grace this book, and to readers of earlier editions who have come forward to discuss their thoughts and offer feedback.

Additional thanks go to Robert Bringhurst, Marilyn Sacks and my wife Beatrice, whose combined editorial skills have contributed greatly to the readability of this book, in particular to Beatrice, for helping keep the unwieldy process on course while all else was going awry.

Finally, I would like to thank the crew of a Tampa-based tug named *Gulf Star*, for help received one dark and stormy night in 1978—and also my aged mother, who boldly purchased one hundred copies of the first edition and still has more than twenty of the darn things in her closet.

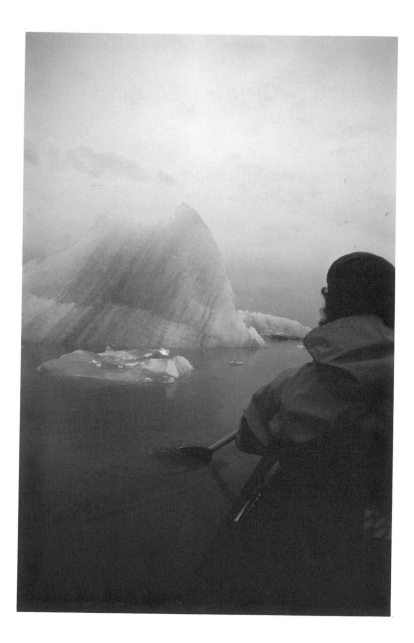

Introduction

Much has happened to sea kayaking since the first edition of this book. What in 1981 was an "off the wall" activity for a few eccentric individuals is now a popular and relatively commonplace recreation for mainstream outdoors enthusiasts. During those intervening years we have seen some extraordinarily impressive kayak achievements, including the California to Hawaii crossing by Ed Gillet and the circumnavigation of Australia by Paul Caffyn. Heroes of the past such as Hannes Lindemann, Franz Romer and Karl Schott have made room for a new generation.

During this period, having turned my passion of twenty years to my livelihood, I have learned a great deal about boats, equipment and safety developments, and have been in constant contact with those pushing the limits of the sport. It has been personally gratifying to watch sea kayaking become established as a recreational activity in its own right, distinct from both whitewater kayaking and canoeing.

My switch from kayak paddler to kayak entrepreneur came in 1980 when my wife Beatrice and I opened what was to become North America's first specialty ocean kayak shop in Vancouver, B.C. and, in 1984, began publication of the sport's first specialty magazine, *Sea Kayaker*. Today there are hundreds of shops all over the continent selling sea kayaks, and articles on sea kayaking continue to appear in dozens of mainstream outdoor magazines. North America has become the most vital and expansive centre of sea kayaking in the world today and its sea kayaking fraternity has created its own distinctive style.

For paddlers this has been a time of much learning and re-learning, and the pool of knowledge and communicable experience is growing almost exponentially. Early editions of *Sea Kayaking* have to date sold over 25,000 copies, but this is hardly an adequate measure of existing interest in kayak touring. Whereas the only books available on the subject at the time of the first edition were Adney & Chapelle's *Bark Canoes and Skin Boats of North America* and two British manuals by Derek Hutchinson and John Ramwell, today there are guides telling you where to paddle and others telling how to camp, forage and cook when you get there, as well as what must be the definitive work on navigation by kayak, David Burch's *Fundamentals of Kayak Navigation*. Also, there are many published kayak travel narratives for stuffing the Christmas stockings of friends smitten by the sea kayak's potential as a tool for adventure.

Much has been printed on the history of kayaking thanks to the research of John Heath, David Zimmerly, George Dyson and Eugene Arima in North America, H. C. Petersen in Greenland and John Brand in England. It is clear from their research that the best traditional native kayaks were extremely sophisticated, well-designed craft from which our modern-day builders have learned a great deal and stand to learn much more. To attempt to cover kayak history is beyond the scope of this book and could only do the subject a disservice. Obviously, we are heirs to a long and complex tradition, one with few surviving masters—just students.

There is now, as there was long ago, a kayak for almost every purpose—from the slender West Greenland-style boat, originally designed for hunting among ice floes, to the 21-foot touring double or triple. Each has its own merits and limitations, and each has its band of single-minded adherents.

My personal preference in a touring single is for a roomy, stable craft around 24 inches in the beam. Although I would pick this for solo coastal cruising, it would not be my choice for day paddling off Hawaii, and I would want yet another craft for cruising with my children. Perhaps more than anything else, it is the very diversity of boat designs available today that makes sea kayaking so overwhelming for the first-time paddler looking to choose the right boat.

I have based this book mostly on my own experience, but occasionally it has been necessary for me to write beyond what I know first hand to present a more balanced picture of sea kayaking when covering such topics as sailing, obscure methods of rolling, kayak surfing and kayaking in sea ice. I have gratefully called upon the expertise of others, among them John Heath, whose knowledge of traditional kayaking techniques was first highlighted in Adney & Chapelle's aforementioned classic.

Because the knowledge required for sea kayaking is so encompassing, I have also frequently chosen to omit the general in favour of the specific. For example, my chapter on first aid ignores such essentials as rescue breathing and the treatment of bleeding, since these are well covered in general publications on the subject. My chapter focusses instead on kayak-related ailments. I trust the reader to already know the basics —for know them he or she must when embarking on a sea journey of some length.

Navigation, camping and general survival are other areas in which I have assumed that the reader is not a novice. The information presented here is geared to kayaking situations and seen from the viewpoint of a kayaker, particularly those problems most likely to be encountered on long kayak journeys.

I have attempted to make this edition of the book suitable for paddlers of all levels. This occasionally creates a need to provide situations with lessons which are valuable to both the beginner and the experienced paddler. In most instances I have elected to present extreme examples in preference to more basic ones on the assumption that all the beginners' lessons are contained within an advanced situation but not vice versa. This is not to imply that paddling storms or wild lee shores or undertaking twenty-mile crossings is the norm: It is not. Indeed, I counsel strongly in favour of a measured approach to new kayaking experience. It is hoped that this book will provide a vision of what is possible to those who bring an adventurous spirit to their kayaking.

Above: Laguna San Rafael, Chile. Below: Maracas beach, Trinidad

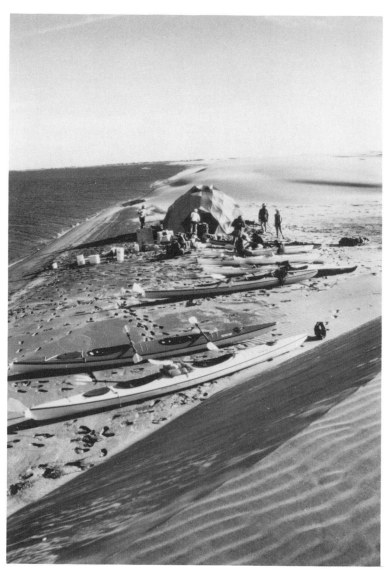

Coastal Baja

I

Equipment

THE BOAT

Sea kayaks are distinguished from river kayaks by a multitude of features for which we have one word: seaworthiness. A sea boat may or may not roll easily, but it must slice through or ride over waves of all sizes, track dependably regardless of the direction of the sea, respond to the paddle in windy conditions, carry your gear, and stand up to continuous punishment from wave action, weather, sand, rocky beaches, sea ice and sometimes very large, very inquisitive fish.

That said, there are still boats of many sorts to choose from, and every dedicated kayaker is his or her own best authority on "the best kayak." What you have to do is choose the right one for your use. There are countless manufacturers, most of them very small operations, and design is by no means stagnant. Nevertheless, the choice at present comes down to two readily available though arbitrarily designated types of boat:

1 Narrow or special-purpose kayaks—usually single seaters designed for speed or liveliness;
2 General touring kayaks—singles or doubles designed for efficient load carrying and greater stability.

Most sea kayaks have a sharp prow and an angular or even

knifelike forefoot. Amidships, the hull is often rounded and flattened in cross section. Farther aft, the cross section resumes its rounded V shape, and the stern itself may be as sharp as the prow. As a rule, sea kayaks have little rocker (the curvature upward of the keel-line towards stem and stern as the boat is viewed in profile) and where it exists, this enhances the manoeuvrability of the craft. A deep, sharp stem and stern allow the boat to track through the waves without yawing under the alternating thrust of the paddle. The rounded section amidships allows the boat to lean easily into breakers, and the partial flattening under the cockpit increases stability. A high prow is found in some designs, including many of the surviving or recorded Eskimo and Aleut boats, a useful feature in ice but of questionable value in open water. In some hulls you will also see chines. These are ridges, angular in cross section, running lengthwise along the hull between gunwale and keel. In fabric or skin-covered boats they are caused by the tension of the skin across a framing rib; a similar feature is sometimes moulded into fibreglass boats such as models where the chine aids turning when the boat is leaned to one side.

Slalom kayaks, designed for quick turns in rivers rather than tracking at sea, have much more rocker than a sea boat, and their hulls are generally flatter in cross section amidships and considerably rounder at bow and stern. A high-volume river boat is often used for surf kayaking and when fitted with a skeg or rudder will sometimes serve for a short sea voyage, but the compromise is not finally a happy one. Away from white water, it is better to have a kayak true to the ancestry of the craft: a boat designed specifically for the sea.

Narrow or Special-Purpose Kayaks

Narrow touring kayaks are usually single seaters between 17 and 19 feet long with an 18- to 23-inch beam. Commonly they may have a rounded hull, hard chine or moderate V hull with very little rocker. Essentially they are coastal craft, and a paddler using them in wind or open water must be comfortable with the technique of rolling. These boats depend upon the skill of the paddler for their seaworthiness. They are, in essence, tippy. (Tippiness, however, is a very relative term and depends upon the paddler's familiarity with that type of kayak as well as personal weight distribution: a broad-shouldered male will have many more problems with balance than a lightweight woman with solid legs and hips, as most of the woman's weight will be close to the centre of gravity.)

The West Greenland and Aleut originals were made from sealskin with a fragile wood and bone frame, but today the best boats in this style are fibreglass or Kevlar. Two popular West Greenland-style models are the Arluk II by Necky Kayaks and the Nordkapp, the latter having been introduced more than ten years ago by Valley Canoe Products in England. Although these 20- to 22-inch beam kayaks have been used on some impressive coastal trips, most notably the circumnavigations of New Zealand, Britain, Australia and Japan by Paul Caffyn and the circumnavigation of the Hawaiian islands by Greg Blanchette, they are arguably best suited for day tripping and lightweight excursions because of their small size and rather wet ride.

Longer, larger and essentially more practical for wilderness touring are the Mariner and Seal, two U.S. designs brought on the market by Matt and Cam Broze of Mariner Kayaks and Lee Moyer of Pacific Water Sports respectively.

The great advantages of narrow touring kayaks are the ease with which they can be rolled and their speedier hulls. (They generally have a top speed of around 6½ knots.) The most obvious disadvantage is their limited stowage space which renders them less suitable for journeys on which food and equipment must be carried in quantity.

The Seal, a narrow, speedy tourer by Lee Moyer

Their most serious drawback, however, is that they are neither stable enough nor roomy enough for real relaxation or even to serve as a platform for photography. They are deadly if their occupant becomes exhausted or incapacitated at sea in severe conditions, unless rafting up is an option.

At the fringe of what can be considered a sea kayak—and not part of the focus of this book—is a variety of specialty boats used exclusively for ocean racing, surfing or both. Most distinctive among these is the surf ski, a long (21 feet), narrow (19 inches) kayak designed for sitting on rather than in. A foot-controlled rudder assists in following seas and cross winds while a quick release belt keeps the paddler in place during turbulence. Not surprisingly, surf skis mostly inhabit the warm waters of Australia, South Africa and Hawaii. The most famous race for this class of kayak is the annual escorted downwind dash across Hawaii's Molokai channel with an average speed that sometimes exceeds 8 knots. In the Pacific Northwest and the Great Lakes, a new breed of sit-in ocean-racing kayak has evolved to give an edge to competitors. This craft is best described as a cross between a down river racing boat and a sea kayak. Examples include the Nimbus Sprint, the Necky Phantom and West Side Boat Shop's Wave Piercer.

Another wrinkle to kayak design for the sport of surfing has been the evolution of the wave ski. To call this planing hulled, sit-on board a kayak is stretching the word's definition, but some manufacturers show bikini-clad ladies paddling them with a beer cooler secured to the stern! In their element on the face of a 12-foot Hawaiian breaker, however, these stubby little craft are clearly the end product of a very specialized line of evolution, and they make surfing in a touring kayak resemble trying to ride a log to shore.

General Touring Kayaks

General touring single seaters are much more prevalent than their narrow counterparts. They are generally shorter—between 14 and 17 feet—and feature a beam of about 23 to 27 inches, yet some, such as the time-honoured Folbot Sporty, have a grand 32-inch beam and are so stable you can stand up in them. The greater stability of general touring boats enables you to rest and relax in them, though in extreme cases it tends to discourage the learning of dependable, more advanced paddling skills. These boats generally have a greater load-carrying capacity than the narrow singles and give a much drier ride. But because they are designed to be paddled loaded, their higher profile can make them vulnerable to wind when empty.

The beamier singles are usually not as fast, maybe a half knot slower than their skinnier brethren, and are more difficult to roll, but they are far less likely to require rolling. Boats in this category include, among many others, the Arluk IV

Cam Broze

Bruce Morris

Above: The Brozes' Mariner is swift and narrow but still built to carry a load; Below: An equivalent load carrier in the doubles is the Tofino by Necky.

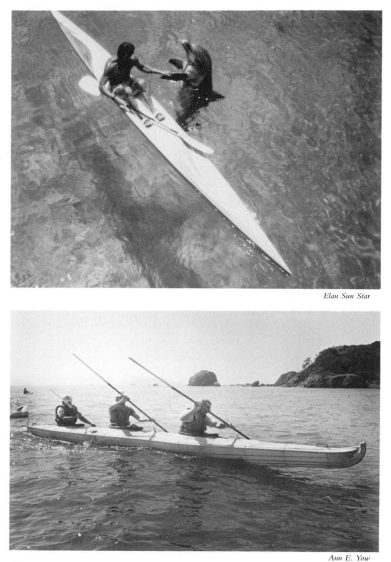

Elan Sun Star

Ann E. Yow

Above: Narrow sit-on kayaks or surf skis evolved for tropical use. Below: Dyson's baidarka replicas cruise the Pacific coast.

by Necky Kayaks, Mariner Kayak's Mariner XL, the Pisces by Current Designs, the Sea Otter 500 by Pacific Water Sports, the Eddyline Wind Dancer, the Easy Rider Eskimo, the Esprit by Northwest Kayaks, the Dirigo 17 by Dirigo Boatworks, the Nimbus Seafarer, the Selkie by Valley Canoe Products, and three rotomoulded polyethylene models: the Nimbus Puffin, Hydra Sea Runner and Aquaterra Chinook.

Having clearly defined two types of singles, narrow and general touring, I will now muddle the distinction by pointing out that there are a number of crossover models of boats which could almost be placed in either category. Some of these, a growing number, include the Solander by Nimbus, Arluk III by Necky Kayaks and Calypso by Eddyline, and the Solstice and Equinox by Current Designs.

The immediate ancestor of the hardshell cruising kayak, single or double, is the collapsible kayak or Foldboat—a design pioneered by the German tailor Hans Klepper around the turn of the century and itself based on originals from the Canadian Arctic. The German models were originally manufactured for lakes and rivers. They have long since lost their pre-eminence in the field to hardshell kayaks of fibreglass and polyethylene, but the suitability of some of these collapsibles for use on the open sea, together with their convenience for travellers, has ensured their continued popularity in Europe and North America.

Today, single and double folding kayaks, featuring wooden or aluminum frames and removable fabric skins, are manufactured by Folbot in the United States, Pouch in East Germany, Nautiraid in France, Klepper in West Germany and Feathercraft in Canada. Sizes range from a 15- to 16-foot length and 26- to 32-inch beam for single seaters to a 16- to 19-foot length and 31- to 37-inch beam for doubles. Such kayaks typically fold down into one to three carrying bags. The only folding kayak that fits the narrow category is the

16½-foot, 19-inch beam Greenlander by Nautiraid. Unlike the natives of Northern Canada and Greenland, who used single-seat kayaks for inshore hunting, the Aleuts of Alaska designed two-seat models for longer, more exposed voyages. These boats, or baidarkas, were given a third cockpit at the instigation of Russian fur traders and used for hunting and trading voyages east of the Aleutians and as far south as Baja California. Today the closest approximations to the larger Aleut craft are the baidarkas built privately by George Dyson of Vancouver, B.C., author of the book *Baidarka* and founder of the Baidarka Historical Society. Using modern materials—chiefly nylon cloth and aluminum tubing—Dyson has built several kayaks with many of the original baidarka features. His triple seater is 28 feet long with a 30-inch beam. It is very stable and can carry a sail. Dyson's experimental fan sail design is most original; ashore the sail can double as a tent. Like its predecessors, this baidarka can carry some 600 pounds of equipment. Apart from the materials used, its greatest departure from traditional design is a sturdy foot-controlled rudder.

With the exception of Pacific Water Sports' three-place Sisiutl and Eddyline's San Juan, the North American hardshell market is at present limited to doubles around 20 feet in length and featuring a beam of 28 to 36 inches. (For two seaters, beams of less than 28 inches are usually reserved for racing boats such as the Elite by Northwest Kayaks.) Among better-known hardshell doubles are the Necky Tofino, Northwest Kayaks' Seascape, the Nimbus Seafarer K-2, Easy Rider's Beluga, the original Sisiutl by Pacific Water Sports and, more recently, their Skookum Chuck. A variety of other models are available in kit form, and some feature a large open cockpit, as is also the case for most folding two-seaters, which come equipped with a large fabric spray deck containing individual cockpits.

CHOOSING A KAYAK

Choosing the right kayak is like buying any other large-ticket item: the world suddenly becomes full of instant experts eager to give you advice and warn you of the pitfalls of this or that feature. Buying on the second-hand market is, of course, usually cheaper but fraught with dangers unless you know precisely what you are looking for. Seeking the advice of friends will usually result in your buying the same boat as they have because they have grown to love theirs and can sing its praises loud and clear; they also have an investment in reassuring themselves—and you—that they made the right choice in the first place.

Buying direct from the builder is probably the worst place to seek an objective opinion, though when your choice has been made, a discount can sometimes be arranged with the smaller builders who do not have a dealer network to support. This lack of objectivity is not to imply that builders are dishonest. They are simply passionately enamoured of their creations and may feel that their design is *the* design for today's kayaker; their conviction can make them a little hard of hearing when you have special needs to be addressed.

By doing the round of designers, you will quickly realize that the so-called experts can disagree spectacularly on such fundamental features as the shape of the bow. I once heard a designer (redesigner might be a more appropriate term since almost all design today is simply a modification of existing design) being asked why he had put a long upswept bow on his kayak. He explained that it was to stop the boat from pearling (nosediving in following seas). The customer thought about that for a while then asked why the other boat he built had a low bow. That too was to stop pearling, he explained a little sheepishly. Certainly there are few clearly right or wrong features—mostly trade-offs and preferences.

Probably the best way to choose a kayak is to visit a sea kayak symposium, one of the major sea kayaking clubs, or a specialty store offering a wide range of models. At the store, seek the general guidance of a sales clerk but don't listen to anything the person tells you about how a boat handles—just take it out and try it. The problem with this system, however, is that a beginner will probably prefer a very stable kayak for a start; later as he or she has become more skilled, the stable boat could feel too dull. So, try a kayaking course, or rent some kayaks with an eye to purchasing. You may still end up choosing the stable boat in the end, but it won't be because you are afraid of the others.

Before you can expect to make sense of the hundred or more models of kayaks currently available on the North American market, indulge in a little fantasy. Cast your mind back to the genesis of your interest in sea kayaking, that dream of how you *see* yourself in a kayak. Maybe it is a weekend tryst to the first secluded cove you and your partner come across; or maybe it is a King Farouk-sized challenge to nature with just you and your little boat dueling the ocean creamers; or maybe you wish to use the kayak for wildlife photography or an evening workout. Got the image? Well, hold on to it because now you have to use that image to find the right boat.

Unfortunately there are at least two other factors that will complicate your choice: your budget constraints and your partner's(s') needs.

As I stated in the introduction to this book, the options available in the late 1980s have expanded impressively from those of the late seventies. We still have singles, doubles, folding boats and rigid ones. Materials include fibreglass, Kevlar, plastic, canvas/lath and nylon/aluminum tubing, plywood and cedar strip. There are both cheap and expensive kayaks, but it is the variety and quality of the new boats that set them apart from those of ten years ago.

Singles

Nowadays, the most popular sea kayaks are rigid singles— the freedom boats for those who seek independence or who are obliged through circumstance to paddle solo. It is also the group with the most diversity of design; so the chance of finding the perfect boat for you is greatest in this category. Couples, however, should keep in mind that two singles will likely cost considerably more than a two-seater.

Doubles

A double is particularly appropriate if you and your partner are of significantly different strengths or if the trip you plan is extremely arduous or to a remote area. After all, you cannot easily become separated from a companion in the same kayak, and two paddlers in a double are certainly a stronger unit than the same two paddlers in singles. However, few doubles can be successfully paddled by one person under difficult conditions, with the exception of down-wind ocean crossings where doubles were chosen by Lindemann and Gillet.

High Volume or Low Volume?

A high volume single kayak is one with a volume of around 18 cubic feet (Easy Rider Eskimo) while a low volume one runs from 10 to 12 cubic feet (Nimbus Solander); there can be appreciable volume differences between two-seaters as well, but not to the same extent. Choosing the right-sized kayak is not quite as straightforward as choosing a pair of shoes since most people select a kayak for the load it carries as well as its personal fit. Others have a clear and unshakable preconceived idea of what a kayak should feel like and they know exactly when they feel it. But choosing a kayak like a shoe is a pretty good place to start since generally if you are a small person (under 150 lbs), you will prefer a

26

small boat, and if you are a larger person (say over 180 lbs), you are going to feel more comfortable in a larger boat. If you had no special load-carrying considerations, you would buy roughly according to such sizing.

For people who are 5 foot 2 inches and sport a pair of size 14 feet, the rule of thumb breaks down. You need a bigger boat to accommodate your tootsies. Even if you have no unusual physical attributes, you may choose a higher volume boat so that you can carry plenty of fresh food along on your trip, or a few bottles of Chablis, or a box of camera equipment. People who fish for salmon from their kayak should consider what they would do if they hooked into a 30-pounder. (They will be glad of the extra stability that usually comes with a higher volume kayak and may judge the trade-off a good one.) Those who feel stiff jointed and awkward getting into a kayak may also be glad of a little extra clearance in the cockpit and deck area.

Conversely, there are 190-pounders who get a great kick out of paddling fast in a sporty kayak, eating freeze-dried food and having waves wash over them every few seconds. They have absolutely no interest in taking pictures from a kayak unless they show crooked horizons intersecting the uplifting profile of their kayak mid-frame. For these people, too, the rules of high- and low-volume choices are accommodatingly elastic. If, however, you find that you are obliged to pile gear on deck because your boat's interior will not accommodate your needs or if you find that you are viewing the waves from the wrong side more often than you should, try a higher volume boat.

Rigid or Folding?

Put simply, you should choose a rigid kayak unless you need the folding quality. The exception to this is where you have a personal preference for the aesthetics of a boat with the traditional internal frame—a boat that performs as silently as the original hunting craft and flexes in the waves like a living thing.

The advantages offered by rigid kayaks are numerous; for a start, there are more of them so the chances of finding the right boat for your needs is going to be greater. They require less maintenance, less care around rocks and less concern for the effects of the elements. They are also usually much cheaper. The reasons for buying a folding kayak, on the other hand, are often as compelling: you may need to break the boat down for travel or to store it in an apartment. Such craft promise you the world of kayak touring in a backpack— Japan, New Zealand, the Aegean, the Caribbean . . .

The price for this versatility is not just measured in dollars; you must nurse your folding kayak over coral or barnacle-encrusted intertidal zones and wipe the sand off your feet and bags before placing them inside since grit beneath the stringers will chafe the hull, rub away at the varnish or jam up the joints of an aluminum frame. They are simply fussier to own and maintain, something to think about as you reach for your cheque book. Assembly time for most folding kayaks is a fairly modest fifteen to thirty minutes.

Those who require more compactness than they would get from a collapsible kayak might consider the purchase of an inflatable kayak. (Audrey Sutherland of Hawaii has forced sea kayakers to take these stubby little craft seriously by paddling more than 5000 miles of Alaska coast in one over several summers.) Apart from being lightweight, inflatable kayaks are the least expensive of folding craft.

For those with a strong preference for rigid kayaks yet a need to reduce their overall length for storage purposes, Nimbus and Easy Rider produce take-apart rigid boats.

Materials

Fibreglass kayaks are usually a combination of cloth, roving and, in some of the more cheaply constructed models, chopped matt. Matt provides stiffness and, when it is thick enough, strength, but results in a heavy and somewhat brittle hull. Most builders now use foam core or an internal keel of either foam or spruce to gain the hull rigidity required for strongly secured bulkheads and optimum kayak performance. The really high tech boats are built with an initial layer of fibreglass cloth to improve abrasion resistance, then layers of Kevlar well stiffened with carbon fibre. Such boats are lighter, stronger and more expensive than their equivalent fibreglass models. Standard weight for a fibreglass kayak is around 55 pounds for a single and 90 pounds for a double.

The resin preferred by the best fibreglass kayak builders today is vinyl ester which is more flexible than the cheaper polyester resins and not as toxic as the tough epoxy resins. Most fibreglass kayaks are protected with a hard abrasion-resistant layer of gelcoat. This is the first layer to be sprayed into the mould and carries the pigment which helps protect the resin and fibres from the damaging ultra-violet rays of the sun. Most kayaks come with a white hull since this shows the scratches less than one of the darker colours. White does not, however, stand out well when the kayak is upside down amid breaking waves. The choice of colour for the deck is basically going to depend upon whether you want to stand out or blend in with your environment. The best colour for visibility is yellow, and the most visible boat is one that is yellow top and bottom.

The rotomoulded polyethylene kayaks are stronger and more economical than fibreglass models. Two principal types of material are used: linear polyethylene and cross-linked polyethylene. Linear is stiffer and cheaper than cross-linked and, in the unlikely event that you split it, it can be repaired with a plastic weld. Cross-linked is softer and tougher and has a slightly waxy feel to it. The best whitewater kayaks are built of cross-linked polyethylene to withstand the impact of river rocks. Repairs, if needed, must be made with a patch riveted over the damaged area.

The disadvantages of polyethylene kayaks are that they are heavier (by about 10 pounds) than most fibreglass models, and they scratch more severely than gel-coated fibreglass. The linear ones also seem particularly vulnerable to denting on roof racks in the hot sun, but dimples can easily be popped out with a stick wedged inside the boat. The life span of polyethylene kayaks, UV inhibitors notwithstanding, is also less than fibreglass, though this is going to vary greatly with the care taken when storing the boat.

Rotomoulded kayaks are made in an expensive nickel, steel or aluminum mould that is heated, usually in a gas oven, then opened to receive a measured amount of plastic granules. This is where science ends and art begins; the mould is then rotated slowly and rocked end for end in such a manner that the melted plastic runs to an even thickness over the inside of the mould as it cools. As the newly formed boat cools, it contracts and must be handled carefully until it has set in its final form.

Wood kayaks are a relatively small part of the sea kayak market. Most are of the home-built variety, either constructed from a kit using sheets of marine grade plywood stitched then glued together or made from thin cedar strips laid over a form and sheathed in fibreglass and epoxy. These kayaks are frequently craft of great beauty and often are surprisingly durable, given the right amount of maintenance. They are fun and inexpensive to build, and indeed this is the most common reason for choosing this type of boat over its less easily damaged fibreglass and polyethylene relatives.

Also popular among home builders are lath and canvas models which can be built from plans and locally available materials. Such boats have an internal frame of wood with 12- or 14-ounce canvas stretched over it which is then painted or varnished. The life of the canvas is around five years, at which time the boat can be stripped to its skeleton, the wood re-varnished and a new skin fitted. These kayaks are lightweight, inexpensive and easy to build, though not exactly bombproof. A tougher hull can be created with the use of hypalon or rubberized cloth.

As we have seen, standard folding kayaks consist of a frame and removable skin. Frames are commonly made of wood or aluminum, or, in the case of Folbot, a combination of both. Ash is the most common wood for longitudinal frame pieces being both durable and flexible. Cross frames of birch plywood are used in Kleppers and Nautiraids. The high tech newcomer to the field, Feathercraft, features a frame of high-grade aluminum with a baked epoxy coating and cross ribs of high density polyethylene.

Wood has the advantage of being relatively easy to repair, though of course there is nothing to prevent you from using wood for temporary repairs to an aluminum frame in the field. The disadvantage of wood is that it can absorb water and swell. Aluminum, on the other hand, suffers from a vulnerability to corrosion and electrolysis—particularly in warmer climates. All folding boats should be disassembled on a regular basis to prevent their metamorphosing into rigid ones. Small metal assembly parts are present on most frames.

Today's most popular hull material is hypalon, with a direct trade-off between hull weight and durability. Feathercraft make an extra lightweight model that uses nylon-covered butyl rubber (their standard model uses hypalon) while Folbot and Pouch opt for a less expensive vinyl composite. Deck fabrics vary widely. Cotton is still used by Klepper and Pouch, and though it is somewhat vulnerable to damage by ultraviolet radiation, it breathes, allowing air and moisture to pass through. This has the effect of keeping the boat pleasantly cool in the tropics since evaporation occurs off the inside, providing a natural air–conditioning system.

Nautiraid and Feathercraft rely instead on pack–cloth or Cordura because they are lighter than cotton, particularly when wet, and both are also waterproof, rot resistant and shrinkproof.

Hull Design

Hull shapes and their significance I confess are aspects of boat building that mostly elude my understanding. Why is it that one successful model is fish form (its widest beam forward of the cockpit) while another is Swede form (its widest beam aft of the cockpit) and yet another symmetrical? What are the key features? My basic ignorance is not for want of trying to understand. I listen, along with the other kayak users, to the explanations of designers and I marvel at their plausible reasons for why the hull was rounded just so, why this or that amount of flare was put in the bow to give added lift at speed and, of course, how each designer went about ensuring that his boat would not pearl as it surfed off the wave. I often find such talk disconcerting because I know that in many cases the designer simply took someone else's design (or borrowed design), padded it out with bondo paste, added a foot of length amidships, changed the shape of the stern, adjusted the pitch of the deck then tried it out to see if it had improved any, and *then* attempted to rationalize the results.

To try and learn something objective about hull design and answer some of the more basic questions, *Sea Kayaker Magazine* sponsored a series of tests on eleven popular models of touring singles within a given length and beam range.

Engineer and kayaker John Dawson supervised the program using the magazine's own facilities and the $2000-a-day test tank at the B.C. Research Institute in Vancouver, British Columbia. Various tests did demonstrate that some boats behaved differently from others, and some startling facts were learned during the course of the study, such as that raising the height of the seat by one inch could halve some kayaks' stability. However, it was also found that some boats that looked radically different behaved almost identically. Almost nothing could be confirmed about basic hull design except for the most obvious stuff such as that long, narrow boats go faster than short, fat ones; and even these differences were nowhere near as great as had been expected.

Computers have not yet provided us with the answer, either. Too often when designers have relied upon the computer for their inspiration, a dog was born—garbage in, garbage out and all that. We just don't know enough to start with. The focus of all our design intelligence to date has understandably been to try and make some sense of what exists, and we seem to be so far from understanding why one hull works while another does not that I doubt I will see the day when we can accurately project our knowledge to design radical new shapes (or perhaps radically ancient shapes) for boats. Today, kayak design still lies mostly in the realm of art and living tradition, and perhaps it is better that way; at least it allows for some imaginative explanations. I also draw some comfort from the embarrassment that must have been felt by the designer of *Magic,* a 1983 challenger to the America's Cup which test-tank researcher Francis Clauser discovered travelled through the water more efficiently backwards than it did forwards, rudder in place and all. So much for science and boat design.

Having made my reservations abundantly clear, let me repeat some of the popular wisdom that has gained credibility: long kayaks (up to around 20 feet) are faster than short ones; wide ones are more stable than narrow ones; round-bottomed boats can be leaned more smoothly than sharply chined or flat-bottomed ones. (Despite optimistic rumours to the contrary, narrow boats have not proven themselves to be more seaworthy than wide ones.) Fish-form hulls are more efficient than Swede-form ones. A deep forefoot makes the boat hard to handle in wind, as does a high bow. A faintly V-shaped hull provides stiffness and aids with tracking when the V is carried aft of the cockpit. Rocker helps with turning; the more rocker, the easier the boat turns but the harder it is to hold on a straight course. A fine entry cuts the waves cleanly but requires above-the-waterline buoyancy to prevent plunging. The stern should have both volume for buoyancy and a fine exit to minimize friction from turbulence.

RUDDERS & SKEGS

A rudder, operated by cables running forward to controls at the paddler's feet, is a useful effort-saver on any sea kayak. It is a necessity on the larger doubles if they are to hold course in cross winds. A good rudder allows you to devote your paddle strokes to straightforward propulsion with an occasional support stroke. For years I paddled a single with no rudder, and I can remember times when, in order to stay on course in a cross wind, I paddled fourteen strokes to port for every one to starboard. A rudder alleviates this problem. In singles, however, a rudder should not be considered a turning device to replace the ability to manoeuvre with the paddle or to control major broaching problems. It is an effort saver for maintaining a course in cross winds, and though some additional drag results, the compromise is a good one.

Kayakers who are proud of their repertoire of paddle

An Australian rudder designed to swing through 270° and lay along the deck.

strokes are sometimes put off by rudders, as if it were demeaning to guide the kayak with the feet. But on a long voyage, or even a short one during adverse conditions, this device can save much wear and tear on belly and shoulder muscles. A well-designed rudder, usually of high-grade aluminum or stainless steel, can always be cocked out of the water where it will be less likely to sustain damage and will not impede the ability of the kayak to be turned sharply while being leaned onto its gunwale. The best combination is to have a sea kayak which paddles well without a rudder but has one anyway.

In doubles, rudder controls can be in either the forward (No. 1) or aft (No. 2) cockpit. The paddler in the No. 1 cockpit has an unobstructed view of the bow and what lies immediately ahead, while the person in the No. 2 position has a more commanding view of the whole boat and a greater sense of control. It is useful to fit auxiliary stirrups to the rudder cables so that they can be operated from either cockpit.

A rudder takes quite a hammering on a long trip and must be strongly built. It should be cocked for negotiating surf or for lying to a drogue, and should kick up automatically on striking a submerged rock. The rudder assembly frequently becomes fouled when towing, though this can be avoided by running the tow line through a short, flexible whip above the rudder or providing a protective on-deck cage to deflect the tow line.

I have to eat most of the disparaging comments I made about skegs in the previous editions of this book. I have, since writing it, paddled kayaks with designs of skegs that worked well, and though I have yet to prefer them over a good rudder, I am impressed. The skeg amounts to a fixed rudder, occasionally adjustable and usually designed to be lifted out of the water. It shifts the pivot point aft in smoothly round-hulled craft such as whitewater boats, and it enhances the tracking ability of more manoeuvrable yet "V"ed touring kayak hulls. The ideal placement for the skeg appears to be just aft of the seat, located in a boxed slot recessed into the keel line of the boat. The blade is raised and lowered with a cord leading back to the cockpit; thus the amount of draught can be adjusted according to conditions. A skeg so placed is almost never lifted clear of the water by passing waves, and this enhances its effectiveness in rough seas. Also, by moving the new pivot point closer to the natural (central) pivot point, the boat becomes much more manageable in wind than it would be if the skeg were placed at the stern.

BUILT-IN BUOYANCY

Without special buoyancy systems, most boats will sink as soon as they fill with water. And even if they don't sink, they will float so low as to be unmanageable. The best buoyancy is usually the most buoyancy, and every opportunity should be made to maximize and back up buoyancy systems. The most effective one is a boat full of foam or air in sealed compartments. More practical because they leave room for gear and legs are a number of other provisions for built-in buoyancy including the air sponsons of some folding kayaks, the blocks of foam some people permanently jam into bow and stern, and the watertight bulkheads, pods and self-draining cockpits found in various models of rigid kayaks. The benefits of built-in buoyancy become especially obvious when one considers the number of inexperienced paddlers borrowing or buying used kayaks from individuals who may neglect to explain or emphasize the need for adequate buoyancy. Over the past few years, the rash of fatal and near-fatal accidents involving insufficiently buoyant boats that sank or could not be re-entered have made this message even clearer. The disadvantages of built-in buoyancy are that it can wear, fail or prove insufficient—and this is why it should not be relied on without back-up systems of waterproof gear bags.

Bulkheads & Hatches

Watertight bulkheads made from either fibreglass or foam slab caulked into position provide dry stowage and structural support as well as buoyancy. To be effective, bulkheads should be fitted as close to the back of the seat and as close to the end of the footrests as possible; this will also ensure a maximum of useable space for loading.

Equipment hatches may be either of the large or small variety. Large hatches—sometimes as large as 10 inches by 14

The pod is essentially a watertight body chamber.

inches—are more convenient and practical than the smaller circular screw-in or pop-on varieties that range from 5 to 8 inches in diameter. The trade-off is one of security: large hatches are usually less watertight than small ones. The choice is yours; how much seepage are you prepared to put up with for the convenience of a hatch which will take a good-sized waterproof bag in one gulp?

The Pod

Developed and promoted extensively by British designer Alan Byde, the pod is a rigid, low volume capsule in which the paddler sits. Permanently attached to the cockpit rim, this watertight body chamber provides buoyancy control approximately 40 per cent greater than that provided by bulkheads fitted in close to the back of the seats and in front of the foot rests of an equivalent boat. The pod's other function is to protect against fold-and-hold entrapment, a situation more commonly seen in white water where the kayak wraps around a rock or bridge support. Under pressure from the flow of the river, the kayak without a pod folds in two at the cockpit and may trap the paddler's legs, whereas the kayak with a pod tends to fold in front of or behind the pod, leaving the paddler clear to escape. This is a problem only likely to be encountered when touring boats are used on rivers or in big surf.

The Self-draining Kayak

This is a rare beast, currently only found, to the best of my knowledge, in the Malibu Ocean Kayak Scupper, a short (14-foot) open cockpit touring surf kayak from California. In this boat, the kayaker sits in a recessed body form on top of the boat. A pair of substantial holes at the lowest point of the recess allows the water to escape, giving the kayak its name. The gear area is divided into fore and aft compartments accessible by large practical hatches. The boat is ideal for warmer climates such as Southern California, Hawaii and Florida. Shortly after the turn of the century, Fritz Fenger's sailing canoe Yakaboo—a sailing kayak by modern-day definition—also featured a self-draining cockpit. Surf skis and wave skis have cockpit recesses so small that they don't even require a drainage hole, only the body of the paddler to displace the water.

SEATS

Nothing is more personal than a kayaker's seat. One individual's source of comfort is another's medieval tool of torture. There are contoured foam seats and fibreglass bucket seats to fit skinny bums and fat bums; there are fabric seats that hang from the frames of folding boats, seats that can slide on plastic tracks, seats that are removable and must be tethered to stop their floating away during capsize drill, and seats that need a hole drilled through them so that water won't collect where you sit. There is, I regret to say, no perfect seat, nor is there a seat that will prove unacceptable to all people. I remember puzzling over one that looked like a Henry Moore sculpture suspended from the tight little cockpit rim of a foreign import. No one could get comfortable on the thing until one day a slim hipped guy with a flat backside walked in and declared it the most comfortable thing he had ever sat on.

Maybe the main point to be learned from this is that as you assess a kayak you should pay only passing attention to the seat. After all, you can change it fairly easily by adding a little ensulite here and a bit of foam there or ripping the whole thing out and replacing it with something that you feel good about. Don't pass up an otherwise ideal kayak because of the seat. Remember too that remaining seated for hours at a stretch isn't something you'll get used to right away, no matter how comfortable the seat; so don't expect too much.

The backrest is another part of the equation worthy of attention, as lower back support makes a significant difference to one's long-term comfort. When I go on a kayak trip, I usually carry so much gear that I end up throwing away the seat and backrest then sitting on my wetsuit jacket and a deflated air mattress, both of which I may want close at hand in an emergency. One of the drawbacks of this system is that you can easily destabilize the kayak by making your seat too high. As mentioned previously, raising the height of the seat by one inch can halve the stability of some touring singles.

SPRAY SKIRTS & SPRAY DECKS

A spray skirt is a skirt of neoprene or elastic-fringed nylon designed to prevent water entering the boat through the cockpit. The smaller the cockpit, the less expansive the skirt and the smaller the chance of the surf pushing it in, or so the theory goes. A large cockpit, on the other hand, is more convenient for entry and makes for easier loading and greater general comfort in the boat. In fact, it seems that a trade-off is not necessary in this case since a well-designed spray skirt can be made to adhere firmly to the cockpit rim of a large cockpit boat. If the spray skirt is fitted with a sturdy zipper which slides from chest almost to the deck, you can enter and leave the boat without removing the skirt—but even more important when the seas are very rough, a zipper gives quick access to your gear without your having to take off the spray skirt. It enables you to close the cockpit the instant you see an approaching whitecap. A spray skirt can be difficult to put on the cockpit at sea, especially if your hands are cold, so it is good to be able to put it on the boat and leave it there. Once you have a zipper sewn into your spray skirt, you will wonder how you ever got along without one. (You may also find it hard to remember what it was like paddling with a dry crotch, unless you have a waterproof zipper.)

A sturdy "panic loop" at the front of the skirt makes it easier to remove. The spray skirt should be attached loosely enough to be removed by a pull at this loop yet tightly enough attached to withstand the pounding of a breaker. Shoulder straps can prevent the skirt riding down on your body and enable you to empty accumulating pools of water from the skirt with a shrug. A useful variation is the anorak which fits around the cockpit over the top of the spray skirt or, like the old Eskimo model, attaches directly to the cockpit, becoming a combination spray skirt and jacket. The anorak too may be fitted with a zipper enabling access to the interior.

Spray decks, found on many folding kayaks, are watertight covers for the enlarged cockpits. Because they cover a large area, it is important that they be securely attached to the coaming of the boat. Turnbuckles are suitable for this purpose, but ideally they should be combined with a further waterproofing system such as a tuck-in flap to prevent waves forcing water beneath the cover. Expansive spray decks for single-cockpit doubles should be reinforced with a plywood frame between the cockpits to give added protection against breaking waves and to prevent formation of the annoying little pool of water which will otherwise gather between the paddlers. The plywood also gives the rear paddler a useful working surface for map reading, meals or the like.

PADDLES

Paddles are such personal items that you must take special care with their selection. The ideal length is commonly considered to be a little beyond the distance from the flat of your feet to your outstretched fingertips, but the preferences of experienced paddlers of my acquaintance vary so greatly that this rule means little. Some things are clear, however. Wider boats call for longer paddles and narrow boats call for shorter ones. Paddle shafts must be strong, oval and well cared for to avoid damaging your hands. Sea kayakers have traditionally used wooden paddles, but recently there has been a shift to synthetic paddles. Under normal touring conditions, tandem paddlers of the same size and strength would choose paddles of the same length. But one of the more common reasons for choosing a double is the imbalance between partners' strengths, and the choice of paddles can go a long way to-

Paddle styles: (upper) Little Dipper, sea-touring blade; (middle) Arctic Wind, Inuit-style cruising paddle; (lower) San Juan, based on a standard racing blade

wards redressing this. The two variables are, of course, length and blade size. Thus if you have a powerful 6-foot 4-inch, 250-pound paddler in the rear cockpit and her 110-pound asthmatic husband in the front, you can give them the same rate of paddling by supplying him with a short narrow blade paddle and her with a long large-bladed one.

To Feather or Not to Feather

When the blades are at right angles to each other, they are said to be fully feathered, and when the blades are in one plane, they are said to be unfeathered. There has been a major swing towards unfeathered paddles during the past few years, and the sale of one-piece paddles to sea kayakers has almost stopped on both the East and West coasts. If you are a beginner, I would suggest using unfeathered paddles. The pros and cons for both are briefly as follows. Feathering reduces windage on the airborne blade when travelling into the wind. With a following wind, however, it is to your advantage to have unfeathered blades and let the wind on the airborne blade help push you along. With a beam wind, unfeathered paddles are again the best choice, since they will catch less wind than feathered ones. Traditional Eskimo and Aleut paddles, which are often relatively long with slender blades, are never feathered.

I myself prefer unfeathered paddles under normal touring conditions, feathering only for gale-force head winds or when exiting through heavy surf where I would want to avoid pushing the back of the blade into the crest of a wave or might need a reflexive brace. This brings up a contentious point. In an earlier edition of this book, I suggested varying the angle of blades according to conditions. This works fine for the more stable doubles, but most people come unstuck when they vary the blade pitch in kayaks which depend upon a reflexive brace for their seaworthiness. (I really appreciated this when I was paddling a particularly squirrelly surf ski in rough seas off Diamond Head in Hawaii.) I quickly had to revert to the feathered blade on which I was weaned to avoid slicing up the ocean and going for a swim. At sea, when the wind becomes too strong to paddle easily, unfeathered paddles are less likely to go spinning out of your hands as the wind catches first one angle and then the other. They are also less likely to catch a sideways gust leaving you with the option of hanging onto your paddle and capsizing or letting go one end of the shaft and losing your stroke. If you have agile wrists, you will be able to retain your grip on the shaft and retrieve the paddle from the sea. If not, you won't have to worry about the angle of your paddle—you won't have one, unless you had it tethered. Another problem with feathered paddles is that over long periods they increase the chance of tenosynovitis, which results from overuse, particularly the twisting motion feathered paddles require. In fact, in view of their few advantages and serious disadvantages, I find it a wonder that feathered paddles ever became popular at all.

Blade shape is another great mystery to most people, and it helps to realize how shapes evolved in order to better judge the most appropriate paddle type for the boat you use and the sort of kayaking you do. The broad square-ended blades, for example, are traditionally whitewater paddles which appear to have evolved from the old square-ended oars popular early in this century. They were broadened to give good control for slalom courses and enhanced holding power in aerated water. The paddles are usually short (less than 7 feet) and feathered to help negotiate the narrow gates of a slalom course.

The large-bladed asymmetric paddle is the most powerful blade because of its size and the fact that the angled tip balances the area of the immersed blade on either side of the spline so as to eliminate any twist. (Twist is also eliminated with a narrow blade.) This paddle is designed for flat water racing boats that weigh 15 to 20 pounds. It is also ideal for light, fast singles when wind is not a factor. It is less than ideal for doubles which can weigh as much as 500 pounds when fully loaded. Here the efficient blade that works so well for the light boat becomes a liability to the joints and muscles of the user. This is a case where the narrower paddle comes into its own.

The narrow paddle evolved in the Arctic, and variations of it were used by all native paddlers, not because they were incapable of manufacturing wider blades, as is sometimes suggested by casual observers, but because the paddles made sense by virtue of their minimal vulnerability to wind and minimal impact on the joints and muscles of the endurance paddler. A wide range of traditional sizes and configurations exist, most of which have yet to be copied by the manufacturers of today's shop-bought paddles. The narrow-bladed paddles that have been produced commercially (True North Quill, Arctic Wind and Little Dipper by Northwest Design Works and Trade Wind by Nimbus) are often too long for the benefits of the narrow blades to be fully appreciated.

BAGS & CONTAINERS

Sea kayaking has almost unlimited potential for people who like putting things in bags and sealing them tightly. A good system for waterproofing equipment is crucial, and in cold climates your life may depend on it. Today, there is a wide range of waterproof bags of different sizes and materials on the market, some designed exclusively for use in sea kayaks. Most seal by means of a flap and dome closure or roll-down top with snap buckle arrangement. Less expensive, and disproportionately less effective, is a series of plastic garbage bags placed one inside the other with necks folded over and tied. If garbage bags are used, they should be protected by a regular canvas bag. Wider boats usually have useful spaces on either side of the seats which can be utilized efficiently if narrow bags are chosen to hold items you may require while paddling. This method is much safer than carrying bits and pieces on deck, and more convenient than carrying them loose inside the boat. Items such as flares, VHF radio, flashlight, diving mask, sunscreen, camera and, of course, lunch can all be stored here and, provided that the bags are securely attached to the boat, they will not be lost should you capsize.

Several manufacturers make tapered waterproof bags

Waterproof bags come in a variety of sizes.

which fit nicely into the bow and stern of the kayak and which can be blown full of air after loading. These are usually sealed by means of a fold-down flap with a Fastex closure and are mostly appropriate for kayaks without bulkheads or those featuring hatches large enough to stuff the bag through. In the absence of bulkheads, such bags should be backed up by a cockpit sock.

Be sure that the tapered bags you use are of sturdy material, that the inside of your kayak is clear of sharp edges and that you have the means to attach the bags to the kayak so that, in the event of a capsize, your equipment will not float

47

A cockpit sock of proofed nylon makes it easy to drain the boat in the event of a capsize.

away. If you are using standard tapered air bags for buoyancy, make sure that they are large enough to occupy all of the space you are not using for your legs or gear in waterproof bags. Small air bags placed at either end of a large boat just occupy valuable storage space and create an axis around which a flooded boat can turn, making it tricky to re-enter without overbalancing again. The ideal location for buoyancy in such a case would be along the gunwale so as to provide a pontoon effect when the boat is awash. With both inflatable gear bags and air bags, make sure that the inflation tubes are long enough so that the bags can be topped up orally while they are in place, necessary when a temperature drop causes a loosening of the bags.

The cockpit sock is one more bag for the last baggable item, the paddler himself. The sock is a pod-shaped waterproof bag, set into the cockpit after the boat is loaded and attached by its elastic rim to the coaming before the sprayskirt goes on. As with the pod, if the paddler fails to roll and is forced to bail out, only the sock fills with water. Rudder controls can be operated readily through the sock. During trials with two socks fitted to a large double devoid of bulkheads, we were able to re-enter and resume paddling within one minute, whereas a rescue in the same boat with only air bags fore and aft failed. It has not proved necessary to invert the socks, which in modern fibreglass kayaks are held in place by a strong vacuum. Sea socks are not appropriate for use in folding kayaks.

The design of food bags will depend on the type of boat you are using. If you are loading your food through a fairly small hatch, you may decide to pack the food containers loosely and use a bag only for carrying them from boat to campsite. In the larger boats, containers may be carried in a wide-mouthed sack or mesh bag enabling you to rummage about inside the bag for the tin which has migrated to the bottom. It is a good idea to have everything stored in some kind of bag. Apart from securing gear during a capsize, it makes carrying easier when your campsite is some distance from the point you were obliged to land.

Special attention should be given to a dry bag for your documents. On the market are several inexpensive plastic and vinyl bags, but these usually have a life span proportional to their economy—not much of a saving when you find your passport or logbook reduced to papier-mâché. Strongly made bags with grommets which allow them to be tied in place are especially useful. So are bags with a separate flotation chamber that can cushion fragile gear or protect its loss through sinking.

REPAIR KIT

Ideally, each boat should carry its own repair kit containing patching materials for deck and hull—be that fibreglass or fabric—as well as needles, thread, assorted stainless steel bolts, nuts and clamps, aluminum or brass rivets and screws of various sizes. Tools should include long-nosed pliers, a bradawl, screwdriver, small hacksaw, sailmaker's palm, whetstone and spare fittings, and a waterproof zipper suitable for the spray skirt together with some neoprene cement or waterproof glue. Several feet of copper wire and some tough monofilament stainless steel wire are also handy, and enough braided stainless steel wire to replace both rudder cables. Most useful of all is a roll of duct tape or divers' airhose tape, which is capable of holding the whole show together (and frequently does). The repair kit should be stored, of course, in a waterproof container.

SAFETY EQUIPMENT

I list here a good deal of safety equipment. To carry it all would be ludicrous, but each article has its use. Just assess the problems you are likely to encounter and take what you are most likely to need, bearing in mind that adequate buoyancy for your boat, a Personal Flotation Device for yourself, a bailing device and a spare paddle are essential to sea kayak safety along with Coast Guard-required light and signalling devices.

Life Jacket or Personal Flotation Device (PFD)
Obviously a non-swimmer would be foolish to go kayaking without a life jacket, but those who go down to the sea in kayaks should know how to swim. The chief value of a life jacket is that it makes swimming unnecessary, allowing the person to stay hunched in the HELP position (heat escape lessening position) and so almost double survival time in cold water.

Of the many life jackets and buoyancy aids on the market, I prefer the old Mae West variety, as used on commercial aircraft, or the diver's buoyancy aid. Whether stowed or worn,

(A) The inflatable Mae West life jacket, and (B) PFD (Personal Flotation Device). Comfortable models of the latter are no longer hard to find and frequently come with useful pockets.

these can be kept totally deflated and out of the way until needed, and then inflated instantly by CO_2 cartridge or more slowly by mouth. Deflated, they are comfortable to paddle in and they fold away into a compact parcel about the size of a lunch box. Because such vests are approved only for aircraft or diving applications, they do not exempt you from the need to carry a coast guard–approved PFD in your boat to satisfy official requirements. Although bulkier and potentially less comfortable, approved life vests do offer a measure of protection against weather and cold water. On the other hand, it can also be said that many of the traditional roles of the life jacket are performed more efficiently by a wetsuit or drysuit, and these provide increased protection against the real killer, which is hypothermia rather than drowning. A deflatable life jacket can be worn handily in conjunction with such suits, and you can swim efficiently by deflating it, or rest when you please by giving it some air. The deflatable jacket's disadvantages are that it requires careful handling to avoid punctures and it is useless if you are struck unconscious before reaching your CO_2 charge—as might happen in surf. Standard PFDs, being more prevalent, are more economical, and good comfortable designs are now easier to find. Although some imported models feature sewn-on pockets enabling the wearer to carry emergency items, such PFDs may not carry U.S. or Canadian coast guard approval. Sewing tabs or pockets onto an approved life jacket may void approval also, exposing you to a potential fine.

Pumps & Bailers

Ideally, a well-found sea kayak needs two bilge pumps: a foot-operated, low-volume pump and a hand-operated, higher-capacity pump. Each pump has its own function.

The foot pump (mostly needed only on folding kayaks with their tendency to leak slightly at the stitched seams) with a capacity of about one gallon per minute, should be mounted so that its intake is at the lowest point of the boat. Its purpose is to keep pace with the seepage from waves washing over the boat or from small hull leaks. It comes into its own during rough conditions when you are taking seas frequently or when for some other reason it is unsafe to pause and bail. This is the case with a strong wind onto a lee shore or in a difficult head wind. Without the foot pump, your boat fills gradually and becomes less stable. You must bail, yet you cannot afford to stop paddling. You do not have to be on a thousand-mile journey to find yourself in this situation; you can encounter such conditions on any day trip.

With a capacity of perhaps 12 gallons per minute, the hand pump is your pump for emergencies. It can be used to drain off routine seepage, but you must stop paddling to do so. Depending on the model, it can be operated through the un-zippered spray skirt, mounted semi-permanently through the deck behind the rear cockpit, or stored inside then taken out and attached to a permanently placed hose with an outlet be-side the cockpit. The main emergency use for this pump is to drain the kayak after a flooding.

Other bailing devices may include your toilet-pot, which we trust will have a generous capacity and can help if you capsize in calm waters, while a sponge will afford you the luxury of reaching the last drops. Hand pumping a narrow kayak after a capsize presents some practical balance prob-lems since it requires the use of the hands both for pumping and balancing. Tricks such as using the pump with one hand while bracing with the paddle across your shoulder and down the other arm cannot be relied upon in rough conditions. Tas-manian kayakers have been using battery-operated bilge pumps for a number of years and claim to be able to empty a flooded kayak in a matter of minutes. The great beauty of such a system is that the boat is emptied rapidly at the flick of a switch while the paddler has both hands free to brace until stability is regained. An electric pump designed for kayaks is now available from a North American source (Eddyline Kayak Works).

Flares, Lights & Reflectors

Each boat should carry its own set of flares. Ideally, this would include several twin star pocket flares with indepen-dent launchers, which may be used as a follow-up to a dis-tress rocket. A couple of large parachute flares such as the Schermuly rockets should be your means of initial contact. The available range includes a very effective maroon star sig-nal flare and flares with radar reflective payloads.

The more flares you carry the better, within reason, but the minimum for a trip on which there is a chance of their being needed is two parachute flares handy and attached to the boat and three pocket flares on your person. I suggest that you plan on three per person though many people would consider this excessive—until they needed them. One smoke flare per boat and a strobe light for night location is also very reasonable. The solo paddler would do well to have all these back-ups.

The routine I recommend for an emergency, such as a capsize in cold water where there is a chance you may not be able to complete a self-rescue in a few minutes, is to fire off your biggest flare right away. When you confirm in your own mind that you are indeed in trouble—and before you begin to feel too cold—fire off the second rocket. These big flares can be seen from as far as 10 or 15 miles, and it could take as long as an hour for someone who has seen it to reach you, so don't despair and don't go firing off your pocket flares unless you can see the rescue boat. The pocket flares are to attract the attention of a rescuer who is fairly close. Such flares do not have a very high visibility since they are in the air only briefly and attain an altitude of no more than 500 feet. (The big rockets can reach over 1500 feet and stay aloft some 40 seconds.)

When choosing pocket flares, avoid the mini-flare packs that have a single launcher and a row of cartridges with screw-in heads. Although these appear to give a greater bang for the buck, they are too fiddly to operate with cold hands, and once you have fumbled and dropped the launcher, you can't do much with the shells. To a lesser extent, the same can be said for the Very Pistol. If you must use this type of flare gun, tie everything together and then to the boat or your person.

For pinpointing your position once the search has been called, you can also use a smoke flare, a strobe or, in the case of an aerial search, marker dye for the water. On sunny days a mirror to attract the attention of distant aircraft and boats can be very effective.

A waterproof flashlight is another handy aid—useful for alerting motor boats to your presence, invaluable for night landings and a coast guard requirement for night paddling. The best I have found is the plastic two-cell diver's light with the screw-on hood. On especially dangerous coasts I sometimes carry an additional, more powerful eight-cell light with the switch taped in the "off" position. Another useful light source is the glow stick—a flexible plastic tube containing chemicals and a glass vial. The contents are mixed by bending the tube to break the vial and shaking. The chemical reaction produces a green light which will last eight hours in temperate climates (more in the tropics and less in the Arctic). Glow sticks provide enough light to make one kayak visible to another almost a mile away, and they enable you to read charts and compass without difficulty. They are not affected by water and produce no heat.

While travelling at night, you can improve your chance of being seen with a radar reflector. This can be conveniently displayed aloft on a fishing rod. It is easy to make a multi-faceted diamond-shaped reflector which folds away flat for storage. Its value is limited on the open ocean since ships will be on the wide range of their radar, but in foggy channels, such as can be found on the British Columbia coast, fishing boats will more readily detect you with such a device.

Checklist of Additional Safety Equipment
— Transistor radio, for weather forecasts.
— A VHF radio, for kayak-to-kayak communication and emergency contact with ships or shore.
— Tow-line, rigged and ready for deployment.
— EPIRB

— Air mattress, miniature life raft or paddle float as a life-saving device and for additional flotation during pump and re-entry.
— Helmet, for dangerous surf.
— Solar still or desalinator, especially for tropical voyages.
— Drysuit or wetsuit, useful mostly in temperate and cold climates.
— Drogue, sea chute and sea anchor.

Radios

A hand-held VHF (Very High Frequency) radio can provide communications to help cope with a wide range of emergency situations. In addition, it can be used for weather reports and telephoning out from coastal wilderness regions, to reassure anxious family members and prevent unnecessary searches. The radios, which range in strength from one to five watts, have line-of-sight capacity which usually translates into 10 to 30 miles depending on the heights of the transmitting and receiving points. They are vulnerable to blind spots caused by mountains and are normally only available in marine band frequencies.

Licences are required for their operation in Canada and the United States, but the requirements are simple and not expensive. To date, several lives have been saved by the timely use of VHF radios carried by kayakers. Almost the entire North American coast is covered by a network of relay stations positioned on prominent mountain tops. I once received a telephone call from a kayaker cruising off the remote Brooks Peninsula. He was a couple of miles offshore with an 8-foot sea running. His signal was picked up by a telephone relay station and connected to the international network. Another source of contacts is the plethora of commercial and pleasure craft that cruise the coast tuned to Channel 16, the international standby and contact channel. These vessels can be requested to relay messages on their more powerful radios.

Aside from its emergency value, a major reason for carrying a VHF radio is for contact between members of the group. If yours is a fairly large party, the first and last boats can be used to hold the group together. (A lower frequency and less expensive CB [Citizen's Band] radio could be used for communication within the group, but CB radios are far more vulnerable to splash damage.) Also, most of the North American coast is served by a marine weather service that transmits constant weather information invaluable for route planning. This service can only be picked up using VHF, and only the VHF frequencies are continuously monitored by coast guard and other vessels.

EPIRBs

Emergency Position Indicating Radio Beacons or EPIRBs are strictly emergency signal beacons which can be either manually or automatically activated when a rescue is called for. There are three classes of EPIRBs: A, B and C. A and B transmit on both 121.5 MHz and 243 MHz, which are monitored by air traffic control as well as the coast guard and the military. C transmits on VHF channel 16 then switches to channel 15 for a homing beacon. (It is a relatively weak signal which shuts down automatically after twenty-four hours.)

A and B are monitored not only by passing aircraft, but also by the SARSAT system (satellite navigation system) which monitors the waters off North American and European shores and can identify your position to within 5 miles. It requires at least two passes of a satellite to fix your position and this can result in a response time of up to three hours, but improvements are imminent.

An EPIRB is obviously a neat trick to carry in your grab-bag of back-ups. Unfortunately EPIRBs are technically illegal for inshore use, and though they are very effective, the coast guard is resisting their more general use because of the ease with which they can be accidentally turned on, thus initiating an unnecessary and expensive search. The kayakers of my acquaintance who carry EPIRBs do so on the understanding that they would happily pay a fine for carrying an illegal EPIRB if it saved their lives. Some kayak outfitters even rent out EPIRBs for about twenty dollars a week.

One of the more dramatic rescues to be initiated by an EPIRB took place off the Oregon coast when the marathon kayaking team of Steve Landick and Verlen Kruger ran into trouble. (Kruger capsized, failed to roll and had his boat blown away by the wind.) Steve turned on his EPIRB then began assisting his companion to shore. In about twenty minutes the coast guard helicopter was upon them, and Verlen was whisked away to hospital. There have been other successful rescues from remote areas from the Aleutians to the Baja—and a number of instances where, because the emergency occurred in a relatively populated area, nobody bothered to respond to the signal believing it was yet another false alarm.

Drogue, Sea-Chute & Anchor

A drogue (sea anchor) is a necessary item on any journey with open sea to leeward; this includes inter-island passages and coastal kayaking with prevailing offshore winds. Its main function is to reduce wind drift at sea, but I have heard of its being used to stabilize entry through surf. It pays to keep the drogue ready for instant use, the end attached to a strong point on the boat. It can then be led through a loop at the bow and back to the deck, where it is folded and held in place by shock cord. The drogue is attached to the boat by approximately 120 feet of nylon parachute cord which, when not in

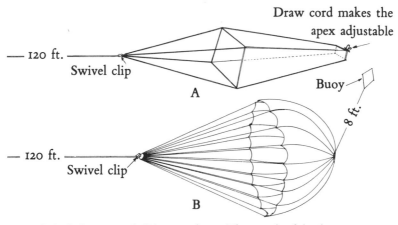

(A) A drogue, and (B) a sea-chute. The mouth of the drogue should be about 18" to 24" diameter, while the diameter of the sea-chute might be 4' or 5'.

use, is carefully coiled and tied to prevent tangles and then tucked inside the folded canopy.

The best material for standard sea anchors seems to be heavy-duty rip-stop nylon or similar fabric which is light-weight and will resist rot if it is stored damp. For a loaded double, an effective size is 36 inches long with an entrance 20 inches square and an apex aperture about 4 inches square. A swivel at the junction of the line and the drogue traces will reduce the tendency to tangle. Most drogues designed for yachts have a trip-line attached to their apex, but for use with a kayak this is not necessary. If the drogue becomes too heavy to retrieve, you need only paddle a little to ease the tension on the line.

A sea-chute is a larger alternative to the sea anchor and is built exactly like a regular parachute. It is more effective at stopping wind drift and indeed it can be so effective as to cause considerable stress in a big sea. With a large sea-chute (5 to 6 feet in diameter), it is important to have a full length of nylon cable so that there is plenty of stretch to absorb the shock. It is also advisable to attach a float to the crown of the chute by a 10-foot line. This prevents the chute from sinking too deep and holding you down into a wave. A short-term alternative to a specialized sea-chute is a parafoil with a restraining float. This can be very effective but may eventually harm the parafoil.

A bottom anchor is hardly standard equipment for most kayaks, but it can be useful if you need to sleep in your boat near shore—either because you are unable to land or because for some reason the land is inhospitable. A small Danforth or Bruce anchor with about 15 feet of chain is suitable. It can be attached to the already rigged sea anchor warp. The anchor also comes in handy if you plan to fish or dive from the kayak. George Dyson frequently anchors his big baidarkas offshore to avoid the hassle of dragging them out of the way of the tide, or to avoid the mosquitoes and blackflies ashore.

CLOTHING

Paddling generates heat, and even in cold climates it usually pays to dress lightly so long as the spray skirt is in place and you are wearing a windproof, waterproof outer garment. The inside layers can be a combination of light underclothing of either polypropylene or wool and a light pile or woollen jersey. Rubber boots are convenient but should be removed for all-day paddles to discourage the formation of mushrooms inside. (Regular dustings with anti-fungal powder will work wonders on these.) On coastal trips that call for frequent exiting through breaking beach waves, wetsuit booties with hard soles may be a practical option to reduce the trauma of getting your feet wet. If you stop paddling long enough to cool off, have something warm at hand to put on. You will need additional clothing as soon as you get ashore, when the closed kayak is no longer insulating you against the cold.

Where there is a likelihood of capsizing (and one could argue that the possibility is always present), consider wearing a wetsuit or drysuit as opposed to an anorak and legging combination. The most popular style of wetsuits are the Farmer Johns (or Farmer Janes). These are tightly fitting overall-style ⅛-inch neoprene trousers with a bib and high back that offer one-piece thermal protection to trunk, crotch and legs. The upper part may be folded down to the waist for summer paddling. A wetsuit functions by holding in a thin layer of water, quickly warmed by the body and insulated from the sea by the layer of foam rubber. Wetsuits are not ideal for trips involving six hours of paddling day after day since they become pretty ripe in a short time. Another point to consider is the necessity to relieve oneself; it can be a tricky business to remove a wetsuit if there is a sea running and no place to hop ashore.

A ⅛-inch Farmer John can be expected to add thirty to forty-five minutes to your functional survival time swimming in cool temperate waters. A neoprene jacket with hood and long sleeves can probably almost double this time, but it is not practical to paddle in and is usually only kept as a back-up to be pulled on in the water. *Note:* In cold water conditions, you will find it almost impossible to put on the wetsuit while swimming, and the importance of anticipating the areas of likely capsize can hardly be overstressed.

The drysuit is a loose-fitting vinyl one- or two-piece suit with latex waterproof seals at all openings and, in the case of one-piece suits, a heavy-duty waterproof zipper across the chest or back. The thermal protection of a drysuit depends on

Drysuits provide the most comfort with the most protection against accidental immersion.

the clothing worn underneath, and therein lies the problem: to be really effective in 50°F water, it will probably require more clothing than you normally feel like paddling in. It is, however, considerably more comfortable than the wetsuit and is probably best thought of as a garment that increases your functional self-rescue time in the water and improves your comfort on rainy days ashore.

A modification of the drysuit is the semi-drysuit made of waterproof nylon with adjustable neoprene cuffs and neck-seal. As with the drysuit, the semi-drysuit depends upon the underclothing layer for warmth. It is, however, not entirely watertight and will admit a certain amount of water through the cuffs and chest zipper when worn in the water. Its effectiveness depends on restricting the flushing through of the precious body-heated water, and it is less efficient than either the wetsuit or drysuit.

The paddling jacket is popular among today's sea kayakers and is often worn in combination with a Farmer John. It consists of a proofed nylon windbreaker with cuffs and neck seals that can be closed against the water. It usually comes fitted with a large kangaroo pouch for carrying personal flares and other useful items such as waterproof matches, a compass, knife, etc. More elaborate versions have detachable hoods as well as underarm vents to minimize the condensation that inevitably occurs. (I have *yet* to find a breathable fabric that is reliably effective in the sea. Most become clogged with salt and grime and lose their waterproof quality within a couple of weeks of coastal use.)

Synthetic pile underclothing is quite good for cold weather trips, but where there is a lot of rain or the waves are giving a wet ride, I still prefer wool. On a six-month trip in Patagonia, which lasted through mid-winter, I finally abandoned my nylon pile underclothing in favour of locally purchased woollen long johns and pullover.

Grant Thompson

Waterproof paddling jackets are evolving rapidly.

One of the joys of warm water kayaking is warm hands. In cold climates you will need pogies or gloves. Pogies are gauntlet mittens designed to cover the closed fists rather than the open hands. They are constructed with a small opening at either side of the fist and a sealable flap across the knuckles so that you can run the paddle shaft in one side and out the other. Pogies will protect your hands while giving you a satisfying barehand grip on the paddle. Many varieties are now available, of either neoprene or nylon, lined or unlined. A neoprene mitten with the palm cut out is also available.

For cold rain and sleet conditions, ordinary leather workman's gloves are usually adequate, and the wet leather gives a good grip on the paddle shaft. I have experimented with silk inner and rubber outer gloves, neoprene gloves and woollen ones, Millermitts (fingertips cut out) and fancy driving gloves, but simple leather work gloves still seem to be the most practical.

Some kayakers also like to wear spats. These are neoprene tubes which seal the cuffs of your anorak. They make short trips more comfortable but tend to encourage saltwater rashes on longer trips. I have several times started a trip with them only to discard them later and allow the water to flow in and out of my anorak sleeves. Spats are redundant, of course, with drysuits, and are already sewn onto paddling jackets.

In the tropics, clothing is mostly for protection from the sun, which for the unprepared can be as deadly as the cold of a northern winter. Cotton is preferable to synthetics. Clothing should be rinsed daily in fresh water if possible to remove accumulated salt. If you are one of those daredevil souls who can look death by skin cancer in the eye, you may get by with a swimsuit during the day; but keep a long-sleeved shirt close at hand for when the sun gets too fierce. A wide-brimmed hat is important no matter how well thatched you might be, and a bandana which can be pulled over the nose and mouth will protect those vulnerable parts. A waterproof anorak and light woollen jersey or comfortable shortie wetsuit should be kept handy for rainy or windy night crossings. You may be surprised how cold such a night can be once you have become acclimatized to the tropics.

If you expect to encounter difficult surf, you may want one more piece of clothing, namely a protective helmet.

LOADING A KAYAK

Normally volume, not weight, is the limiting factor when loading a touring kayak. Although the manufacturer may claim that a boat will carry 250 pounds, the volume of items such as tents, wetsuit, food, clothing and sleeping bag may reduce the effective load to as little as 100 to 150 pounds in a small kayak. A large double can comfortably carry 250 to 300 pounds of regular expedition equipment.

How a kayak is loaded is largely a matter of personal preference, but there are some general points to bear in mind. The kayak must ride evenly in the water for normal cruising comfort. A bow-heavy boat will plunge into waves and be awkward to steer in a following sea, whereas a stern-heavy one will behave badly in side winds. However, if you know you are going to be punching into a head wind all day, it is to your advantage to make the boat light on the bow so that it will rise easily to the waves. Load the objects you will require least frequently in the extremities of the boat, of course, and leave those required at sea or during a lunch stop to be packed last. Everything, both inside and outside, not stashed away in bags should be lashed to the boat. A caution here: a kayaker who recently capsized on an extended trip discovered that his boat could not be flipped upright because of the weight of the gear hanging from various strings beneath it, including an anchor! All had to be cut away before the boat could be successfully righted.

Nautiraid

Loading kayaks can be an art form, particularly for the military.

Spare spray skirts, fittings and emergency food supplies should be pushed as far forward as they will go. Tie a trailing cord around the neck of these bags so that they can be withdrawn without having to crawl inside the hull. Heavy objects like canned food, water containers, etc. should be stored along the keel of the boat and some heavy object such as a diver's weight belt kept until last to correct the final trim.

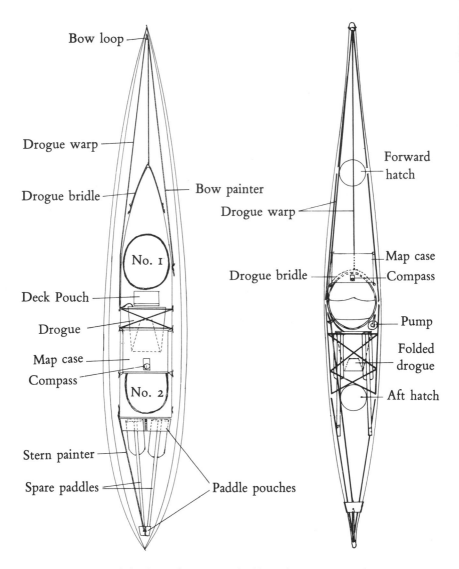

Bow loop

Drogue warp

Drogue bridle

Bow painter

Drogue warp

No. 1

Deck Pouch

Drogue

Map case

Compass

No. 2

Stern painter

Spare paddles

Paddle pouches

Forward hatch

Map case

Compass

Drogue bridle

Pump

Folded drogue

Aft hatch

Deck loading of a cruising double and a narrow single.

The Deck Cargo

A well-loaded sea kayak carries the absolute minimum on deck. Nothing which is not firmly tied down should be there unless you can afford to lose it. Some people like the deck crisscrossed with nylon webbing and shock cord. Convenient as it may be, though, elastic shock cord is not reliable enough for permanent attachment in rough water, and you will eventually lose equipment stored under it.

It is my opinion that the only objects on deck during a kayak journey should be spare paddles (in secure holders); a drogue, fully rigged and stored beneath a map case which is made fast by means of small cleats at all four corners; and a kangaroo pouch (easily glued to the spray cover) for miniflares, sunglasses, sweets and the like. Perhaps the only object loosely held by shock cord could be a canvas sack to hold fish caught during the day.

A sea-going kayak should have secure loops at either end to which are attached 10-foot bow and stern painters. (The bow line will serve as the paddle leash.) These painters are normally tied off to cleats on each side of the cockpit(s). A variety of additional sturdy cleats can take the shroud, stays and sheets of a sail rig. When paddling open water or lee shores, I rig a 120-foot running line through the bow loop ready to take a drogue or regular anchor.

Don't carry your water bottle on deck. It is far too valuable to risk losing, and besides, it would heat up in the sun. Rocket flares and flashlight are best stored close inside where they cannot be carried away by a wave or knocked off by another kayak when you are rafted up, and where they will stand a better chance of staying dry.

The after-deck is a tempting place to deposit your treasures, since it is the area least swept by the sea, but it is also the place where you are least likely to notice equipment breaking free. You can even carry rucksacks on the after-deck of some kayaks, at the price of stability, but this is not advisable during rough or windy conditions and certainly not on open water.

If you plan to rely on a paddle float for self-rescue, you will also require rope or webbing paddle holds to secure your outrigging paddle.

Carrying a Loaded Kayak

Frequently you will have to move a loaded kayak up or down the beach, which can be hazardous for both boat and self. A loaded double often weighs as much as 400 pounds. Dragging that much weight can damage the hull, and having to push and pull such a heavy load up the beach could strain your back, even if you slide the kayak on seaweed or roll it on small logs.

If you have four people in your party, the best way to carry a loaded boat is to have two people on each side support its weight on two straps made from nylon webbing slung about 3 feet in from the bow and stern. These straps may be as short as 4 feet, with toggles for the hands, or long belts which run over the shoulder and are held in the offside hand. In either case they enable you to carry the boat more safely, as your powerful leg muscles do the heavy lifting.

One person at each end is much less desirable but often necessary because companions are not handy to help you, or because the surf is too hazardous to leave one boat in it while lugging the other. This method of carrying is probably responsible for more injuries to muscles and discs than anything else on a kayak journey. It can also put great stress on a boat, not to mention relationships. If possible, remove the heaviest gear from amidships before lifting. Good sized hand toggles at bow and stern will make your carry more comfortable.

One person, or two people with a strop, can move a heavily loaded kayak up the beach by taking one end of the boat and walking it around 180 degrees, then returning to do the same with the other end. As soon as your boat touches the beach, you can begin this process by lifting the bow and floating the stern up the beach on a wave. To reduce damage to the pivot point, slip a piece of board or an inverted skillet underneath, and let the boat turn on that. Remove or cock the rudder to avoid damage.

A set of wheels that can be taken apart for stowage inside the boat is a very useful item for carrying a kayak on and off ferries. Presently, kayakers are permitted to wheel their craft without charge aboard the government ferries that ply the British Columbia, Alaska and Washington coasts. This may be true in other areas as well.

KAYAK MAINTENANCE

The amount of time you spend on kayak maintenance will depend on what type of kayak you have. As we have seen, folding kayaks require the most attention while a rudderless plastic or fibreglass kayak requires the least.

UV the Destroyer

Probably the most destructive element for a plastic or fibreglass kayak is direct sunlight. Ultraviolet rays alter the composition of the hull material so that it becomes brittle and eventually weakened. The process will likely take six to twelve years (we don't really know with modern plastics since they have yet to stand the test of time) depending on the strength of the sunlight, the composition of the hull material and protective layers such as gelcoat or UV screen waxes.

Ultraviolet rays can be even more destructive to soft skin boats. I have seen folding kayak decks that were literally falling apart after less than two years' exposure to constant tropical sunshine and salt water.

To protect your kayak from the ravages of ultraviolet light, store it carefully in the shade when not in use, and polish fibreglass kayaks with an ultraviolet inhibiting wax. I know of no way to protect canvas from ultraviolet rays though some of the new fabrics found on modern folding boats have improved UV resistance.

Water the Infiltrator

Plastic and fibreglass boats are mostly immune to damage from water, but folding boats and lath and canvas kayaks are another matter. Water soaks in through any small scratch in the varnish and may travel inches on either side. Fungus soon follows, and in no time greyish stains mar the golden hues of the ash and birch. Water left on the skin of canvas boats is a breeding ground for fungus and rot which can destroy a skin in weeks. Certain death for a folding kayak is to leave it upside down on the lawn over winter or store it outside so that autumn leaves lie wetly on its shaded surface.

When you have finished using your folding kayak, dry the skin on the frame (to avoid any chance of shrinkage), dust down the inside with French chalk then store it in a cool dry place such as the attic of your house or in a cupboard. If there are rats or mice around, store the skin in a mouseproof box since the little bleeders sometimes develop an expensive taste for synthetic rubber. The frame should be inspected at the beginning of each season for signs of water seepage, and every few years the old varnish should be sanded off and new coats applied.

Salt the Consumer

Salt corrodes and consumes your metal fittings. Aluminum-framed folding kayaks can seize up in a matter of months if left assembled in tropical waters. You can almost watch the little cauliflowers sprouting out of the affected joints. Dismantle the boat every month or so and wipe the metal to metal joints with an oily rag. On one trip I literally had to replace all the aluminum rivets on the frame of an Aerius 20 after only four months of kayaking in the tropics. Foot pedals and rudders need constant attention to prevent their seizing up. Combining metals distantly spaced on the electrolytic scale results in sometimes spectacular electrolysis as one metal consumes another. Sacrificial zinc anodes in the bilge might be a consideration if you are doing a long tropical trip with an aluminum-framed boat.

Heat the Exacerbater

All of the above destruction becomes a more serious problem as the temperature increases. Decay and corrosion are much slower in the Arctic. With heat, electrolysis speeds up: fungus grows on everything that sits still and lots of things that don't; metals ulcerate in a matter of weeks. Prevention requires that you treat your folding boat with fungicides, wash it down with fresh water, and let it dry off as often as possible in a well-aerated space. Plastic and fibreglass kayaks only really need an occasional rinse out with water and diluted fungicide and some WD40 on moving parts such as the rudder and rudder controls.

Checking for Leaks

Leaks can be difficult to find, particularly in fibreglass kayaks. Begin by checking the hull for small impact fractures. These can appear as soft spots in the gelcoat or a spider web of small cracks. No hole may be visible but under pressure, water will find its way through. This type of leak can be repaired with a small fibreglass patch on either side of the fracture.

73

If no fracture is found in the hull, check the following possibilities:

1 Seams—Kayaks with plastic extruded seams between the deck and hull are difficult to build without leaks. To locate them, run a hose around the seam and watch to see where the water comes through. If that does not work, you may have to fill the kayak with water. (Support it well first.) Mark the spots then re-fibreglass them on the inside.

2 End plugs—This is a solid area at each end of the kayak designed to strengthen the tips and provide a solid anchor point for rudders, bow loops, etc. The plug is formed by pouring a mixture of fibreglass resin and micro-balloons into the end of the vertical kayak. Sometimes the plug cracks as it cools, and when holes are drilled into it, water can seep in through the hair cracks in the plug. This can be fixed by making a second pour of a small quantity of resin.

3 The coaming—The coaming is usually attached to the deck of the kayak with an epoxy putty. Sometimes this cracks, falls out or was never put in properly. A hose squirted up under the lip of the coaming will reveal any leaks, and fresh putty can then be applied without having to remove the whole coaming.

4 Bulkheads—To check the bulkheads, fill the mid-section of the kayak with water and mark any leaks with a felt pen. Repairs are made with either fibreglass patching strips or Sikaflex caulking compound applied to both sides of the bulkhead.

Note: with all the above repairs, the kayak surfaces must first be dried carefully.

Storing for Winter

After your folding boat is dried, powdered and tucked away under your bed, take your plastic boat and store it right side up on a flat surface with small wedges under the bow and stern to maintain the rocker. Don't put it on two sawhorses for three months or you may find that you have some permanent grooves across your hull in the spring, particularly if you are storing the boat in a heated room. Storing outside is not good for any self-respecting kayak either, particularly in snow country. I know of some rather sad-looking kayaks dug out from under a pile of wet snow that fell from the roof of a house which was supposed to be offering it protection.

Car Topping

For most of us, the roof of our automobile is going to be the riskiest place we are likely to place our kayak. The potential for total destruction of the boat is considerable; for example, you have the overhang—frequently not visible in the rear view mirror. You back up in order to extricate your vehicle from a parking space and drive the stern of your kayak into the brick wall of the supermarket. If you drive a small car and paddle a large double, it is probable that sooner or later you will impale a Winnebago at a traffic light. I have personally broken a kayak from whiplash when I drove over a curb, not realizing that an inch of rain had accumulated in the bilges overnight.

But perhaps the most spectacular way to do in your kayak is to leave the bow-line trailing so that the front wheel of your car drives over it. Even at modest speed, the effect of this is devastating.

As a final possibility, consider the brace of kayaks that you notice floating alongside you on the freeway. These boats, which originated on your roof, are floating free because your cheap roof rack has chosen this moment to release its grip on the gutters of your car. Combining an overload problem with a failure to secure the boats fore and aft or a reliance on rubber bungies is definitely something to avoid.

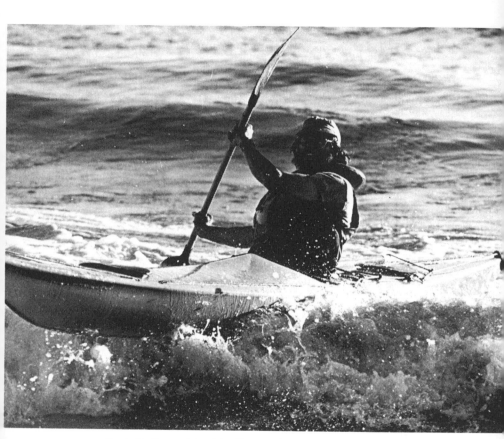

Paul Caffyn and his Nordkapp riding in on a wave on the coast of New Zealand.

2

Technique

PADDLING

The key to paddling for hours at a time is to develop a relatively effortless paddle stroke. This is not possible against strong head winds, but for most other situations, you can ease up on the power as the boat reaches cruising speed. The ideal stroke for steady sea kayaking is a moderately wide, balanced push and pull, with the paddle shaft about 45 degrees to the horizon. The hands are usually held about shoulder width. For cruising, unlike racing and slalom kayaking, most of the effort is exerted from the waist up, back braced lightly against the backrest while the knees are wedged in firmly beneath the deck and the feet are braced against the foot rest. The legs and feet are important both for balance and as the roots of power for the stroke. In the narrower kayaks, the bracing of the legs is more critical than in the large stable ones.

To get the paddle stroke right, reach forward an easy distance with the paddle so it enters the water no more than blade depth. Maximum power is exerted during the middle third of the stroke, sweeping out slightly (as demanded by the length of the paddles if they are not to go too deep). This outward sweep will give increased stability. Withdrawal begins as soon as the blade enters the final third of its stroke and is achieved simply by reaching into the next stroke with the opposite paddle blade. Power applied during the last third of the stroke wastes energy by lifting water unnecessarily. The leading arm should punch steadily forward—elbow not quite straight—levering the blade through the water against the pull of the other arm. The fingers of the upper hand should be relaxed and open, the fleshy part of the thumb and palm pushing against the shaft of the paddle. As light a grasp as possible should be maintained with the pulling hand.

On long trips, avoid paddling with unnecessary force. In doubles, seek a harmonic rhythm with your partner and the condition of the sea, and try not to succumb to the temptation to race with the boat steaming away alongside you. (But if your day is almost over, *then* you can scream "race you to the beach!" and take off in a wall of spray and thrashing paddles.)

Your travel speed is going to depend on how everyone is feeling as well as on the prevailing conditions. On a long trip at sea, your energy will ebb and flow. Sometimes, for no apparent reason, you will feel like going for it; other times, you will barely be able to push one paddle ahead of the other and you'll wonder why you didn't take up sailing instead. Ride high on the good times by all means, but try not to burn yourself out in mid-crossing. Plodding on with leaden paddles becomes somewhat easier too with the knowledge that the next stage of the cycle is bound to be a good one.

Conserve energy by remembering that you have it. A good trick to try near the end of a long day is to imagine you now have to turn around and paddle all the way back again. (It's great when you realize you don't have to.) Frequently, your energy will evaporate as soon as you make a landfall, and until experience has taught you better, you will be quite convinced that you are incapable of paddling another mile. But if you *had* to paddle back, your energy *would* last. You really have a choice: to let go or to hang on to that energy. The more you hang on to it, the more amazed you will be by the apparently infinite amount at your disposal.

78

Alone on the sea, your paddle rating (cadence) will be as variable as the conditions and your mood. In a head wind, it will be long and slow with power applied nearly all the way, sometimes rating under thirty strokes per minute. With a fresh following breeze, you will be doing over sixty, using a chopping, shorter stroke, and your boat will race along. Your seating position too will vary—first forward then back, on one cheek then the other—anything for a change.

With wind and waves abeam, lower your stroke and lean into the wind slightly. The resulting wider sweep stroke on the leeward side will alter the rating slightly. These adjustments will occur automatically as you get used to the conditions. If the waves are big and breaking, a great deal of stability can be acquired by accentuating the regular paddle stroke into the breaking crest, and this may alter your rating as you hang back or jump your stroke to anticipate the whitecap.

Variations in the rating may also occur when running with a good following sea. The waves will alternately push your boat with the crests, then drag heavily at it in the troughs. This speeding up and slowing down can be exhausting. Surfing these waves is good fun, but over distance it is usually best to strive for a steady rhythm.

Chaotic seas, such as those off steep-to lee shores, demand a very rapid rating; you may almost have to sprint through them. Quite likely you'll feel like doing that anyway. You should make your stroke short and quick, providing extra stability in the unpredictable waves. A faster rating leads to faster reactions, readier support strokes and less time spent in unreadable water.

Apart from regular paddle strokes, which offer most of the stability a sea kayaker requires, there is a variety of technical manoeuvres, known as paddle braces, which may be useful.

PADDLE BRACES

Paddle braces are strokes that maintain the balance and control of the kayak. Their importance and relevance increases as the beam of the kayak diminishes and conditions become rougher. They run the gamut from the reflexive slap support stroke for times when you nearly "trip" to the deliberate sculling support stroke. They are valuable skills for all paddlers, particularly those with kayaks sporting a beam of less than 25 inches, though even with a beamy double, a sound brace can make the difference between coming through the surf line on top of or underneath your kayak. To be effective, braces must be a natural, automatic reaction to a situation on either side of the kayak, be it the sudden cresting of a breaker or the twist given your kayak from crossing an eddyline. They are the tools by which you turn the paddler/ kayak combination into a seaworthy unit.

Sculling Support Stroke
This stroke (see p. 88) provides a constant support for a stationary kayak. It stabilizes the boat for operations such as re-entry. The procedure is to lean the boat slightly to the side on which you intend to gain support, which should be the weather side when conditions are rough. (Leaning downwind increases the chance of capsize.) The paddle is stretched abeam the boat and the blade sculled back and forth on the surface, face down, taking enough weight to give stability. This action is most effective if hands are moved about 18 inches back along the shaft towards the airborne blade. This stroke deserves plenty of practice so it won't cut water and send you swimming. It is a useful stroke for emergencies or where an extraordinary amount of stability is required.

Slap Support

As its name suggests, this is a straightforward recovery stroke in which you smack the paddle face (or back) onto the surface to regain lost or threatened balance. It is not used frequently by sea kayakers, but it is a necessary reflex to develop. The only tricky part is to be sure to slap the face, not the edge, of the paddle onto the water; if you have been varying the feathering of your paddles, your reflex slap just may not be of much help to you. A more common variant of this is to blend the slap into a regular stroke, thus providing recovery power without breaking rhythm. The paddle blade will return to the surface at an angle, so in fact your slap support will lead easily into a sculling support stroke.

The Floating Paddle Brace

The floating paddle support enhances stability for a move such as rearranging your seat or retrieving a water bottle from inside your cockpit. It is particularly helpful for beginners who find themselves sitting in an unfamiliar or unstable kayak. Simply float the blade of your paddle out on the surface of the water at right angles to your boat. The shaft at the base of the near blade rests on the coaming while the control hand, wrist held straight, holds the paddle near the centre of the shaft. This has a stabilizing effect both psychologically and physically. The paddle is well placed to scull gently back and forth or to provide a softly sinking platform if you need sudden support. A most useful feature of the floating brace is that you can remove your hand from the near end of the paddle to perform simple tasks.

The Low Brace

This is a brace suited to gaining support when a small breaking wave catches you suddenly abeam. Thrust the blade (in the case of a spoon-shaped paddle, use the back of the

Above: The High Brace. Support is from a downward pull with the power face of the blade. The elbow on the non-bracing side is kept in close to the body and the hand is below eye level. Below: In the Low Brace, support is from a downward and forward push with the back of the blade. Wrists are kept straight for strength.

blade) out onto the turbulence while leaning some of your weight onto the shaft, much as an alpinist will gain three-point support by leaning on an ice axe during a glissade. The strongest brace is one using the straight-backed fist pushing downwards onto the paddle shaft close in to the paddler's waist and in the stern quarter. The result is a very stable position so long as the boat is sliding sideways and the paddle blade remains on the surface.

The High Brace

The high brace is better suited for coping with stronger breaking waves such as surf where your paddle can be thrust into or onto the turbulent internal hydraulics. It differs from the low brace in two principal ways: firstly, during a high brace, it is the face of the blade that is the working surface. The second point is key to the safe execution of this brace and involves the position of the paddler's elbows, which should be held in as close as possible to the body so that the hands hang off the shaft rather than pushing down on it as in a low brace.

This brace has sometimes been shown held high so that the paddler is literally hanging off a paddle held above his head. This technique has resulted in a large number of shoulder dislocations. The strongest position to place the paddle is in the forward quarter. Any backward angle on an outstretched arm will increase the risk of dislocation.

A high brace can be incorporated into a normal paddle stroke simply by turning the blade from the vertical to the horizontal position if a wave hits in the midst of a stroke. Indeed, it can be argued that there are really only two strokes—forward and backward. The forward strokes use the face of the paddle while the backward strokes use the back of the paddle. Every stroke—and every brace—is some modification of these two basic movements.

Above: The Sweeping High Brace (Forward Sweep). Leaning makes turning easier by raising the kayak's bow and stern from the water. Below: The Sweeping Low Brace (Reverse Sweep). A steeper blade angle gives more turn, but less support for the lean.

John Heath

Greenland sculling positions

Greenland Sculling Braces

John Heath's research has brought to light various sculling braces traditionally used by Greenland paddlers. Unlike standard braces, where the purpose is to help the paddler avoid immersion, Greenland sculling braces explore the halfway zone between up and down in a way that leaves the torso largely immersed. There is the Greenland Side Sculling Brace and the Back Sculling Brace. (Another method, the Chest Sculling Brace, has been excluded from this discussion because the bracing position required can only be sustained for very short periods.) I leave the description of the Side Sculling Brace and Back Sculling Brace to John Heath:

In the Side Sculling Brace, the kayaker lies in the water more or less on his side, with the paddle at right angles to the axis of the kayak. The torso is twisted slightly with the upper shoulder nearest the kayak, and one leans as far aft as one comfortably can, both of which serve to keep body weight near the kayak. The paddle is extended outward from the kayak at right angles, as seen from above, and most of it is under water at an angle to the surface—as seen from either end—of about 30 degrees, although the angle can vary widely. The hands hold the paddle across the chest with both palms facing up against the face of the inboard blade, knuckles facing the paddler. The inboard hand, which will serve as a pivot point for the sculling motion, grips the blade near the inboard end.

Everything said about the Side Sculling Brace applies to the Back Sculling Brace, except for the body and paddle positions. In this brace the shoulders are twisted in line with the theoretical centerline, or axis of the kayak, and since the paddle is held across the chest, it then extends toward the bow, parallel to the axis, instead of at right angles to it. The body position also positions the paddle more or less parallel to the surface.

The torso need not be held close to the kayak, because with the shoulders twisted in line with the kayak axis, it is easy to keep most of the upper body except the face, hands and abdomen under water. The buoyancy thus gained enables one to loaf for several minutes using this brace.

MANOEUVRING

An efficient rudder is a great asset to a kayak at sea. As previously discussed, it saves energy by eliminating the need to constantly lean the kayak or break the paddle rhythm for corrective strokes. It also reduces the chance of your pulling a muscle through uneven effort. But a rudder should not be relied on for manoeuvring single kayaks. Instead, there is a simple repertoire of strokes that will handle 99 per cent of your needs and should be learned thoroughly.

To adjust your course to starboard, just ease up on the starboard paddle stroke and sweep a little wider with the port stroke while tilting the boat gently onto the port side. To alter course more drastically, skip the starboard stroke altogether and sweep wide to port with the kayak hard over on the port side.

Stern Rudder

This will give you a sharper turn. A stern rudder involves reaching back with the paddle so that the back of the blade presses hard at the passing water, pulling the bow of the kayak around to the paddle side. You lose headway with this stroke.

Reverse Sweep

From the stern rudder position, you can sharpen the turn further by leaning out onto the paddle while at the same time sweeping the blade out and forward across the surface of the water, easing off power as the paddle enters the forward quarter.

A reverse sweep alternating with a forward sweep on the opposite side will normally turn a single kayak in its own length and is known as pinwheeling.

The Sculling Support Stroke (left) and the Sculling Draw Stroke

Cross-Paddle Turn

The turning circle of a double may be tightened by a cross-paddle turn. In order to turn sharply to starboard, for instance, the rudder is held hard over while the No. 2 paddler leans back into starboard stern rudder position and then executes a reverse sweep. At the same time, the No. 1 paddler does a forward sweep on the port side. This procedure will normally turn a laden double in its own length.

Sculling Draw Stroke

On occasion it is desirable to move a boat sideways. The stroke required resembles the sculling support stroke in many ways, but you bite deeper with the paddle while hanging off the shaft in much the same way as you would during a high brace. Keeping the blade in the water at an angle of about 55 degrees, draw a series of Zs, one on top of the other, and you will draw the boat abeam through the water. This manoeuvre is useful to bring one boat alongside another for a lunch stop, a discussion of charts, or to pass something across. An indispensable stroke when positioning your boat to assist a swimmer or capsized fellow kayaker, it is also handy for docking.

88

SAILING

To a kayaking purist, paddles are for paddlers, sails are for sailors, and motors are for maniacs. Even purists will agree, however, that an improvised sail on a kayak can be of great benefit in some survival situations since it enables the paddler to conserve strength and cut water intake by reducing effort. In truth, kayak sailing is a sport in its own right—one that was once very popular in the United States and Europe and can be a lot of fun. Sailing can provide relief on long trips; indeed, many of the longest sea kayak expeditions have relied on sail. In 1923 Karl Schott paddled and sailed a Klepper down the Danube to Greece, around the Mediterranean to Suez, and across the Arabian Gulf to India. In 1928 Franz Romer sailed across the Atlantic in a specially built 21-foot single Klepper, and in 1956 Hannes Lindemann repeated Romer's feat in a double. In 1987 Ed Gillet sailed and paddled from Monterey, California, to Maui, Hawaii, in a fibreglass two-seater. The three transoceanic crossings took between fifty-six and seventy-two days.

If you intend to sail your kayak for more than running with the wind, some modifications will be necessary. A keel, centreboard or leeboards, or at least some substantial ballast, is needed. Several manufacturers sell sailing rigs and leeboards specifically designed for their own models of kayak.

A most remarkable example of sailing kayak was the *Yakaboo,* designed by the American Frederic Fenger, early this century. The 17-foot, home-built craft boasted such features as a self-draining cockpit, watertight bulkheads with hatch covers, a mobile, retractable centreboard and 6 feet of sleeping space. It carried 80 square feet of canvas on twin gaff-rigged sprit sails, and could sail itself so well that on Fenger's 1911 trip from Grenada to Saba in the West Indies a rudder proved unnecessary. All alterations to course were achieved

The Yakaboo: Frederic Fenger's ketch-rigged single kayak, 17' long with a 36" beam

by manipulation of the main sheet and centreboard, and Fenger sailed to windward successfully, crossing the rough inter-island passages of the Lesser Antilles against the trade winds in approximately half the time it took my friends and me when we paddled the route sixty-seven years later.

In 1969 a friend and I followed the path of three survivors from the Australian Commando Group X, who had tried to escape by kayak after a raid on Japanese Singapore during World War II. (One made it to Timor before being caught and executed.) Our kayak, like that of our predecessors, was not rigged specifically for sailing, but a square of parachute silk hoisted on a spare paddle provided a welcome relief from paddling in the scorching heat of the South China and Java seas. Twice we travelled over a hundred miles between land-falls—journeys we would not have attempted without the sail. On another trip, in the Caribbean in 1977–78, we intended to use sails as a back-up in the event of a storm blowing the party out to sea from the Windward or Leeward islands. Our plan, rather than attempting to fight the northeast trades and the equatorial current back to the islands, was to rig a tent fly on the spare paddle, then turn and run 500 miles southwest to Venezuela or Colombia. As it happened, we held our course and no tent-fly sailing was required.

Parafoil Sailing

The parafoil, developed by Jalbert of Florida, is ideal for sailing a kayak. It eliminates the need for a mast—that source of purchase which can result in a sudden capsize when normal sailing rigs are fitted to kayaks; and it packs away to the size of a shirt. The boat is literally drawn along by the pull on the string. Given that in a head wind it is usually more efficient to paddle than to tack, the use of a downwind rig such as a kite will offer no serious limitations. In fact, the parafoil can offer assistance to a loaded kayak up to 80 degrees off the wind.

*George Dyson's extremely seaworthy three-man baidarka, whose sail
doubles as a tent*

Generally, kites come in two sizes—9 or so square feet and
15 square feet. I also have a 30-square-footer (which can almost lift me off the ground in a 25-knot wind), but 15 square
feet is adequate to pull even a loaded double when the wind is
10 to 20 knots, and this size is about as big as one can launch
from the boat. To launch these smaller kites, I turn the kayak
down wind on the rudder, then hold open the tubes on the
leading edge of the kite. As wind fills them out, the kite lifts
and the lines trail through my fingers to the apex, then eventually to the single line.

Smaller kites are easier to launch than larger ones and can
be set successfully in winds as low as 5 knots. Under such
conditions, however, the kite has no pull and is more of a
frustration than an asset. (If you wish to use winds of this

strength, you would be better off with a spinnaker type sail.) For kites of 15 square feet and over, 10 knots is the minimal useful wind though some assistance can be gained from a 7-knot breeze. In winds exceeding 20 knots, however, you may do better with a small kite stabilized with a tail.

It certainly helps to have a rudder on the kayak for parafoil sailing, though it is possible to steer with the paddle if you attach the parafoil cord just forward of the cockpit. This, however, can be dangerous since, unlike regular sailing, if you *did* happen to capsize, your kite would keep on pulling, and you could find yourself on a long swim after an upside down kayak that has just been relieved of your weight. Some safety suggestions for using a parafoil are:

1 Don't attach the kite string to the kayak without also tying yourself to the boat.
2 Always attach your paddle to the boat (it is too easy to lose it from the deck lines), and always carry a spare.
3 Keep a sharp knife or safety razor handy in case the kite has to be released suddenly.
4 Use a lightweight spool so that the kite will fall and not fly on if released.
5 Attach a small piece of styrofoam to the kite tail to prevent it from sinking should it fall into the sea.
6 Avoid pulling hard on a submerged kite since you may damage it.

For proper flying, the kite must be correctly adjusted. This is best done on land with about 30 feet of line out. All the bridle lines (shrouds) should first be evenly tensioned. This will require repeated launchings and readjustments. Try to tighten the lines evenly on opposite sides of the kite. If you find that it flies off to one side, loosen off the lines on the favoured side or tighten those on the opposite side. The angle of flight can also be adjusted by shortening or lengthening horizontal rows of shrouds. The optimum angle of flight is about 60 to 70 degrees: too high and the forward pull is reduced, too low and the kite swoops and plunges excessively. A tail made of strips of cloth will help stabilize the kite in high winds.

The ideal point of attachment for the kite string to the boat will vary according to the angle off the wind you are attempting to run. For example, if you are planning to run down wind exactly, attach the line close to the bow. As you move off the wind, the point of attachment is moved back until it is at the cockpit. This can be achieved by running the line through a clip which is fastened to a rope loop that can be pulled forward or back. Hold the kite reel in your hand to retain a feel for the pull being exerted on the boat and keep a knife handy to cut the line free if you are unhappy with the way things feel and cannot pull it in.

Although the kite may be flown on 500 feet of line or more, it requires a lot of work to bring it in again; 75 to 100 feet is usually adequate.

SURFING AT SEA

In a following sea, when the combinations of wave size, wave shape and boat speed are just right, your kayak will catch the wave and you will find yourself surfing. With practice, you can judge the right moment to throw your weight forward, paddling hard to hitch such a ride. The tell-tale is your bow. Anticipate its burrowing into the wave that has just passed, then haul on the paddles. As the next wave comes up on you, it will lift your bow clear. You can help further at this stage by throwing your weight *back* while increasing your rating as the boat speeds up. Then for a hunded yards or more you can be swept along in front of the wave—at up to three times your normal speed.

The wave passes; your run dies and the boat drags down the back of the wave into the trough. This is not the time to ease up paddling if you want to catch the next wave. Watch your bow, put on full power and throw your weight forward again.

Surfing can heavily tax your strength, but it is a good way to pick up miles at sea and can be grand fun. There will come a time, however, when the fun ceases, the waves suddenly become unmanageable (bad weather seems to sneak up less obtrusively from astern) and you realize, with sudden misgivings, that instead of your playing with the waves, they are playing with you. If you have a boat loaded with fancy equipment (not least your feet) which you are anxious to keep dry, and if the water looks cold and the land is still miles away, you will probably want to alter the rules of the game. When the next big wave builds up on you, stall by back-paddling a stroke or two just at the point where, before, you would have thrown your weight forward. This should not slow you down too much, and it will help prevent that agonizing uncontrolled descent and the distressing high speed broach across the face of the wave, with your weather paddle clawing up the slope towards a wall of green and white about to envelop you.

If you still find your boat being picked up by the waves (a turn of the tide could be steepening their faces) and if you are no longer able to brace comfortably into the breaking crests, you may have to consider a holding action. Turn and face the oncoming crests, paddling into them as they break, and allowing yourself to be blown backward (with occasional help from your paddles). If the wind is strong enough to blow up a sea like that, you will probably still be making in excess of

2 knots with your course lying to sternward. Open sea waves can carry very hard-hitting crests. The only ways I know to tackle the really big ones are:

1 Paddle right through them.
2 Take them side on with your paddle stuck into the turbulence, just as you would come through beach surf.
3 Lie to a drogue.

Once, in very rough water during a night crossing of the Mona Passage, between Puerto Rico and the Dominican Republic, our kayak was hit by the full force of an ocean breaker while I was busy hand-pumping the bilges. (We had no foot pump.) I sensed the presence of the crest above us and managed to zipper the spray skirt closed just as the wave struck. It came down exactly on our stern, and the force was numbing, as if we had just been struck by a ship. We were swept forward at a phenomenal speed, breathless in the wall of flying spray and totally out of control, managing merely to wing a paddle out on each side as a token gesture. There were four of us in two doubles, and we had been keeping close company. When we shakily regained our equilibrium after that wave, we were so far away from each other that we could barely make out each other's lights.

3

Seamanship, Self-Rescue & Assisted Rescues

Seamanship is the art of living according to the rules of the sea. It is what this book is all about, and it requires, along with knowledge, a healthy respect for the sea and a knack for predicting the unpredictable. It means committing yourself to the problems of the voyage, from initial planning through final execution, with a complete acceptance of responsibility for your actions. Your seamanship is the measure by which you partake of the wisdom of the sea.

DAILY PLANNING

Daily on a kayak expedition or a trip of any length, you will face the questions of whether and when and where to paddle. These are fundamental questions, always worth re-asking. And as always where the sea is concerned, there are no fixed rules; the variables make every situation totally different. Your choices will depend on the condition of your party, where you are in the world, where you are on the coast, your sense of the weather and the nature of your intended landfall, how far you will have to paddle to your destination and how much farther you will have to paddle if you miss it or are unable to land. Timing may be a critical factor, and you may have to choose between a night or daytime trip. A major fac-

97

tor to consider will always be the weather and, more specifically, the wind: its direction, strength and likely development. Tides, currents and surf may also play a prominent role in your thinking.

Normally your group will get together for a pre-departure discussion of conditions and the day's schedule. This is the time to talk over all possible problems and decide on a bail-out plan. An escape route should be an integral part of any day's planning. Sometimes one is simply not available, and it is particularly important that this fact be realized before you set out, not after an emergency occurs. Such knowledge will greatly affect your decision to travel or to stay on shore. If your group consists of equally experienced members, you will all be able to decide on the best of several probable alternatives. If, on the other hand, you have one knowledgeable leader, this meeting becomes critical in a different way. It allows the group to learn from the leader and understand the reasons behind the decisions. The problems may require less laborious discussion in experienced groups, but a bail-out plan should still always be established and a rendezvous point agreed on, to be used if the group is accidentally split. Unintentional separations can occur under the calmest water conditions, so before leaving the shelter of a bay, you should agree on your exact destination and a compass course. Even if you can see the land you are paddling to, rain and fog may quickly obscure it. Everyone in the party should know the course and the goal.

When circumstances allow, it helps to take a day's pause before a big crossing. Spend the time resting, watching weather and currents closely, talking with local fishermen and eating plenty of good food. Getting the boat and equipment ready in advance is a part of the mental preparation, as is talking over details of the route with your companions—if you have not already worn the subject out. Take some time to compose yourself and quietly go over the chart so that when the moment to push off arrives, you are totally focussed on the problems to come and have a sound knowledge of what to expect.

TAKING ADVICE

Don't be intimidated by reports of currents that run at terrible speeds, but don't dismiss them either. Just treat all advice on currents with suspicion. Few sailors can report accurately on the speed of currents they have experienced, and seldom do their estimates err on the slow side. This may be because in a motor vessel they usually have far more power available than you do. Likewise, your faithful copy of the government *Coast Pilot* or *Sailing Directions* must be regarded only as a general guide to inshore navigation, not as a bible. For all their survey ships and research stations, navies and coast guards often know precious little about currents.

The best you can do when planning a major crossing is to combine all you have heard and read with what your eyes tell you from the cliff top. Judge each source of information critically against your own experience, then make your decision. Don't let anyone do it for you unless you are listening to a kayaker more experienced than you are, or to someone whose credibility you know to be utterly beyond doubt. Yachtsmen's advice must be tempered with your knowledge of kayaks. Commercial fishermen tend to be scornful of sea kayakers, and their advice is often full of gloom. Skippers of ocean-going ships seem to be either all for you or totally against you. Their advice is usually sound, but remember that they don't know the inshore effects of currents, and their ships behave *quite* differently from a kayak in rough seas. Landing sites in particular are a subject on which you cannot unquestioningly accept the word of those who have not studied the coast from a kayak. It may be helpful, though, to cross-examine yachtsmen by asking such questions as: "Can you get ashore in a dinghy?" or "Is it safe to swim in the surf off that beach?" This approach may alter their frame of reference and yield a more useful answer than the general question, "Is there any protection on that shore?"

Remember too that visibility from a kayak is far less than from a yacht or fishing boat, so a sandy cay or rocky reef visible at 15 miles according to yachtsmen may not be visible until 7 miles from your boat.

GROUP TRAVEL

If you are travelling as a group, always stay close enough to maintain communication—unless you have made some other arrangement which everyone clearly understands. During darkness, staying close enough usually means staying within earshot of the other boats and being able to see their lights clearly. Daylight allows travel within hand-signalling distance on fine days, but you should be close enough to respond to likely emergencies during rough conditions.

Although each kayak carries a compass and chart and each person knows the course, it is usually best if one boat leads. This will help to eliminate the tendency that crews or individual paddlers have to pull apart, each convinced they are on the right course. I regard this as very important. Diverging compass courses can result from compass differences if some metal or electrical circuit is nearby, but mostly they occur as a result of one paddler compensating slightly more or less than the others for the effect of each passing wave. It is the sort of thing which can become irritating for everyone concerned, and quite often no one is really to blame—yet the distance can become so great between boats that communication is hampered, and someone ends up having to paddle back half a mile to vent off resentment. Another advantage to one boat following the other is that, should the lead boat wander off course, the deviation can quickly be corrected by the other paddlers. It is good for morale if the role of lead boat is changed frequently.

It is the responsibility of the lead boat to see that no one is left too far behind. If you have more than two boats in your group, try to keep one of the strongest paddlers or teams of paddlers at the rear to help in emergencies and to encourage weaker members. Juggle the crews of doubles so that no boat has two weak paddlers. The point of having a team is the additional security the presence of other boats can offer and the pleasure of their company. If you are all going your own ways and not looking after each other, these advantages are cancelled out and you might as well have made your voyage alone. When travelling as a group on a windy day, an ideal formation is as a line with each boat spaced two boat lengths astern and two to windward of the one in front. This formation enables each paddler to watch the nearest boat astern while at the same time keeping an eye on approaching waves. Your blind spot in wind lies astern and to leeward.

RESCUE

Fundamental to safe sea kayaking is a reliable method of self-rescue. It is not good enough to rely on the platitude that there is safety in numbers. Sometimes there is, but it is a fool who bases his capsize recovery entirely on the assistance of companions. The following pages will discuss the Eskimo roll, alternative methods of self-rescue and, finally, assisted rescues.

THE ESKIMO ROLL

This is the first line of defence against falling out of an up-turned kayak for those with suitable boats. It is, however, a mistake to rely on the Eskimo roll alone, and one should always be capable of performing an alternative self-rescue. Remember, needing to roll is usually a sign of failure to manage the conditions, and those same conditions will be there to greet you when you come up. Your back-up system should be secure enough to cope with the conditions that knocked you down. Also, no matter how deft your roll, if you capsize while you have the spray skirt open and your arms inside the boat rummaging for your lunch (a very likely time to capsize), rolling is not going to help you much.

Some kayaks roll easily (some roll too easily!) and others can be rolled only with great difficulty. Some of the surviving traditional Eskimo kayaks are plainly not designed to be rolled, and it seems clear that the Eskimo roll was by no means a universal technique among those who invented and perfected the kayak.

The Pawlata Roll

There are many ways to roll, and it does not matter very much which one you choose so long as you can do it consistently with your loaded boat. Probably the simplest and most reliable is the Pawlata or extended-paddle roll. It is possible to co-ordinate it for use in doubles, but the practice is not common. For slender singles, the Pawlata is ideal since at sea you have plenty of time to position your paddle carefully, a luxury that whitewater kayakers do not always enjoy.

To learn to roll properly, you are going to need a little help from your friends, or better still, from an instructor. When you are upside down with water up your nose and your world out of focus, it is extremely difficult to be your own best critic on the finer points of the angle and depth of the

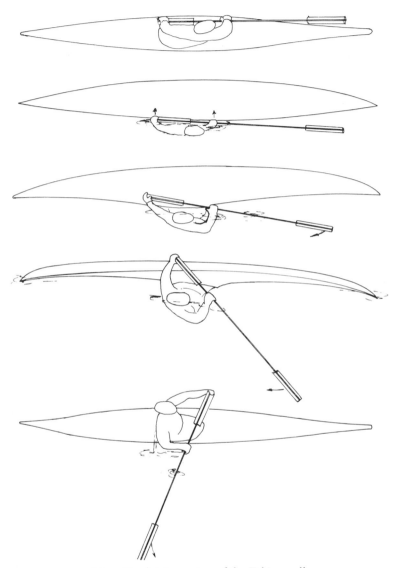

Hans Pawlata's version of the Eskimo roll

paddle blade. There are several exercises which can render your first roll a less desperate affair; for a start, you can get used to escaping from an inverted kayak—just in case you should change your mind about rolling some day. Capsize the boat and control your panic. Count to five slowly, then feel for the spray skirt release tab. Count another five seconds then pull the spray skirt free and do a gentle, unhurried forward roll out of the boat and up to the surface. It is good to know you can come out of your boat without tearing away the deck or leaving your knee-caps behind.

Next, with a friend standing waist deep alongside and holding your hands, capsize and pull yourself upright again. You will find that it pays to flick the hips sharply, leaving the head and shoulders to follow. Do this until you can come up easily and without a struggle.

When it's time to make your first attempt at rolling:

1 Lean forward, hold the blade of your paddle in your left hand and, with your right hand, hold the shaft at about the midway point. The paddle is placed along the deck, extended blade towards the bow on the port side, the blade horizontal and facing upward. The right wrist is turned and dropped so the back of your hand faces outward.

2 Capsize the boat and, when you have stabilized upside down, sweep the blade of your paddle towards the surface. At the same time, lean out towards the paddle while pushing the left hand forward and up.

3 Levering the blade against the water at the same angle as that used for a sculling support stroke, sweep the paddle out from the boat. Your head and shoulders will be drawn closer to the surface. As your body begins to break water, pull down hard with the right hand, give a flick with the hips, leaving head and shoulders until the last moment then sculling forward with the paddle for final support.

I would like to rely on the knowledge and experience of John Heath to supplement this section on the Eskimo roll with three examples of techniques developed by native kayakers: the Standard Greenland Roll, the Greenland Storm Roll, and the Alaska King Island Roll.

The Standard Greenland Roll

This historically significant roll is at the basis of both the Pawlata and Screw rolls. John's description follows:

John Heath

The solid lines indicate the starting position for a clockwise roll. Holding the paddle as shown, lean forward and to starboard until the kayak capsizes. Turn the illustration upside down and you will get a fish-eye view of the fully capsized position. To right yourself from this position:

1. Position the paddle to a planing angle by rolling your wrists.
2. Sweep the paddle outward in a planing arc, thus lifting your body to the surface.
3. Complete the roll by lifting your hands while applying opposing hand pressures and dragging the blade inward.

The Storm Roll

This roll is of interest because it leaves the kayaker in a stable, low profile position at the completion of the roll. As the name implies, it evolved for use in storms, and knowledge of this technique probably saved the lives of a large number of Greenlandic hunters. Explains John Heath:

> This method brings one up leaning well forward with the paddle extended to one side in a paddle brace. By keeping low, with the paddle extended, one can rest, or scull if necessary, to prevent another capsize.
>
> The basic movement of the Storm Roll is similar to the Standard Greenland method in that it consists of a sweep and a lift by using the paddle as a lever.
>
> But in the Standard Roll, the torso sweeps back with the paddle and the lift is done in a chinning attitude with the palms facing upward. In the Storm Roll, the torso does not sweep with the paddle, and the roll is finished with the paddle against the foredeck with the palms facing downward.
>
> 1. To practice the Storm Roll, lean far forward and keep the torso, head and arms as low as possible. Hold the paddle flat against the side of the kayak, below the starboard gunwale, parallel to the water surface and as far forward as possible with the right hand holding the blade near the end and the left hand holding it short of the middle. (This applies to a Greenland or other narrow unfeathered paddle.)
>
> 2. Capsize to the right.
>
> 3. To recover, push the aft end of the paddle forward, upward and inboard so that the knuckles brush the bottom of the kayak, keeping the blade flat against the kayak. At the same time, the left hand is brought outward in a sweep past the head, with the leading edge of the working blade at a 5- or 10-degree planing angle to the water surface. As

the right hand moves across the kayak bottom, the kayak rolls under it, so that the roll is completed with each hand at its respective gunwale and the paddle extended to the left in a brace.

The critical stage of recovery is illustrated below.

John Heath

The start (solid lines) and finish (broken lines) of a planing sweep are shown head-on. Success is almost certain if you have surfaced by the time you have completed the 90° sweep.

The King Island Roll

This roll was developed by King Islanders who usually used a single-bladed paddle. It is included here, because many kayakers carry a two-piece sectional paddle on the after deck where it is accessible to roll up with in the event of the loss of the main paddle. Also, in the event that a paddle breaks, the paddler can use the King Island roll with the remaining blade.

Before capsizing, the paddle is held horizontally in front of the body, with the blade to the left, parallel to the water surface. Capsize to your right.

Turn the illustration on page 108 upside down, for a fish-eye view of your capsized position. The arms are extended during, or immediately after, the capsize.

John Heath

To right yourself, sweep your paddle forward along the path shown by the arrow (illustration viewed upside down), the leading edge of your blade towards the surface of the water in order to gain lift.

Other Rolls

With practice it is possible to roll up with all manner of aids such as a flat board, a knife or even your hands. These techniques have evolved from necessity and any one of them can be considered a back-up to the failure of some other system. However, the need to roll at all usually indicates that the paddler is in major trouble and that the overwhelming conditions will remain after the roll has been completed. Unless the cause of capsize was falling asleep, the paddler is going to be in a weaker position than before the roll. The real value of a repertoire of rolls may well be the development of such fine paddling skills that there is little likelihood the rolls will ever be needed.

Note: A 1.5-square-foot ethafoam sandwich about 4 inches thick slipped over the paddle blade will assist greatly with early practice rolls by keeping the paddle close to the surface and providing solid support. This float can then be stored close in behind the paddler where it can be reached and used to hand roll the kayak in the event that a paddle is lost or broken.

A list of instructions such as this is a poor and probably bewildering substitute for learning from an expert who can see your mistakes and guide you clearly. Most instructors will have their own favoured variations of the roll. What matters is that you find a version that you can successfully perform when you have to.

OTHER RECOVERY METHODS—*Some Good, Some Not So Good*

In this book I would like to emphasize self-rescue techniques *other* than the Eskimo roll because a back-up technique is mandatory for sea voyages, and because workable alternative techniques are too often neglected.

The alternatives taught by most kayak schools in the past involved the use of one or two other kayaks in a variety of routines with code names such as T, TX, H and HI. These techniques are somewhat misleadingly known as *deep water rescues* and basically involve hoisting a flooded kayak across the decks of two others. They have their place as training for novice parties in calm water with empty boats, but they are often absurd techniques for the touring kayaker. They cannot be reliably performed with a loaded boat, and they are unreliable during the sort of conditions likely to cause a capsize. I have myself instructed unsuspecting Outward Bound pupils in these techniques, using the unconvincing line that "with a little more practice you will be able to do it in rough water." That is wrong and dangerous advice.

I repeat: under rough conditions with loaded kayaks, most one-kayak-across-the-other, swimming-pool coaching methods of rescue simply do not work. Fresh from the factory, a sea kayak may weigh as little as 40 or 50 pounds. Laden with gear and awash from a capsize, it can easily weigh a thousand pounds. A quarter of that weight cannot be lifted by two kayakers in calm water, much less be controlled in a raging sea.

Another method sometimes advocated for sea work is the Eskimo bow rescue. In this procedure, the capsized individual (we'll refer to a man) remains seated in the inverted boat, confidently thumping the upturned hull with his fists to attract the attention of his pals. He then sweeps his arms backward and forward in the hope of finding a friendly bow upon which to hoist himself smartly out of the water with a flick of the hips and, doubtless, a loud gasp. Again, this can be an interesting exercise. The weakness of the plan (which, incidentally, works fine in a swimming pool) is that in a touring situation it would normally take a good deal more than thirty seconds for a companion boat to be manoeuvred into a position of assistance. I doubt that a man who has accidentally capsized at sea will hang around upside down hoping that his mates will make it before he runs out of air.

Another technique sometimes advocated is the upside-down re-entry for the kayaker who, though capable of rolling, has failed to do so. In this case the individual dives and re-enters the boat upside down (provided the gear has not shifted to prevent this). The spray skirt is then replaced carefully, the paddle manoeuvred into position and the roll executed. This again works fine in swimming pools, but it is more of a stunt, a step beyond competence at rolling. Of course, the conditions that caused the capsize in the first place will still be there when you come up, and chances are the cockpit will have scooped up a tub full of water that destabilizes the boat. It is by no means a method for those who, because of exhaustion or extreme conditions, have just failed to complete the much simpler Eskimo roll.

Note: Ideally, the self-rescue method that you rely on as back-up to your Eskimo roll should leave you in a more stable position than you were in when you capsized.

Cold Water Self-Rescues

During capsize drill in 50°F water, even wearing a Farmer John wet suit, Vancouver paddler Duncan Murray discovered to his amazement that he had lost the functional use of his arms and fingers after only seven minutes in the water. In tropical waters the loss of dexterity would be unlikely to occur for three or four hours. Obviously, your margin of safety is going to be drastically affected by water temperature, and your technique for getting back into the boat should reflect this.

During a cold water capsize the priority, after having air to breathe, is to reduce the rate of body heat loss. This means getting out of the water as soon as you can. Start the process by recognizing that you are in a potentially life-threatening situation. Grab your wetsuit jacket and the largest rocket flare you have and haul your upper body out of the water across the upturned hull. Fire off the flare while you still have the dexterity to do so, then struggle into your wetsuit jacket (unless this involves removing effective protective clothing).

Your next move will depend on the type of boat you have, the amount and placement of buoyancy, the rescue aids you carry and the methods you have practised; and practise them you must, for it is not enough to simply carry a pump, paddle float or Sea Seat. You must be able to use your aids readily under moderate conditions if you are to have a hope of using them effectively under extreme ones.

The more stable your kayak, the easier the self-rescue, all other things being equal. The more buoyancy you have, the more stable the boat when it is awash. Obviously then, a beamy single with a pod or sea sock is going to be a lot easier to re-enter than a narrow single with loose-fitting air-bags, or, worse, with no buoyancy at all.

A most sobering exercise is to dump your kayak and try to re-enter it with 6 inches of water in the cockpit. Even with none of the destabilizing slosh and splash inside the boat, you would still find it difficult to maintain your balance astride the cockpit. When you adopt the more efficient low profile technique of hugging the after-deck while you insert your legs inside the cockpit then twist your body into the seat, you will still find it hard to re-enter reliably. Given the sort of conditions that cause a capsize in the first place, it will soon become clear that you have discovered a formula for disaster, since each time you fail (and get colder) diminishes your chances of success on the next attempt. Your priorities are: get out of the cold water, and stabilize the kayak enough to pump out the water. Here's where the rescue aids come in.

Outrigger Self-Rescue

This rescue, popularized by Matt and Cam Broze of Seattle, involves using a rigid foam paddle float or twin-chambered inflatable bag designed to slip over the blade of the paddle as an outrigger to provide sufficient stability for the paddler to re-enter the kayak, attach the spray cover and pump out the water. It requires carrying the paddle float

Cam Broze

Outrigger Self-Rescue

device together with a deck-rigging configuration capable of quickly securing the paddle blade to the boat.

METHOD

1 Right the kayak.
2 Secure the paddle blade to the after deck (down wind).
3 Attach the paddle float to the blade.
4 Position yourself forward of the paddle shaft then swim your upper body onto the stern deck, face down with most of your weight supported on the paddle float.
5 Insert one leg into the cockpit then the other and twist around into the seat.
6 Reattach your spray skirt.
7 Pump out the boat.
8 Retrieve your paddle.

APPLICATION: Suitable for rough water self-rescues by paddlers in singles or doubles, this is the most dependable back-up to the roll that I know of.

LIMITATIONS: The rescue requires practice to clarify the

routine and develop a feel for the balance. In addition, there appear to be conditions of surf and strong currents against strong winds which make this rescue nearly impossible to complete. In surf you would do well to concentrate on getting ashore.

Sea Trek Paddle Float Rescue

This aid rescue is similar to the Outrigger Self-Rescue and was developed by Will Nordby and Bob Licht of San Francisco. Like the Broze method, it uses an inflatable paddle float, but does not attach the paddle to the kayak.

METHOD:

1 Bail out of the kayak and right it.
2 Swim to the downwind side of the boat.
3 Slip the paddle float over the blade and inflate it.
4 Position yourself aft of the paddle shaft. (*Note:* This may vary depending on the boat you use.)
5 Hold the base of the other paddle blade tightly against the back of the coaming with the hand close to the cockpit so that the paddle is held at right angles to the kayak. The other hand grasps the edge of the rear hatch or deck rigging.
6 Swim up onto the after deck and hook the feet over the paddle shaft close to the float.
7 Keeping most of your weight on the outrigger, step into the cockpit with the nearest leg.
8 Move your second hand onto the paddle shaft and then, transferring most of your weight onto your hands, slide your second leg up the paddle shaft and step into the cockpit.
9 Hold your hand position while leaning on the outrigger then rotate your body into the seat.
10 Replace the spray cover then pump the boat dry.

APPLICATION: This method is suitable for moderate conditions where a very quick rescue can be performed.

LIMITATIONS: It requires considerable upper body strength, agility and dexterity to perform the rescue. If the hands are very cold, you could find yourself unable to grip the paddle shaft effectively. (Use the Broze method discussed above.) In very rough conditions, you may also find it difficult to hold the paddle at right angles to the boat or indeed hold it at all. But this method's main disadvantage, compared to the fixed outrigger method, is that the flooded kayak is much less stable after re-entry. An option would be to switch to a fixed outrigger once re-entry was complete, a simple matter given the correct deck rigging.

The Inflatable Cushion/Raft Rescue

This system involves inflating a raft or mattress which is large enough to hold the paddler clear of the water or to be used as a support for an outrigger brace. One such device (the Sea Seat) was developed by Professor John Hayward of the University of Victoria in British Columbia. It consists of an orally inflatable cushion with a lanyard for attachment to the kayak. (A miniature life raft such as those used by downed pilots is another viable rescue/survival device for kayakers. It has the advantage of being inflated by compressed air. Unfortunately, such rafts are seldom available on the civilian market.)

METHOD:
1 After a capsize, remove the folded Sea Seat from its storage pouch (which will ideally be on your person) and clip it into the deck rigging near the cockpit.
2 Fasten the paddle to the bow line or paddle leash.
3 Lie across the upturned hull of your boat to reduce heat loss.

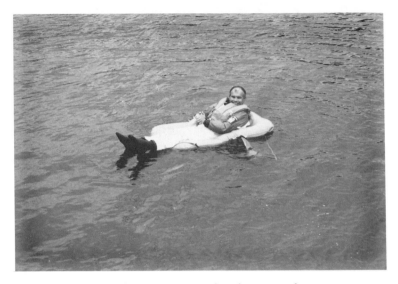

The Ecomarine sea kayak rescue raft

4 Inflate the Sea Seat (two to four minutes) then
  a lay the paddle across the Sea Seat and onto the back of
    the coaming of the boat, using the Sea Seat as an over-
    sized paddle float, *or*
  b climb onto the Sea Seat and draw it close enough to the
    boat for it to be used as a refuge from the cold water
    while you pump.

APPLICATION: This is a good back-up system for really cold water or where you might have trouble pumping the boat dry such as with some of the large-volume folding doubles. A strong case can also be made for having a Sea Seat along when you have children in the kayak. During a scenario of this type, the child, whose rate of heat loss is much greater than that of an adult, could be "stowed" on the inflated seat while the adult attempted to re-enter the boat.

LIMITATIONS: Blowing up the seat orally is hard work and loses precious time. Some sort of compressed air system would be a significant advantage. The Sea Seat also requires a considerable amount of agility, upper body strength and technique to mount successfully so practice is recommended. A larger, more stable self-inflating device would be a great advantage.

Note: In any of the above three rescues, if unmanageable conditions caused the capsize then you should seriously consider maintaining the outrigger or Sea Seat in position alongside the boat until conditions modify.

It should be clear by now that I favour self-reliance as both your first and second line of defence against a capsize. This is not to deny value to systems that use the presence of others when they are around but rather stresses that the first back-up system of rescue you learn should be the one you can perform alone.

ASSISTED RESCUES

Paddle Stirrup Method (PS Rescue)
This rescue requires the participation of at least one other kayak. It is a refinement of Lee Moyer's sling rescue, developed by the Sea Kayak Association of B.C.

METHOD:
1 The rescue kayak pulls alongside the capsized boat on the upwind side.
2 The paddles are laid across the upturned hull and held in the crook of the rescuer's arm. He then reaches across the hull and rights the boat.

3 A sling made with about 6 feet of floating rope is slipped over both paddles close to the side of the flooded kayak using a cat's paw knot.

4 The capsized paddler swims to the downwind side of the two boats, puts one foot in the sling, steps up and slips one leg into the cockpit then the other with a turn around into the seat.

5 The spray skirt is fitted and the boat pumped dry.

Note: a modification of this rescue can be used to recover an unconscious or incapacitated paddler, though for this situation it helps to have a third boat in the raft in which case the sling is dispensed with. The rescuer, gaining support from the upturned boat, leans over, grabs the swimmer by the belt or seat of the pants then hauls him/her across the two boats. Such a rescue is a great deal easier when done from a double with its extra hands and added stability.

APPLICATION: The sling method is a particularly good rescue for someone with poor upper body strength or very cold hands and arms since it relies upon the powerful leg muscles to lift the swimmer out of the water and into his/her boat. It is also a good method for an experienced paddler to administer to a novice since it is simple and can be done with a fully loaded kayak just as readily as an empty one. The rescuer remains in a stable position throughout the rescue and can assist and orient the shivering wretch who has just been hauled from the ocean.

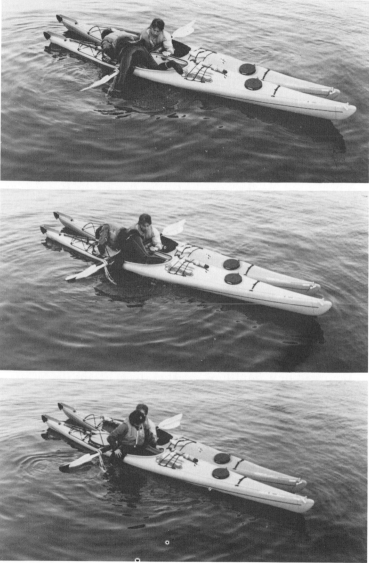

The PS Rescue

Grant Thompson

LIMITATIONS: This rescue is limited to moderate, choppy conditions because of the hazard of having two boats rafted in close while the seas are rough. It requires a piece of equipment (the rope loop), and there is always the risk that the person in the water will poke his/her leg through the sling and become snared. In addition, the risk of breaking paddles is high when heavy people are to be rescued.

Pump & Re-entry (Doubles)

There are two versions or stages to the doubles pump and re-entry method. The first works well for moderate seas and has been used by the Special Boat Section of the Royal Marines since World War II. Stage two is essentially the same technique adapted for use in heavy seas or very choppy water.

Stage 1

1 Once capsized, each partner checks that the other is swimming clear, that both paddles are accounted for and that the boat is not in danger of being blown away.

2 The No. 2 (stern) person gives his/her paddle to No. 1, who swims to the bow. No. 2 then mantleshelves onto the upturned hull amidships, reaches over, grasps the far gunwale and flips backward into the water, pulling the kayak over with him/her.

3 No. 2 then re-enters by climbing astride the after-deck while No. 1 steadies the boat by hugging the bow.

4 No. 2 then steadies the kayak with a sculling support stroke while No. 1 lays across the cockpit then, facing down and backward, slips into the cockpit and twists into the seat. As far as possible the person re-entering should check first to make sure that dislodged gear is not blocking access.

5 Spray skirts are secured; the boat is pumped and bailed dry.

If you are in a lightly loaded double, there is a useful alternative for step 3 of this method. Both kayakers dive and come up with their heads inside the boat and their shoulders in the cockpits. They inflate their life vests when necessary then grip the coaming and give a synchronized push on one side while holding firm to the other. A light boat flipped in this way will have less water inside and will therefore be faster to pump and more stable to re-enter.

If a second kayak is standing by during re-entry, you will be able to brace your paddles across the two boats, steadying the empty craft and giving you a convenient grip as you hoist yourself out of the water, or use a Paddle Stirrup rescue.

The sea, however, has a way of playing havoc with the straightforward antics of this stage. You will find that waves constantly sweep over the waterlogged kayak, defying your attempts to pump it dry. The problem is invariably that the boat is too low in the water. In warm climates, one or both of you is going to have to get back into the sea to lighten it. In cold water, you must have a wetsuit or drysuit on to consider such a move. If you have no such thermal protection and do not have an inflatable raft, your best bet is to stay in the boat, sealing it as best you can—and pumping like hell.

Stage 2: The Extreme Procedure

1 If the boat rides too low with your weight on board, re-enter the water, leaving the spray skirts in position on the boat. (Spray skirts with zippers make this especially easy.)
2 Unless fresh water is going to be in short supply, your water containers should be emptied then shoved back inside to give extra buoyancy. Air mattresses can be partially inflated inside the boat, and heavy objects such as weight-belts and canned food can be ditched or transferred to another boat. All this is so that you can pump water out faster

Breaking waves make for the most difficult rescue conditions.

than it sloshes in, and of course the tighter your boat seals, the fewer problems you will have.

3 No. 2 ties off the No. 1 spray skirt so no water can enter (the bow painter can be used for this), then ties off the No. 2 spray skirt around the hand pump—unless you are using a built-in hand or electric pump, in which case both spray skirts are tied off.

4 Only when the kayak is pumped dry and floating high should you attempt to re-enter it as described in Stage 1.

A second kayak can help considerably during this operation (particularly by keeping the swimmers out of the cold water), but be prepared to handle it unassisted.

Note: Buoyancy is the critical factor in any pump and re-entry operation. Anything you can do to increase it will help.

Earlier in this chapter I mentioned a series of group rescues which, although I personally don't trust them for laden kayaks, have their place on club trips particularly with lightly loaded boats under moderate conditions. These include the TX, HI, and more questionable All-In Rescue.

The TX Rescue

This is a rescue for two paddlers, one of whom capsizes well within the level of capabilities of the other. It can also be used by an experienced paddler who comes upon someone in difficulties in a canoe or kayak since the system does not depend heavily upon the experience of the capsized paddler.

METHOD:

1 The capsized boat is left inverted so as to trap as much air as possible as it is manoeuvred into a position at right angles to the hull of the rescuing craft.
2 The rescue paddler snatches the bow of the capsized boat over the fore-deck of his own kayak as quickly as possible so as to minimize the amount of water entering the cockpit.
3 The swimmer helps manhandle the upturned kayak across the deck of the rescue boat, rocking it from the bow to help remove the excess water.
4 When the boat has been drained, it is rolled over and slipped back into the water. The kayak can then be re-entered using the Paddle Stirrup method.

LIMITATIONS: This method is not appropriate for loaded boats, doubles or rough conditions. It is also destructive of spray skirts and fibreglass kayaks and can injure fingers and hands.

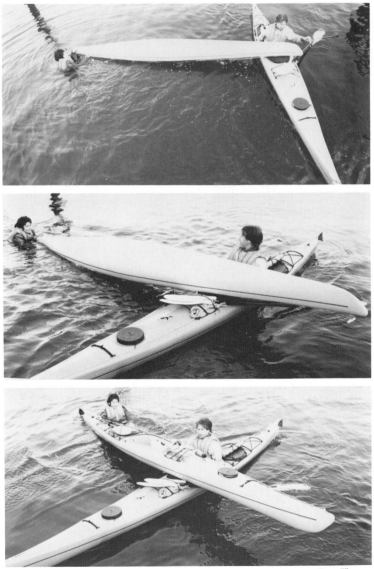

The TX Rescue

Grant Thompson

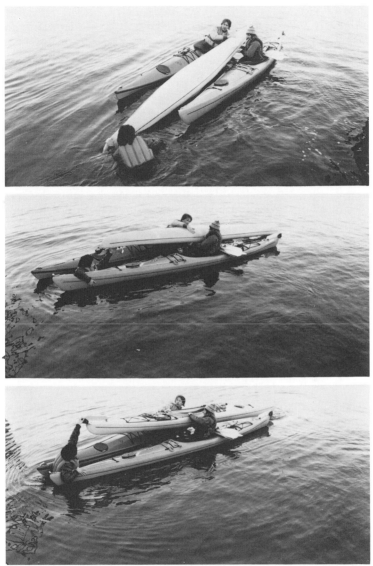

Grant Thompson

The HI Rescue

The HI Rescue

This is a rescue for one of three kayaks. It got its name not because everyone involved sits waving at beachside spectators but because the boats, when seen from a rescuing helicopter, will look either like a squished H or an impacted I (or maybe a K or an N depending on the frequency of large waves). It can also be used to rescue kayakers or canoeists outside your group since, when conditions are fairly calm, it can provide a stable platform.

METHOD:

1 The capsized boat is kept upside down.
2 The two companion boats come alongside, collect the unfortunate's paddle and form a bridge between their two cockpits with the bundle of three paddles.
3 The capsized boat is hauled between the rescue craft then lifted across the bundle of paddles assisted by the swimmer, who is hanging off the bow of one of the rescue boats. Rocking timed to coincide with passing waves will remove most of the water from the boat.
4 The boat is then turned over and re-launched between the two "nurse" kayaks.
5 The paddler re-enters.

APPLICATION: This is a fine rescue for teaching a group of novice paddlers how to work together or for building character. With practice, it can be performed quickly under moderate sea conditions.

LIMITATIONS: The method is not appropriate for loaded boats, doubles or rough conditions. It can damage the paddle shafts, even in extreme cases breaking the whole bunch. Perhaps its worst feature is that if the swimmer lets go of one of the rescue boats in a strong wind, the whole contraption could take off faster than he or she could hope to swim.

The All-In Rescue

This rescue is designed for the situation in which an entire group is blown over by a gust of wind. It is assumed that all are close enough to pull their boats together.

METHOD:

1 Keeping all the boats in a group, select the one which is riding highest and use it as the fulcrum for a modified TX rescue.

2 With one swimmer on each side of the most buoyant boat, heave the bow of the boat to be emptied across the up-turned hull.

3 When the cockpit is sitting on the hull of the pivot boat, rock gently to empty both ends of water. (Take care not to let air escape from the pivot boat.)

4 Right the emptied kayak and assist the paddler into it using a stirrup from a paddle held across the two boats.

5 The rest of the boats are then emptied using the TX rescue or a pump and re-entry Paddle Stirrup rescue.

Note: It is necessary to get the strongest, most competent paddler out of the water first since that person will need to do the remaining rescues. The next person back in a boat should probably be the most hypothermic.

APPLICATION: This is a desperate, last-ditch system for group rescue. Its usefulness is considerably greater in warm water than cold.

LIMITATIONS: This is definitely a flawed rescue, and my principal reason for including it is to highlight its limitations since it is often advocated as a viable system by people confusing classroom exercises with the realities of the sea. For a start, it is extremely unlikely that any party that is all blown over at one time will be close enough to stay in contact, much less pull the boats together. To attempt to do so would just waste valuable time and energy which would be better used performing self-rescues. Secondly, it has almost no chance of being performed with a loaded boat, let alone a double. Thirdly, it leaves people floating idly in the water waiting their turn. In cold water these people only have ten to twenty minutes of being functional, and when their time comes for a TX, they might as well be using stumps instead of hands. Even training with this method runs the risk of creating some potentially tragic illusions about safety.

I would suggest that the most useful procedure for a situation where all the boats are blown over by a squall is to have every person perform his/her own self-rescue; this enables the successful ones to go around and assist the rest with Paddle Stirrup rescues.

The Curl

The curl is a useful technique, apparently developed by English instructor and author Derek Hutchinson for draining water from a partially waterlogged kayak, a condition known as Cleopatra's needle which, if not treated promptly, might leave you sans kayak.

METHOD:

1 The cockpit of the partially submerged kayak is hooked with the hand or foot of a swimmer gaining support from the bow of a rescue boat, and slowly lifted until it lies parallel to the rescue boat. This need not require a great deal of strength so long as none of the boat is lifted out of the water.

2 When the cockpit of the submerged kayak is close along-side and slightly in front of the rescue boat's cockpit, the swimmer leans across the rescue boat's deck and, turning

Grant Thompson

The Curl is useful for emptying a seriously flooded boat.

the flooded boat on its side, grasps the cockpit rim, palms uppermost, elbows braced on the rescue boat. With the two boats touching, the swimmer slowly leans back, breaking the air seal and allowing water to flood gently out of the cockpit. If care is taken with the use of leverage, and enough time is allowed for the boat to drain slowly, most of the water can be eliminated.

3 During the last phase, the rescuing kayaker can assist by leaning gently away from the now partially emptied kayak so that almost no strength is required by the swimmer.

APPLICATION: This is useful for a seriously flooded kayak, but only, of course, when there is a second kayak standing by. It can be incorporated in a number of foreseeable rescue scenarios where it may be necessary to remove most of the water from a boat with poor buoyancy before attempts are made to re-enter it.

LIMITATIONS: The curl works better with small light singles than with large doubles since the latter require both paddlers to "curl" simultaneously in separate cockpits across the rescue boat.

Swimmer Rescue

In the event that a kayaker has to rescue a swimmer, there are several alternatives depending upon the type of kayak being used, the size of the individual being rescued and the skill of both parties. Basically, all involve getting the swimmer out of the water and onto or into the kayak. This is much faster than towing a person and greatly reduces heat loss.

METHOD:
1 Be sure the swimmer is neither panicking nor likely to disobey your directions.
2 Hold the kayak stern to the wind. This position gives you a view of both the swimmer and approaching waves as you look back.
3 Instruct the swimmer to crawl over the stern of your boat onto the after deck to a point where his/her head is close to your back. Your passenger should be lying face down as low as possible with his/her legs over the side to enhance the stability of the kayak.
4 Paddle to safety.

APPLICATION: This method can be used for rescuing a kayaker whose kayak has sunk as well as rescuing a swimmer or board sailor in difficulty. Long distances can be covered, especially if the swimmer's legs can be lifted out of the water.

LIMITATIONS: As previously stated, much of the success of this operation depends on the kayak, kayaker and swimmer involved. Kayaks with low, buoyant sterns are more suitable than those with peaked, low volume ones. A 105-pound person is obviously going to threaten the stability of the kayak less than a 280 pounder, and a 34-inch double is going to require a lot less balancing than a 20-inch single. A great deal also depends upon the paddling skill of the kayaker since someone with a really strong brace could get to shore with an epileptic walrus on deck. There is also doubtless a limit to the degree of turbulence in which it is practical to attempt this rescue, though this too can be countered by the determination of those involved, or the use of special equipment such as life rafts.

The swimmer's ability to crawl onto and balance on the after deck of the kayak will be affected by the degree of hypothermia present. If the swimmer is barely able to move, you may find it easier to assist if (s)he crawls up onto the forward deck. This position does not enhance the handling of the kayak, but it gives you a better idea of the victim's condition. Rudders and deck equipment can also injure or impede a victim's efforts.

Note: Any self-rescue or group rescue must be practised in rough water and controlled conditions to be sure it works for you. In the case of group rescues, practise sessions should give participants an opportunity to experience the various methods from the perspective of both the rescuer and the victim.

B. & G. Epting

4
Navigation

This chapter is not designed to teach basic navigation. For that I would refer you to *Fundamentals of Kayak Navigation* by David Burch. The chapter assumes familiarity with chart and compass, and a degree of competence in basic navigational skills. With that as a basis, it discusses some special difficulties and their solutions using minimal equipment. The kayak, remember, is the smallest, simplest ocean-going craft there is. What I have to say here may well raise the eyebrows of navigators schooled in the methods of a modern navy, but the kayak handles very differently from a motor vessel. The apparent "bush navigator" approach of the following pages is not meant to repudiate precise navigation; rather, it is an acknowledgement of its limits when applied to kayaks at sea.

Most kayak navigation is done by dead reckoning, which in my terms is navigation as an art rather than a science. It involves the use of nautical charts, a watch, dividers, compass, protractor and a great deal of knowledge of weather, tides, currents and wave patterns, all rolled into what eventually becomes an elusive "feel for the sea." You will also need another commodity which can't be found in the chandlery—the knack of turning the answers to old problems into the solutions for new ones. Good dead reckoning means being constantly aware of your approximate position then using the techniques at your disposal to check and clarify that position. To be unsure of your position on any part of a routine coastal paddle is inexcusable. From your chart, you should be able to anticipate the next problem or the next safe landing. If you find yourself making repeated navigational errors, then brush up fast on your map and compass work.

TOOLS OF THE TRADE

Nautical charts are too large to handle in a kayak. They should be cut carefully into one-foot squares and water-proofed *both* sides with clear adhesive plastic. Take care always to include a section of the corresponding latitudinal degree markings so that you can accurately measure distance. Where possible, include a compass rose and make a note of relevant warnings to mariners. For plotting on a plastic-covered chart, use a chinagraph pencil, which can be erased with a cloth or the back of your hand.

British Admiralty charts are usually reliable for deep water readings and sometimes for shallow water ones, but a kayaker cannot always depend on the latter, nor can you always rely on the existence of old landmarks. I have known charts on which not only towns but also whole islands are omitted, lights misplaced and marked channels nonexistent. Perhaps the early cartographers reasoned that the waters were too shallow to interest navigators, but in-shore details are of paramount importance to the kayaker. National Ocean Service charts are usually more accurate, as they are often drawn from aerial photographs. Ordnance Survey or topographical maps are more reliable for land detail such as roads, buildings and contours, and where they exist, these maps may be used in conjunction with your chart.

It is not good enough to hold your chart to the deck of the kayak by a piece of shock cord. You cannot afford to lose it of all things. A waterproof folder with a clear plastic window through which the chart can be viewed should be attached firmly to the boat forward of the cockpit. If shock cord loops are fitted to its rear corners, this cover can extend over the spray skirt, where it will offer added protection against breaking waves while holding the chart in the most perfect position to be read as you paddle. The basic orienteering compass is adequate for a kayak. It can be slipped inside the map case through the velcro-sealed entrance at the rear end of the case. It will eliminate the need for a protractor and is accurate enough for you to paddle to within 5 degrees of your intended course—which is as good as you can reasonably expect from a kayak. Orienteering compasses are inexpensive, and because of their low profile, there is little chance of their being knocked overboard.

Keep a pair of brass dividers in the map case so that you can quickly and accurately check distances during the day. It is a good idea to do this frequently against the clock until you have developed a firm sense of speed without constantly having to calculate it.

A diver's watch is ideal for a kayaker and vital for estimation of distances at sea. There are many inexpensive models which are quite adequate.

A radio direction finder (RDF) takes navigation beyond dead reckoning, but it is a useful aid to navigation in certain parts of the world. The coasts of Europe and the U.K. as well as the Bahamas and North America are covered with set frequency transmitters, and a small RDF carried in a kayak can fix your position by tuning in on two of these. I dare say it won't be long before such navigational equipment is available in pocket calculator size.

A sextant and tables is another possible aid for those crossing open ocean or running the risk of being blown out to sea. I have never carried either an RDF or a sextant on any of my trips, though I could have used them on a number of occasions to confirm my dead reckoning. The sextant may also be used for calculating distances by measuring the angles to summits of known altitude, but the bulk of the instrument and its tables makes most kayakers think more than twice before bringing one aboard. Hannes Lindemann carried two air force surplus sextants on his Atlantic crossing but finished the epic trip by dead reckoning after losing both in capsizes. Ed Gillet had better luck; he managed to maintain his course to Hawaii precisely and arrived with both his sextants.

TAKING RANGES & BEARINGS AND ESTIMATING SPEED & DISTANCE IN THE WIND

Most sea kayaking is done within sight of land, and the simplest method of locating your position is by ranges or transits. Choose a pair of stationary objects which you can see and which are shown on your chart; then watch for them to *range,* or line up, as you paddle by. A line drawn through the objects on your chart will match the range line through the objects, and your position is necessarily somewhere along that line. If you can gauge the distance to the objects, you can gauge your position. If you combine the range line with a compass bearing on a third object, the intersection on your chart of the range line and bearing line will give you your position exactly. Even without the compass, you may be able to find two simultaneous ranges, and the intersection of these two lines will again give you a plot of your precise position (see page 137, example A). Buoys, remember, are likely to move, and should therefore not be used for ranges or bearings if accuracy is required.

Attentive coastal kayakers draw up dozens of mental transit lines as they paddle along. They will notice one object passing another on the shore, and not only will they have

During coastal travel, keep tabs on your location by a series of fixes using ranges (A), bearings (B), or both.

fixed a mental range line but they also will be able to estimate from it how fast the current is running and how much the wind is affecting them. In short, through a vast number of what eventually become automatic ranges, a kayaker can gather a total picture of his/her progress.

The use of a compass in a kayak introduces some new and exciting ways to make mistakes. Only if you always pack your kayak the same way and always keep the compass in the same spot can the compass deviation be reliably known. The fact is, though, that you will probably have to move the compass around in order to take bearings. And if you put your flashlight on deck to examine the needle which is to guide you through the foggy dark, your needle will probably be following you instead of the other way around. The solutions to these problems are to load all ferrous metals and radios well clear of the compass and to use a chemical light. With the objective deviation hazard minimized, you will be able to dedicate yourself to a sometimes far more fecund source of error—your use of the instrument.

Some orienteering compasses can be conveniently adjusted to compensate for local variation. Take care to correct either the compass or the bearings you take with it, but not both.

Normally a navigator would transfer the bearing to the chart with a parallel rule, and it would be nice to have one aboard, but most kayakers don't and will try to do it by eye —with the aid of two fat fingers and a thumb. This is another source of considerable error! As a substitute for the awkward parallel rule, a perspex grid about 10 inches square can be stored conveniently inside the map holder. Or you may choose to use a combination protractor–plotter instead, correcting all bearings to true and working the protractor against a convenient longitude line.

A useful way to get an approximate idea of your position during a crossing is to get your line of travel by means of a bearing on your point of departure or destination, then estimate your distance along this line by multiplying your time by your known speed of travel. The obvious weakness in this formula is the great variability of "known speed of travel." The following table is a series of estimates based on a standard ten-hour paddle with approximately five minutes' rest each hour and about half an hour for lunch, except in the case of high head winds, where the estimates assume that you must snatch food while paddling. Corrections for current must naturally be made according to conditions.

	Wind Speed in knots	Kayak Speed in knots	
	20 – 30	1.50 – 0.75	
HEADWIND	15 – 20	2.25 – 1.50	
	10 – 15	2.50 – 2.25	
	5 – 10	2.75 – 2.50	
	0 – 5	3.00 – 2.75	
	0 – 5	3.00 – 3.25	
	5 – 10	3.25 – 3.50	
STERN WIND	10 – 20	3.50 – 4.00 ⎫	Surfing
	20 – 30	4.00 – 5.00 ⎭	

A beam wind will usually affect your course, not your rate of travel, unless it is so strong as to interfere with your paddling. Winds forward and aft of the beam naturally have an effect on your speed which varies according to their angle.

OPEN CROSSINGS

The open ocean is normally a friendly environment for a sea kayak. Waves are regular and predictable, winds and currents tend to be constant. Island hopping, which often includes open water, can be trickier, however. You may have a variable current or tidal flow to contend with, disturbed seas on each side of the crossing near land which is exposed to bad weather, and also the big wave exposure of open sea. Part of your planning when island hopping is to gain a clear picture of what the tidal flow will be doing. If local tide tables prove inaccurate, keep a close watch on the ebb and flow yourself. Follow the phases of the moon so that you will know when to expect the strongest flows. When you are on the move constantly, you will become as familiar with the phases of the moon and the state of the tide as you normally are with day and night.

Paddling a kayak from one island to another across open sea poses some of the more serious navigational problems you will normally have to face. Let's assume your group is camped on a calm bay on the sheltered side of an island and you plan to paddle 25 miles to a high island due north, a major crossing by paddling standards. You know that there is a steady one-knot current running from east to west and that the wind is forecast at 10 to 15 knots from the east-northeast.

A knowledge of your cruising speed under varying conditions is vital. This information is best obtained not from the foregoing table but from frequent observations and calculation of *your* average speed over a whole day of reasonably constant conditions. A measurement of your speed over an hour or two is meaningless for longer-distance calculations.

Let us say that in the past you have calculated your average speed to be 2.5 knots under conditions such as our hypothetical crossing. You know that the 25 nautical miles will take you ten hours. (I would call that eleven just to be on the safe side.) It gets dark at seven o'clock in the evening so you want to be in by five—in case you have to search for a landing or you find yourselves delayed. Counting back eleven hours, your scheduled departure will be for six o'clock in the morning. If your group takes the normal two hours to get away in the mornings, that means getting up at four o'clock.

There is a way of estimating the allowance you will have to make for that one-knot current: take a piece of note paper and draw a line BC of appropriate length for the current, at 1 knot to the inch. At a right angle to BC, draw a line BZ of indefinite length. Now lay the ruler so that the zero mark is at C and your paddling speed (again at 1 knot to the inch) is on the line BZ. Mark the point where the lines cross as A. The

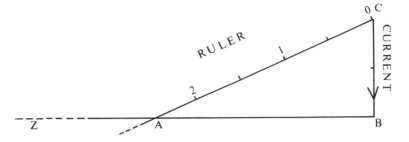

angle BAC is your necessary correction, and the length of AB tells you how far over ground you will travel in one hour.

Alas, life is not so simple. Because of your slow cruising speed relative to the current, not to mention the current's variability, you cannot rely on being able to maintain this course. There is usually an allowance to be made for wind, but even neglecting that for the moment, you must take the calculated correction for current as a guide only—one which has to be constantly checked.

Let us assume, for example, that you depart on schedule and paddle down the sheltered coast to the nearest point of land to your destination. After a brief pause to see that the bilge pumps are sucking water and the spray skirt is correctly secured, you head out into the rough water. Coming from the open sea, the waves are 6 feet and lumpy off the headland because of the current and rebound effect. Paddle steadily on your intended course (in this case due north plus or minus the magnetic variation for the area plus the angle BAC) for a distance of about a half mile. That should take you about ten minutes. Then sight along the shaft of your paddle to your destination (or your departure point, if your destination is beyond the horizon or is obscured). Hold the kayak to your course (as corrected for current) while making this sighting. Then lay the shaft of your paddle across your compass; you should get a reading against the shaft which corresponds to the *uncorrected* compass course plotted on your chart. If it does not correspond, correct the set of your boat to the current until it does. Watch carefully for changes in the current flow. Do you expect it to ease up or change direction with a change of tide? If so, you should know when to expect that change.

Note: It is prudent to err on the weather side of the current and wind during the first part of such a crossing since it is much easier to correct for an overestimation of current than for an underestimation. Once you have decided on a set for the crossing, check it at least once an hour using your paddle shaft. The presence of shoals can greatly affect the speed of the current—pushing a 1.5-knot surface current to as much as 4 knots on occasions. Your chart should show these shoals. Their worst effects can often be avoided by skirting them upstream.

Should rain or haze obscure land, you must combine your total knowledge of all forces affecting your passage then hold your course accordingly. Have faith in your reasoned decision. The inability to see where you are going can rapidly undermine confidence if you are not prepared for it. Changes of current are difficult to spot unless related to some stationary object such as land or a buoy, but an experienced eye can sometimes detect them from the altered shape of the waves. In fog, your ears will alert you to the proximity of surf, and in rain, visibility is normally sufficient to avoid danger.

Here is an unhypothetical example of navigating by the paddle shaft. There is a 21-mile crossing from Trinidad to Tobago in the West Indies, known as the Galleon Passage. It has a steady current of 2 to 2.5 knots. Our party paddled it at night, going from Toco lighthouse on Trinidad to Scarborough lighthouse on Tobago. Both lighthouses were visible the whole way except during brief squalls. Our allowance for the current was frequently as high as 70 degrees from our intended course. Total crossing time: nine hours. Although use

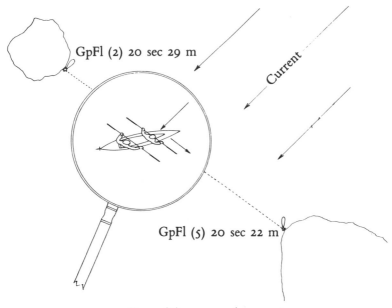

GpFl (2) 20 sec 29 m

Current

GpFl (5) 20 sec 22 m

Ferry-gliding across the current

of the compass became necessary in squalls, most of the time
we simply lined up the two lights along the paddle shafts and
varied our set to keep them in line—exactly as a river kayaker
would ferry-glide from one bank to another.

A different approach was needed on the next leg of that
particular journey, where the distance was far greater: 80
miles of open sea to Grenada, in the Windward Islands. Departure was from a point 65 miles east and 50 miles south of
Grenada, paddling due north so as to allow the current to
carry us onto the island. This was considerably safer than
ferry-gliding as it gave more sea room to correct for unexpected delays—which could not have been made up had we
been down-current. Rain obscured our destination until
twenty-five hours after leaving Tobago. As soon as a land

sighting was made, the course was adjusted to keep up-weather of the island, thus assuring seaway for the latter stages of the paddle—a particularly necessary precaution in this case because of a shoal to the southwest, which causes the current to accelerate with nasty overfalls and a poor chance of fighting it back to the island.

MORE ABOUT WIND

Wind can affect the sea kayaker even more than current, but paddle-shaft navigation works for judging its effects as well. The east-northeast wind on our hypothetical crossing a few pages ago could be very difficult for a northbound kayak unless it is fitted with an effective rudder to counter the infuriating tendency to turn into such a wind despite every paddling technique you can apply. In this example, however, you would be paddling almost exactly east-northeast by virtue of the allowance you are making for the current, so you need not correct course for the wind at all. You need only take into account that your average speed will be somewhat reduced. The wind, we said, was forecast at 10 to 15 knots, so you could expect it to cut your speed by at least half a knot.

Should the wind swing more to the east, however, you would need to increase the angle of your set by a few degrees to compensate. Just how much allowance you make will depend on a variety of factors, including the weather outlook. Are you trying to gain seaway (getting upweather of your destination)? Has the wind been on the increase? And what is the condition of your party?

If the island to which you are paddling is steep-to and mountainous, be prepared for disturbed gusty winds near the shore, with williwaws, downdrafts and blasts coming from odd directions as a result of the funneling effect down valleys.

One such downdraft is the infamous White Squall off the southern end of the island of Dominica, which recently struck a 60-foot yacht so savagely that she was laid hard over. Water flooded through her open hatches and she sank in seconds.

Landforms such as Cabo Froward in the Strait of Magellan so disturb the flow of winds that williwaws, twisters and appalling downdrafts are almost daily occurrences. Indeed, in blustery weather half a dozen or more williwaws may play about the cape at one time.

You cannot expect real progress against a wind in excess of 30 knots. You will barely hold your own against one of 40. But if you paddle at sea long enough, you will sometimes have to contend with even higher winds, especially in squalls, when you may have to settle for a ride backward until the gust eases—at which point you can resume your forward crawl.

One of the worst aspects of really strong head wind is that it prevents you from pausing. Assuming your normal speed is 3 knots, a one-knot headway in a strong wind means that you will be blown back at 2 knots if you stop. Seen another way, it means that half an hour's pause in a strong wind demands another full hour of paddling just to regain your previous position. Such conditions can be soul destroying, and these are the situations in which you will be grateful for a small-volume, foot- or battery-operated bilge pump, or a large sea-chute, or both.

Normally one would be well advised to avoid making inter-island crossings such as our hypothetical one in winds exceeding 20 knots if they are from the forward quarter. From anywhere astern, however, such a strong breeze may be a great asset—although you will still need to make allowances for drift depending on how close abeam it is blowing.

NAVIGATING IN THE PRESENCE OF COASTAL WINDS

In general terms, coastal paddling may be classified according to whether the wind is onto the land (a lee shore) or off the land (a windward shore).

Unprotected lee shores are normally dangerous. They are usually visited by heavy surf and may be bristling with rock or coral reefs. The safest thing to have under the surf, of course, is a nice sandy beach. Whenever you are obliged to paddle a lee shore, plan your arrival for certain daylight and choose as a landing site a sheltered cove or an area protected by an offshore reef. This may not always be possible, and heavy surf may make landing at your intended destination too risky. In that case—if there is no nearby alternative—you have either to continue paddling throughout the night and find a safe landing at dawn, or to search until dark, then anchor offshore and wait until dawn to see what your choices are. Be warned, however, that you should not count on your anchor if the wind is strong, and it is extremely dangerous to attempt to land on an unknown lee shore in the dark.

The sea off a lee shore is usually rougher than open sea, and chaotic rebound waves develop if the coast is at all steep-to. If it is a gently sloping beach, the waves will steepen long before they break. Stay well beyond the line of breakers and keep a weather eye open for the rogue wave which may peak a hundred yards farther out than the rest.

Although it is undeniably dangerous, the lee shore does not hold the same terror for kayakers as it did for the sailors of the old windjammers, whose ships were often swept onto the rocks when they ran out of seaway. Even modern yachts which can beat effectively to windward must take care never to be caught in a gale on a lee shore. You are less at the mercy of the wind in a kayak, but being caught on a lee shore during gale conditions could force you to run unfamiliar surf if there are no good landings within reach, and that is a situation to be avoided if possible. Lee shores without protected harbours should be attempted only when the weather is stable.

Windward shores are more forgiving. The water is calmest here, and hazards are more easily seen and avoided. When approaching a small island from upwind, you should land if you can on the windward shore. Even if you *are* able to land on a lee shore because of moderate conditions, you may get stuck there if the wind freshens during your stay. When approaching a strange island in the dark, always do so from the windward shore.

The danger of windward shores is the sometimes strong offshore wind which can blow small boats to sea. This is frequently the cause of fatal miscalculations by the inexperienced who see that the water "looks so calm" close in to land. The farther out you get, the rougher the sea may become and the harder it may be to return. If the wind is really strong, you may not be able to return against it from only a few hundred yards offshore. You can paddle a windward shore during high winds only by staying very close to the land. Under such conditions, don't be tempted into taking the short route across a wide bay.

DEALING WITH COASTAL CURRENTS

The sea is seldom without a current along the coast of an island or continent, and you can save a lot of effort if you know what this current is doing. Although annoying, a contrary current on a coastal paddle does not necessarily condemn you to stay in camp. It usually means that you should paddle close ashore to gain the benefit of eddies and backflows (though this is not possible on rough lee shores). Even where there *is* a current close inshore, it is frequently slower than farther out to sea. In some cases, shelter can be gained from strong currents by paddling inside the line of kelp or inside a coral reef. Going *with* the current, on the other hand, it is faster to stay well clear of the shore. Entering bays in this case only causes you to get caught up in backflows.

The trick, obviously, is to know when to paddle close ashore, when to paddle out, and, if you are paddling inside the current, to know just how far you have to enter the bays to avoid the head-on current yet not to lose distance by entering the counterflow too deeply. Your instructions are written on the surface of the sea. Once you realize they are there, they are not difficult to read. Belts of currents can be seen from their effects on the water surface, enabling you to turn tightly into a current flowing your way. Close inshore, snags, kelp, lobsterpot buoys or lines of flotsam may reveal the flow of back eddies which can be of assistance to you. As a cyclist's knowledge of hills becomes more intimate than a motorist's, so your knowledge of currents will become more intimate than other mariners'. Few other craft can navigate in water less than 6 inches deep. And the kayak's slow cruising speed and light weight make an occasional bump on a boulder quite inconsequential if the sea is calm.

NAVIGATING ESTUARIES AND HEADLANDS

Rounding a steep-to headland produces the greatest difficulty for those travelling against the flow of the current. It is off the headland that the current runs strongest and closest to shore. Usually there is no alternative but to sprint around into the relatively still water of the next bay. On a rough lee shore, the current around a prominent headland will produce very turbulent conditions well out to sea. The winds will be stronger, and williwaws may occur. In short, headlands are crisis points in coastal kayaking.

Estuaries also produce a variety of surprises for the unwary. Most problems occur in the higher and lower latitudes where tidal variations are greatest and current speeds can get very high if the estuary extends far inland. Where it enters open sea, the tidal outflow from what may basically be a small stream can acquire the proportions of a mighty river. In some places, speeds can exceed 15 knots. Overfalls, upsurges, bores and whirlpools develop, and where the flow meets big ocean swells, rollers form a barrier of destruction. When approaching unknown estuaries, look well ahead for the white water then do what you must to avoid it.

Ferry-gliding is the normal way of crossing a fast tidal flow in an estuary. If you have to make ground against the flow and can't wait for a tide change, stay in as close to shore as you can. If you are going with it, get out in the middle and enjoy the ride. When entering a fast flow from still water, either enter at an angle considerably sharper than that which you will adopt to ferry-glide the stream or lean downstream as you enter the current. This prevents water piling up on the deck and causing a capsize.

NAVIGATING AT NIGHT

Try to avoid paddling by night along unknown coastal waters unless there is a bright full moon or the coast is well marked with lights and lighted buoys. As already mentioned, there are times when night paddling is desirable, but these are usually for open sea crossings or familiar waters. Extra care must go into the planning of night crossings if you are pad-

dling towards an unlit shore. If you can arrange to depart before dark, do so because it will allow you to check your drift
against the land before you lose sight of it.

Paddling with your head bowed to the compass all night
can be unpleasant. It can also be unsafe, as you will to some
extent lose your feel for the sea and increase the risk of
seasickness. When the stars are visible, it pays to select one in
line with your course and paddle towards it fifteen minutes or
so at a time, then select another if the movement of the
heavens requires you to do so. Few things can be more en-
chanting than paddling across open water on a starry night
with bursts of phosphorescence glittering on your paddles
and streaming off the wet deck. On cloudy nights, you have
little choice but to paddle with your eyes to your compass,
but when the wind is steady, you may get relief by simply
holding a constant angle to the wind and waves. But beware
of gradual shifts in the wind, made noticeable by its coming
to odds with the waves.

The collision rules do not mention kayaks, but they require
of a rowboat, "*whether under oars or sail, to have ready at hand a
lantern showing a white light, which shall be temporarily exhibited
in sufficient time to prevent a collision.*" In addition to a diver's
flashlight, I advocate that each boat carry a chemical "glow
stick." When we first experimented with these glow sticks,
we carried them on the stern of each kayak. In a following
sea, however, the light was frequently beneath the water for
seconds at a time and on one occasion, a huge fish struck one
kayak a blow which the unfortunate paddler described as like
being rear-ended at a traffic light. (I have since learned that
glow stick lures are popular with deep sea fishermen.) After
that, we wore the lights in our hat bands. This increased the
effective range of the sticks and provided us with a fine light
by which to read the compass.

The great unwritten rule of the sea says that kayaks must

12/21/2018 6:21 PM   **Sales Receipt #109549**
Store: 1   Workstation: 1

Time Tested Books
1114 21st Street
Sacramento CA 95814
(916) 447-5696
website: www.timetestedbooks.net
email: info@timetestedbooks.net

Cashier:

Description 1	Qty	Price	Ext Price
SEA KAYAKING- D(	1	$9.95	$9.95 T
		Subtotal:	$9.95
Local Sales Ta>	8.25 % Tax		+ $0.82
	RECEIPT TOTAL:		**$10.77**

Credit Card: $10.77
Visa

Thank you for shopping at Time Tested Books!
No Cash Returns
Keep price sticker intact and receive 50% trade
credit towards used book purchases

109549

get out of other people's way. Lighted or not, your kayak is too small to be seen easily, and you won't appear on most radar unless you are flying a radar reflector. Neither this nor anything else will give comfort in the presence of fast craft such as speedboats, hydrofoils or hovercraft, whose very speed sometimes makes their course almost impossible to predict accurately enough for a kayaker to take effective evasive action. In these cases you will have to rely on your guardian angel and white light, and hope that they are keeping a good watch. This is not to say that big ships cannot be scary and don't travel deceptively fast. They do; but a ship's course is more constant, and at night you can tell her direction by the lights—red for port, green for starboard, and the bow light always 15 feet lower than the masthead light. You know all is well so long as you can see only the green or the red light with the two white lights spaced comfortably one before the other. When you see both red and green, and the two white lights one above the other, it is time, or past time, to move quickly.

SNIFFING UP LAND

When paddling over the horizon to a large city or town at night you will usually see the loom of the lights—a glow in the sky—long before you see the lights themselves. The chart will usually indicate the outline of the town, and you can take a useful compass bearing on the glow in the heavens. The loom of a lighthouse too is usually visible well beyond the limit of visibility of the light itself. Your chart will indicate the range at which the *light,* not the loom, can be seen on a clear night. Lights in places such as the Bahamas, Latin America, Southeast Asia and the Middle East cannot be relied upon.

Convection clouds are flat-bottomed fluffy clouds which form above low land masses in the tropics. The morning sun heats the land faster than the sea, and the hot air goes straight up, forming a cloud when the dew point is reached. In the Bahamas, you often see a fluffy replica forming directly above the landmass; cloud replicas are most distinct around noon. These airborne models can be so accurate that they show the individual bays which lie below. By late afternoon, the image will usually have merged into more general cloud, but these too may tell a tale because their bellies reflect the pale turquoise water of The Banks.

Mountain clouds (cumulus rain clouds) often hover around the peaks of high islands, especially in the tropics, on otherwise clear, cloudless days. They too may be seen long before the land itself.

Winds and waves may also indicate the presence of obscured land. A flat island may not be visible from a kayak more than 5 miles distant, but look for waves which seem smaller than you would expect from the existing wind over open sea. If the waves are smaller, their fetch (that is, the distance over which the wind raises them) may be shorter, indicating the presence of an island or reef to windward.

An old transistor radio containing an internal dipole antenna can be used to locate the direction of a known radio station. Rotate the radio until it gives the best reception. The station then lies on a line at right angles to the dipole. With luck you will know which way to head along this line.

5

Weather

Generally speaking, kayakers set their own limits on the weather—or, more precisely, the wind—in which they choose to paddle. I don't know the limit of a well-found sea kayak, though I have approached what I believed to be my own limit a number of times. Yet always the limits are nudged forward with the use of better equipment and the application of more skill and determination. Who can say where they lie, or even be sure there are limits at all? I suspect that this is the hidden quest of the dedicated sea kayaker—the answer to those unanswerable questioners who, without hope of comprehending, ask why you paddle in the first place.

I say only that if you feel compelled to push your limits in wild weather and rough seas, you must not set out to do it on trips with less experienced people. If you are organizing a group, it pays to view weather defensively. Situations with odds acceptable to one person testing mind and body at sea are often best avoided by a heavily loaded flotilla crossing from one island to another.

It is nice to know, however, that should you be caught in a real blow, all is not lost. There is an excellent chance of survival in a well-found kayak if the paddlers know what they are doing and nobody panics. I once ran before a storm into harbour at Picton, New Zealand, where the weather station was recording winds of 96 knots. We were not blown away and did not lose our paddles or anything else. In fact, the heavily loaded boat handled beautifully. We just clutched the paddles, crouched low and guided her into harbour on the rudder. In the Windward Passage north of Haiti, four of us in two boats were once caught 20 miles from land in a tremendous storm at night. Preceded by a waterspout over a thousand feet high, the wind at one stage did a full 360 degree turn in one hour, and the rain and flying spray were such that it was almost impossible to see the light on the other boat though it was so close that there was a constant risk of collision. Lindemann and Romer survived days of fierce storm at sea when they crossed the Atlantic, and many an epic has no doubt been silently endured by hundreds of dedicated sea kayakers the world over. What I am saying is that with care, knowledge, skill, the right boat and plenty of faith in yourself, you can come to terms with the sea in most weather.

If you have doubts about the conditions, usually the best thing is to paddle out and look. Remember, seas are often more chaotic and difficult near headlands and on steep-to lee shores, so you may have to go out a way into the open sea. If you are a party, however, and you as leader have any doubts at all, be prudent. Return and wait for better weather. You can be pretty sure that those with less experience will be having far more doubts than you, and their very lack of confidence can only increase their vulnerability. (Some novices, on the other hand, are totally fearless even when faced with disastrous conditions, and these people can be equally dangerous to themselves and their companions.)

Part of your trip planning should be a visit to your library to study the weather patterns of the area, in particular the nature of the prevailing winds. Local mariners usually know nothing about the capabilities of kayaks, but they too can be full of valuable tips on the weather. They can tell you the special weather warning signs of the region—mist forming on such and such peak, or the significance of an unusual shift in the wind. Their descriptions of local weather are also likely to be more vivid than the dry jargon on official forecasts.

Let's face it, though, value your forecasting ability as you may, your most reliable and commonly available aid in predicting the weather will be your radio. Before entering an area, record the times and frequencies of marine weather forecasts. Get a weather check before any major crossing or lee-shore paddle. In civilized parts of the world, a phone call to the local weather bureau, coast guard or airport will supply you with exactly the information you require, but if you are in the wilderness, you will have to rely on what you see around you to forecast your own weather. (Sometimes even in remote areas your radio will pick up useful satellite information on the location and movement of air masses.)

WIND ORIENTATION

Weather systems entering the area, bringing shifts of wind which would make a crossing hazardous, will likely be your prime concern. Nature provides warnings of these approaching systems. High cirrus clouds (the effect of a jet stream) usually indicate the approach of a low pressure system still a day or two away. Lenticular clouds threatening more immediate high wind, or a suddenly forming high haze, may also reveal a drop in pressure as a new weather system pushes in. Still other signs are a haze ring around the sun or moon or layers of cloud running at different angles to each other.

In the northern hemisphere, depressions contain winds at the lower levels that blow counterclockwise, whereas at higher altitudes (3 to 10 miles) winds flow more or less steadily from a westerly direction. Thus by examining the movement of upper and lower cloud levels during unstable weather, you can locate yourself relative to the depression and make an enlightened guess at future weather trends.

Weather prediction from wind orientation is illustrated on the opposite page. The dotted line represents the equator, the horizontal arrows represent the prevailing high-altitude westerlies, and the circles show the wind patterns of low-pressure systems nearer the earth's surface. At point A, if you stand with your back to the wind you will be facing north. The high clouds will be coming from your left, and the odds are that the weather will worsen. At point B, you will see the cloud layers moving in opposite directions, a sign that you can expect more of the same weather. At C, if you stand with your back to the wind, you will be facing south and will see the high clouds coming from your right—a sign that the weather may soon improve. At D, high and low clouds would be moving in the same direction, meaning more of the same weather. In summary, back to the wind, watch the high cloud; from left is bad, from right is good; forward or backward means no change. Not all low-altitude winds are depression winds, of course, so wind direction alone is not enough on which to base your forecast. To an observer at point C, a north wind is good news, but not all north winds in the northern hemisphere portend good weather.

In the southern hemisphere, where low-pressure systems circulate clockwise instead of counter-clockwise, the same prediction rules apply, but observations must be made while facing into the wind instead of away from it. Thus at Point E, an observer facing north into the wind would find the high cloud coming from his left—an indication of worsening weather. At F, the high and low clouds would be moving in the same direction, meaning more of the same weather. At G, facing south into the wind, an observer would find the high clouds coming in from his right, auguring well. At Point H, the high and low clouds would seem to be moving in opposite directions, and it would be reasonable to expect no immediate change in the weather.

North

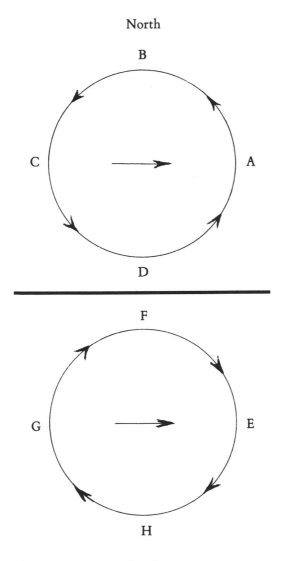

South

BAROMETER

After your transistor radio, a barometer is probably the most useful aid to weather prediction you can carry. But the barometer offers no easy answers to weather forecasting. It tells only the present pressure. It's up to you to make an informed guess based on past pressure and apparent trends. Certainly there is a well-established link between low pressure and bad weather, and the patterns of pressure change can make your prediction better than a wild guess, but even with the knowledge provided by hundreds of barometric pressures over a wide area, the weather services of the world can't claim to have it tabbed—so don't expect too much from your single location readings. Seen in the context of all the other changes going on around you, however, including your wind orientation observations, the behaviour of your barometer should give some meaningful clues.

In the tropics, where the only fluctuation you may get for weeks is the pulse of day and night, a sudden plummeting of pressure is sure indication that you are in for a severe storm. On the coast of northern British Columbia, Norway, southwestern New Zealand or Patagonian Chile—the lands of the eternal lows—a low barometric pressure may be much less significant, and you will make your decision to paddle or not to paddle according to the wind and wave conditions on the shoreline you hope to travel.

In the temperate zone, where most kayaking is done, there are certain pressure patterns whose predictability makes them worthy of comment. A long steady rise from 980 millibars to above 1020 millibars is a good indication of a stable period of fine weather. Sudden rises seldom lead to long fine periods. A steady fall indicates a more general deterioration. But such rules of thumb should be only one factor in many on which to base your predictions of future weather.

Animals

Animals seem to know when bad weather is approaching. If we humans have lost this sense (though I am by no means sure we have), we can at least keep an eye on other creatures and pay heed to their warnings.

Birds become nervous and more twittery than normal when a big storm is pending. Gulls huddle together on shore, sometimes flying well inland where they squat nervously in the fields or crowd the beaches on little islands.

Sandflies go on an orgy of feeding, and their increased presence is most definitely noticeable.

Mosquitoes tend to be thickest *after* a storm, but if you are in a badly infested area, their pre-storm enthusiam is also noticeable.

Porpoises have the remarkable trick of leaping clear of the water then slapping down on the surface with a report like a rifle shot when a storm is imminent. Seeing this, fishermen on the west coast of New Zealand reckon a storm will break within twenty-four hours. I have observed the coincidence there and also in Chile.

Frogs—ah yes, frogs. Such sensitive little creatures. No serious sea kayaker should be without one. Have you ever noticed how excitement and croaking runs high in the frog pond just before the weather is about to break? If you don't have a frog pond near your campsite, why not take a frog along in a mason jar and seek its advice on the weather every morning. It might prove considerably more reliable than some of the other forecasts you will be listening to.

TROPICAL WEATHER

The tropics, regardless of what the tourist brochures may say, are loaded with unsettled, wild weather. Much of this can be anticipated from a study of the weather patterns and an understanding of the basic causes of tropical weather formation; here are a few generalities.

The tropics are an area of prevailing easterlies, usually in the form of the southeast or northeast trades, and you would do well to go with them if possible. In Southeast Asia, the western Pacific and Indian oceans, monsoons have a profound effect. The January monsoon, for example, will provide fresh northeasterly winds until as late as March. A period of southwesterly winds takes over between April and October. Unfortunately, these monsoons don't always follow the textbooks. I have encountered weeks of near gale-force northeasterlies along the coast of Java during August.

In Southeast Asia and Indonesia, typhoons strike most frequently between October and December as the July monsoon weakens.

In the Caribbean, December through May is the period of strongest trade wind activity. June through October is the hurricane season, and though the storms are terrible when they strike, they are mercifully rare and the intervening weather usually has long periods of calm.

Severe squalls (known as waves) may cause prolonged unsettled weather in the tropics. Visually these resemble the low pressure bad weather of the temperate regions, though there is no barometric variation.

Hurricanes & Typhoons

Let's hope that as a sea kayaker you are not going to be caught out by a hurricane. Unless it forms right over you (in which case you will know about it as soon as the weather satellite), your radio should give you at least a day's warning of its arrival—but don't count on it; keep your eyes peeled for natural signs. If you are in a populated area, you will certainly get the message even if you miss the radio broadcasts. Birds have nothing on people when it comes to flapping! A storm warning of square red flags with black square centres hoisted one above the other at the port entrance (or, at night, a white light between two red lights) is customary, and warnings will usually also be broadcast on a public address system. The sky itself will also be plastered with warnings, and the tension will be considerable.

Nature's hurricane warnings:

1 Unusually high swells coming from the direction of the hurricane;
2 Dramatic cirrus displays;
3 A spectacular drop in the barometric pressure;
4 An ominous calm period;
5 Darkening skies which gain a coppery hue;
6 Waterspouts or tornadoes on the right front quadrant six to twelve hours before the arrival of the big winds;
7 Panic among the sea birds;
8 Rapidly increasing wind as the storm approaches;
9 Your weather frog's voice becoming tremulous.

The hurricane is a circular storm (spiralling inward counterclockwise in the northern hemisphere, clockwise in the southern hemisphere) with winds which may exceed 200 mph. The devastation is staggering. The sea level may rise over 12 feet and waves are very destructive. Kayakers will have their work cut out surviving on land. Pity help you if you are caught by one at sea, but if you are, you will not be the first. Franz Romer died at sea in a large hurricane in 1928. He had just crossed the Atlantic by kayak and had survived two other hurricanes in the course of his crossing.

WEATHER IN THE SUB-POLAR &
COOLER TEMPERATE ZONES

Some of the finest kayaking routes are found in the colder latitudes. After all, the kayak is originally a cold weather craft.
It seals around your waist, encasing the lower part of your
body in still air which acts as an insulator. (Open the spray
skirt, however, and the chill factor increases dramatically.)

Western Canada, Alaska and the eastern Arctic, Labrador,
Greenland, Scandinavia and Scotland all provide fine cold
weather kayaking. So do Patagonia, the Falkland Islands and
the southwest coast of New Zealand. These areas have in
common a vulnerability to polar air masses with most of their
weather coming off the sea. All were once heavily glaciated,
so their coastlines now offer excellent protection and great interest for kayakers in a maze of fjords and rocky islands.
These areas are subject to constant storms, and a kayaker
must be prepared to paddle in all but the very windiest of
weather or risk waiting weeks for it to clear. Such latitudes
are the breeding grounds of the low pressure systems that in-
vade temperate regions. They can produce snow showers in
mid-summer when the sun hovers in the sky for twenty
hours a day and the nights don't really get dark at all, whereas
in winter you have barely six hours of dim light in which to
paddle and the routine of making and breaking camp is done
in freezing darkness. One would normally try to avoid paddling during these winter months, but if you are well prepared, there is no reason why you cannot do so.

Patagonian weather, like Alaskan weather, comes mostly
from the west, but north and south, of course, are reversed in
their significance. Storm winds blast the area from the northwest and bitter polar air masses occasionally sweep in from
the south. The southerly wind following the passing of a low
pressure system foretells fine weather. Wet westerly winds

drop hundreds of inches of rain a year on the tangled mossy forests of the mountain valleys and feed the great Patagonian icecap with an endless supply of snow. The needle of your barometer will mostly oscillate between 980 millibars and 1000 millibars with only the occasional high taking over for a day or two. You mustn't be disconcerted, though, by the bottom dropping out of the glass. Patagonian paddling is so protected that you can almost always find a calm side of a fjord to travel—and as that veteran of Patagonian exploration, the late Eric Shipton, once remarked, "If you wait for good weather in Patagonia, you'll never do anything."

Katabatic Winds & Williwaws

Williwaws result from high winds being deflected by steep land masses. They occur most frequently off headlands that are backed by high mountains or on the fringes of the lee of a high island. These are hardly unique to Patagonia, though the name originates from the region. It is the Yahgan word for the wind squalls of the Strait of Magellan. Some of the healthiest specimens may be found frolicking off Cabo Froward. A williwaw manifests itself as a blast of wind, sometimes twisting, sometimes falling out of the sky as a downdraft and rushing across the sea in a wall of spray over 200 feet high. As it travels it collects water from the wave tops and appears as a white cloud. You can hear williwaws coming; at night this is all you have to judge their approach. When they hit, lie low, leaning well into them and holding your paddle so that it is not caught by the wind. In an unstable boat, a low profile paddle brace to windward will improve stability. In a stable one, hold your paddle hard against the deck or, if it is feathered, in the water alongside, on the windward side of the boat. This reduces the chances of having it blown out of your hands.

Katabatic winds, or bora, are the result of the drainage of

cold air from high ground under the influence of gravity. A vast reservoir of cold air gathers over the icy interior and is tripped by a light offshore wind. It gathers momentum as it avalanches towards the sea. Katabatic winds are common in Greenland, Alaska, Norway, the Antarctic and the Adriatic.

Such a wind once struck our camp on the shores of the Strait of Magellan. It was a still, moonlit night, and the only warning we had was an eerie howl which brought us out of our tents. The wind almost blew our camp inside out on the first blast. For two hours it slammed into us, then, as suddenly as it had started, it stopped and there was silence. It is unlikely that vessels at anchor with an eye to protection from the west would have survived that devastation from the east.

TEMPERATE WEATHER

The temperate zone, lying as it does between the perennial lows of the subpolar latitudes and the tropical high pressure systems, is the area of greatest unpredictability. It is also, however, the area where you are most likely to get skilled assistance with your weather forecasting, since it is home to the world's most technological civilizations. Here your most important piece of weather forecasting equipment definitely will be your radio or telephone line to the weather office, but you should take care to stay in tune with the signs of nature yourself, since sometimes the edge your guess may have over the weatherman's is that you looked at the sky that morning.

By the way, don't underestimate Mediterranean weather. The summer winds can be fickle and devastating, making long crossings more hazardous than in areas where the wind remains steady. Summer is surely the best time to paddle in the Mediterranean, though I have kayaked there myself only during the winter. It was excellent training for Patagonia— katabatic winds and all.

6

Reading the Sea

Almost everything a kayaker needs to know about the sea is written there in a code of colours, swirls, patterns, shapes and sizes which reflect the weather of the moment and may indicate weather to come. This code can tell you the character of the sea bottom and how far beneath the surface it lies. It can tell you of currents and tides. It can even tell you something of the nearby land. Foremost among the messengers of the sea are the waves—complex pulses of energy which move relentlessly through the oceans. Waves originate chiefly from the action of wind passing over the water but can also be formed by water flowing over an obstruction, or by earthquakes and landslides (tsunami waves). Their energy is ultimately lost through dissipation as heat—either gradually, due to viscosity, or abruptly, as the wave breaks. With windblown waves, the larger they are, the faster they move.

Remember, though, that what moves is the wave, not the water. The passage of a wave through water does not result in any net movement of the particles of water except where the wave is breaking—and there is little movement even then, as the crest tumbles and carries a small surface flow after it. Only the wave energy crosses the seas; the particles within the wave move in a circle, returning more or less to their original position when the wave has passed.

The waves you will encounter on the open sea will seldom be simple and uniform even when they all appear to be travelling in the same direction. Some waves are obviously larger than others, and there are moments when the sea almost seems to flatten out. This is the result of waves of different sizes, and therefore different speeds, alternately complementing each other and cancelling each other out. These waves have different origins, and their interaction is highly significant for the kayaker trying to get through a line of breakers. By careful observation, a pattern of big and small waves can sometimes be discerned, enabling you to anticipate the arrival of the next set of big ones and sneak through before they hit. Frequently, however, no reliable pattern emerges.

Let's have a look at the more common types of wave and how they affect a sea kayaker.

OCEAN SWELLS, WINDBLOWN WAVES & CHOP

Ocean swells are raised by the wind, but their stormy origin may be hundreds of miles distant. They may exceed 1500 feet in length, from crest to crest, and travel at speeds in excess of 30 knots. As they approach the shallows near land, these great waves steepen and slow. When their height reaches roughly one-seventh of their length, the crests topple and the waves crash ashore as surf.

On the open sea, these waves normally pose little problem to a kayaker. They just slip by, occasionally obscuring the land and other paddlers. They become a problem if you happen to be where they are forming in the midst of a storm; then they can reach their critical height at sea and their crests go plunging down their 50-foot slopes, enveloping all in their path.

Swells also cease to be slumbering giants when they run against a strong current. Under such conditions, the leading face of the swell is undercut, steepens and the crest crashes over as a plunging breaker or ocean roller. Such waves form in the shallows off harbour entrances when there is an out-flowing tide, and can occur in the currents of the Gulf Stream and off the east coast of Africa and Japan. This situation is certainly to be avoided since it is extremely difficult to judge the size of the rollers without getting too close. Other places to watch for them include shallow banks fringing deep ocean, and in the estuaries of large-volume rivers which flow into open sea. If you cannot avoid these waves, you must handle them as you would surf: head-on if you are going against them, broached-to on a paddle brace or even with a pre-emptive roll (to reduce their destructive impact) if they are abeam.

Windblown waves differ from swells only in that they are smaller and formed locally. They build and die relatively quickly in the open sea, being readily cancelled or altered by a change of wind. They are of shorter wave length than the ocean swells and move correspondingly more slowly.

Their size depends upon the wind speed, fetch and length of time the wind has been blowing as well as on the composition of the water, which in some of the most interesting ocean-kayaking areas is anything but constant. In places, the sea may contain hundreds of square miles of fresh surface water, which will cause waves to form more readily and more steeply into the sort of chop one might expect to find on freshwater lakes.

A chop forms where the fetch of the wind is short and equilibrium has not been reached. Such conditions occur in a harbour on a windy day. Chop offers little serious threat to a well-found kayak, though it can be most unpleasant. Steep 3-foot waves are just big enough to throw a bucket of cold water in your face every five seconds when you are paddling into them.

INTERFERENCE WAVES: RIPS, OVERFALLS & CLAPOTIS

A current setting over a shallow, irregular bottom, or two currents intersecting one another, will often cause a patch of chaotic water called a rip. As the currents responsible for these rips are often tidal currents, the rips are often called tide rips—not to be confused with the so-called riptides, better called rip currents, which are found on beaches. Tide rips and their attendant eddies and whirlpools are notoriously common among the archipelagoes of British Columbia and Alaska, where some but not all of them will be marked on your charts.

Rips are composed largely of standing waves. These are waves which "jog in place," moving up and down while the current flows through them. Standing waves are normally more sharply peaked than travelling waves, and the water in them is for the most part moving up and down and side to side instead of rolling in stationary circles. When these waves break, either from wind action or from the force of the current flowing through them, the result is called an *overfall*. These are regularly encountered in Alaska's Alexander Archipelago.

When a wave strikes a steep cliff, either obliquely or directly, it is reflected as if from a mirror. The rebound waves may pass right through the incoming waves, if their crests and troughs do not coincide, but the confused sea which results can make for hair-raising paddling. When the crests of such contradictory waves *do* coincide, however, their amplitudes combine, creating huge standing waves, again much steeper than travelling waves. This phenomenon is called *clapotis*. (The same word is used on French charts to mark tide rips.)

Off the northern tip of New Zealand, where major wave

patterns collide in deep water, clapotis is regularly seen. The pinnacling waves formed here have so much vertical power that they can throw a laden kayak clear out of the water. In the Grenadines, between Isle Ronde and Carriacou, is an 8-mile crossing known, for good reason, as Kick'um Jenny. Here the waves often enter both from the Atlantic to the northeast and the Caribbean to the northwest. They strike the steep cliffs at Diamond Head and rebound into a four-way chaos of pinnacling waves for miles out to sea. A current setting side-on at 2 to 3 knots complicates matters still further. The resulting illegible confusion can be very rough going in a kayak.

When the current is running hard against normal ocean waves, the wave length shortens and the faces of the waves steepen, causing the crests to tumble. This is another form of overfall, and it too can be very unpleasant for a kayaker. In milder form, however, such conditions usefully betray the movement of the current. Even out of sight of land you can detect a change in the tidal flow from the altered angle and length of the waves. In a kayak during dark night crossings, if the wave patterns are not too confused, you may even hear or feel this change through the seat of your pants.

When the waves become smoother and more rounded than you would expect from a certain wind strength, it is reasonable to expect that they are running *with* the current, though this is more difficult to identify. When the wind blows across the current, the wave length is normal, but the crests are twisted slightly as they break, with a tendency to form toppling pyramids.

A wind blowing against the waves is usually a temporary situation, since waves are normally a product of the wind. When a sudden wind change occurs, however, there can be a period of chaotic seas as the new pattern establishes itself. This is not normally a threat to a kayaker, though it is nice to be prepared for the change when it occurs. Local wind blowing against heavy swells has little effect on the direction or size of the swells. Instead, smaller waves will travel on top of the long swells regardless of their direction. Mostly the chaos caused by wind against waves should be taken as a warning that something unsettling is happening to the weather.

BREAKERS

The way a wave reacts upon reaching land depends on the depth of the offshore waters, the nature of the land and the angle at which the wave strikes it.

Plunging breakers, or dumpers, form where there is a steeply shelving drop-off to open water. There is little shortening of wave length as the wave approaches the shore, and typically there is only one row of breakers that curls and bursts directly onto the foreshore from which the spillage of the previous wave is rapidly receding. From seaward the ferocity of these waves can be gauged by the explosive quality of the break as the air trapped within the plunging crest is compressed and then expands, throwing sand and gravel up with the water. Perhaps the most dangerous plunging breaker is the one that forms on shoals or coral reefs.

Spilling breakers form where the offshore gradient is gentle and their energy is dissipated gradually. On the north coast of Java, the gradient is so gentle that the waves reach their critical depth miles offshore, and getting out through the surf in the morning can mean a one-hour battle against breakers. Spilling breakers are probably the most manageable for a kayaker, since they lack the explosive quality of dumpers. They also allow you to judge the water depth, since their height declines shoreward in fixed proportion to the depth of the water. (The effect of the tide can be important when plan-

Plunging breakers, or dumpers, are recognizable from seaward by their violence. They occur where the beach drops off steeply. Avoid them if possible. If you must land in dumpers, try to sprint in on the back of them and scramble out of the danger zone.

Spilling breakers can usually be identified from seaward by their long sweep towards shore. The gently sloping bottom against which they form may be visible on your chart.

ning your landing or departure through these breakers. Where the tidal range is great, you may have plunging breakers on the beach at high water and spilling breakers for a quarter of a mile when the tide is out.)

On occasion you will encounter a third type of breaking wave, which occurs when the beach slope just exceeds the steepness of the wave. Then, instead of plunging, the wave surges up the beach, breaking as it climbs.

The distinctions between plunging, spilling and surging breakers are frequently blurred, however, and more than one type of breaker can often be seen on the same beach.

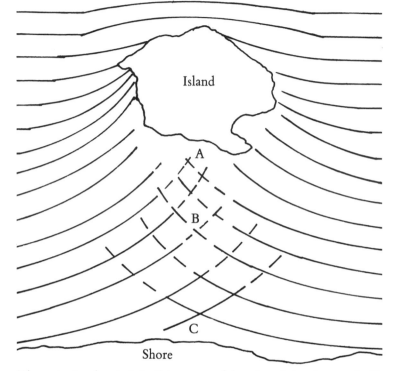

The water is calmest at A. B is a zone of clapotis and chaotic seas. At C, the converging wave patterns focus energy on the shore, creating difficult surf.

When waves reach land and their energy is not dissipated as breakers, they are variously affected according to the nature of the land and the angle at which they strike. A small island, for example, causes the waves to change direction and bend around the land mass, spreading their energy as they do so. Standing waves sometimes form behind and somewhat beyond the island, at a distance about equal to the diameter of the island. Here, if the water is shallow and the bottom sandy, a bar will form. When paddling inside such an island it is advisable to choose a course in close to the island. Inside this "wave shadow" is usually the most desirable place to make a landing. The approach from behind the wave shadow, of course, should be avoided since converging wave patterns are likely to create a difficult, breaking sea.

BOOMERS

On exposed coasts, barely submerged rocks can be spotted by the heavy swells which break upon them. But suppose the rock is 10 feet beneath the surface and is not quite uncovered by the average passing swell. A wave larger than usual comes through, the top of the rock is exposed, and the crest folds over and virtually explodes on the rock. This is known as a boomer, and it is a common danger for kayakers paddling a rocky lee shore exposed to open ocean. Watch at least a mile ahead to locate boomers. Eventually you will make an automatic mental note of any breaks in the wave pattern, just as a hiker will note obstructions on the path. Deeply submerged rocks may catch only one wave in twenty—but if you are on that wave you will be taken by disastrous surprise.

Some basic rules for avoiding boomers are:

1 Check the chart well in advance and know when currents are likely to push you onto an infested area.
2 If you are paddling through shoal waters, keep a keen eye for and remember the position of all isolated breakers near your course.
3 Avoid patches of kelp which, at higher latitudes, probably conceal rock.
4 If you see rock beneath you, sprint clear.
5 Watch out for waves peaking unusually sharply. They could be "feeling bottom" on a submerged rock.

In the tropics, isolated coral heads can produce boomers. Their position can sometimes be seen from a darkened patch in the sea. Because kayaks frequently travel where no other craft would go, you may find yourself in incompletely charted waters. Besides, coral grows, and charts based on fifty-year-old surveys cannot be relied upon to show inshore coral patterns.

WAVES & WIND SPEED

Waves are the principal tell-tales of the weather at sea, and are used to categorize weather conditions. Waveforms and wind speed as ranked on the Beaufort scale are as follows:

Beaufort Force	Wind	Sea	Wave Pattern and Paddleability
0	0–1 knot	Calm	Monotonous kayaking, risk of hyperthermia in the tropics, old wave patterns only, smooth surface.
1	1–3 knots	Light air	Slight relief from heat unless the movement is from astern; scale-like ripples.
2	4–6 knots	Light breeze	Comfortable kayaking. Small wavelets.
3	7–10 knots	Moderate breeze	Large wavelets; crests start to form and break with clear foam. Good kayaking weather.
4	11–16 knots	Good wind	Small waves becoming longer. Whitecaps. The comfortable limit for novice kayaking.

5	17–21 knots	Strong wind	Large waves form; whitecaps are numerous. Weather for experienced kayakers.
6	22–27 knots	Very strong wind	Breaking waves begin to streak; williwaws near headlands. Try to avoid this weather.
7	28–33 knots	Near gale	Moderately high waves with streaks and spray flying from their crests. Definitely outside the realm of normal kayaking.
8	30–40 knots	Gale	High waves, dense streaking and flying spray. This is the practical limit for kayaking (no progress into it).
9	41–47 knots	Strong gale	High waves start to tumble, dense streaking; the paddler is blown backwards.
10	45–55 knots	Storm	Very high waves; long, overhanging crests tumbling. Survival situation running or lying to a drogue.
11	56–63 knots	Violent storm	The sea is white with spray; huge waves. The kayak is running before the wind or lying to a drogue.
12	64–71 knots	Hurricane	The air is filled with foam and spray. Visibility from a kayak is near zero. Running with warps astern is probably your only practical option.

The preceding table assumes a steady wind on the open sea. In the case of coastal waters and onshore winds, the condition of the waves will be very different, and a kayaker unassisted by technology will have to estimate the wind strength from the appearance of the water surface and the performance of trees, if trees are visible. Gusts are more frequent close to steep land, and their velocity is especially difficult to estimate.

TIDES & TIDAL CURRENTS

As there is no shortage of manuals on compass and chart work, so there is no shortage of books on tides and tide prediction. I assume on the reader's part some knowledge of the theory of tides and an ability to use tide and current tables. It is one of the pleasures of kayaking, however, to go where no other boat can go, and this often means going where no tide and current table is available. At the same time, the kayak, with a cruising speed on the order of 3 knots and a top speed of perhaps 5 or 6, is highly susceptible to the effects of tidal currents. (As a boat which frequently spends the night on a beach, it, like its paddler and sleeping bag, can also be vulnerable to the tides.) Current and tide predictions of some sort are indispensable to coastal kayaking, especially in the higher latitudes. This all adds up to the fact that the sea kayaker must develop the primitive sailor's wary and attentive eye for what the water and the moon are doing.

If you are paddling under an opaque Alaskan overcast, your lunar sightings may be few, but if the moon can be seen at all it will foretell much about the state of the tide. Spring tides, of course, come with the new and the full moon. Neap tides occur when the moon is neatly cut in two, at the first and third quarters. The moon's effect increases at perigee (when it is nearest the earth) and decreases at apogee (when it is farthest away). When the perigee coincides with new or full moon, which happens at least twice a year, the tidal range will be greatest: the high waters will be especially high and the adjacent low waters especially low—perhaps several feet lower than the lows shown on your charts.

High water can be expected a couple of hours after the moon crosses the meridian. At new and full moon, this means somewhat after noon and midnight. At the quarter moon, when the tides are smaller, it means somewhat before. Successive high and low waters are likely to be about equal when the moon is riding the equator. In the Pacific and Indian oceans, the tides tend to be wildly *unequal* when the moon is "in the tropics"—that is, when its orbit runs to the Tropic of Cancer or Capricorn. What this means in terms of the visible declination of the moon naturally depends on where you are when you're looking, but the changes of declination are easily seen, and your tide table should include a lunar calendar which will help you get the hang of it. In thick weather, this calendar alone will give you much of the information you need for seat-of-the-pants tide prediction.

When you have the luxury of using the tables themselves, remember that the predicted heights and times can be drastically altered by high winds. Prolonged or severe barometric drops are generally accompanied by an increase in the tidal range, and a sudden or sustained rise in atmospheric pressure will usually reduce the range. These factors too will cause the tides to depart from the tabulated heights and times.

When you have to negotiate a long passage in which the sea is peaceable only at high or low slack, keep an eye on the tables for a standing tide. This phenomenon occurs when a relatively low high water is followed by a high low water, usually followed again by a low high tide. For hours in such a case the tide may scarcely budge.

Standing tides are common at the quarter moon on the Pacific coast of North America. In other areas, such as the Gulf of California and the South China Sea, the tidal cycle routinely runs at half speed, with only one high and one low water per day, all month long.

Often the item of real concern to a kayaker is not the tide itself but the tidal current. In many narrows and passages along the coast of British Columbia, for example, tidal currents reach 10 to 15 knots. The tide and current tables give accurate current predictions for many of these channels, but the fjords and passages most tempting to the sea kayaker are often precisely those for which no predictions are published. A copy of the relevant U.S. *Coast Pilot, British Admiralty Pilot Guide* or *Canadian Coastal Sailing Directions* will often give you a general idea of what to expect. Remember, though, that the coast pilots and pilot guides are not written with kayaks in mind.

Whatever your sources—the *Coast Pilot,* published predictions, advice from local fishermen or casting bones—it is useful to have an advance notion of the set (direction) of flood and ebb currents, their maximum velocity and the approximate times of slack water. The current may peak anywhere from two to five hours after the turn, but an interval of a little over three hours from slack to peak is most common. The zero current, at the turn, may last only a moment, but for some time before and after the turn, the current will be negligible. How long this slack period will last depends on how fast the current is running when it peaks. At neap tides the current may not be running anywhere near its maximum spring-tide velocity, and the duration of slack water may be much increased. As a general rule, if the current peaks at 2 knots, there will be a period of about sixty minutes at slack water when the current runs at no more than half a knot. If the peak rate is 4 knots, the half-knot slack period is likely to last only about thirty minutes. For a 6-knot current, the half-knot slack may last about twenty minutes, for an 8-knot current, fifteen minutes and for a 10-knot current, only ten minutes.

In the archipelagoes of Alaska, British Columbia and southern Chile, the intricacies of tidal currents are such that, by careful planning, a kayaker can paddle around an island on the flood current to a point at which the tidal currents diverge and, arriving there at high slack, can continue the journey at once, riding the ebb.

With a few significant exceptions, the current will run fastest where the water is deepest. When you are forced to buck the current, therefore, you will usually find it easiest to do so by paddling close ashore. Where shoals or a shallow bar obstruct the main flow, however, the shallow-water current will be faster, not slower, than the deep-water flow. Tide rips and overfalls frequently form in such circumstances, and the current can push you mercilessly through a forest of jagged standing waves. Headlands protruding into the flow will also accelerate the current, creating patches of very swift water called tide races. If you are obliged to cross a tidal current, the narrowest part of the channel may therefore be a poor choice. Up-current from a headland or shoal the flow is likely to be less hazardous.

Tide entering a shallow channel may break into a steep-fronted wave called a tidal bore, whose speed is dependent on its height and the water depth ahead of it. Tidal bores may form on expansive mud flats and in tidal rivers. They occur on the coasts of Britain and France, and large ones regularly form in some of the major river entrances of India, Asia and North and South America. A bore 25 feet high advances up the Amazon during spring tides at speeds sometimes exceeding 12 knots. Where bores exist at all, they are usually regular features and will be mentioned in your *Coast Pilot*. The large ones can be very dangerous, though smaller ones may provide excellent surfing.

OCEAN CURRENTS

The ocean currents are like great eddies between the continents. They rotate clockwise in the northern hemisphere and counterclockwise in the southern hemisphere, driven by the spin of the earth and the force of the winds. They have a profound effect not only on tidal flow but also on climate and weather. The relative warmth of the Japan current, for example, is responsible for the mildness of the sea-level temperatures in southeastern Alaska. Ocean currents such as the Gulf Stream off Florida or the Kuroshio off Japan may exceed 4 knots, throwing up dangerous seas when opposed by a strong wind. In the West Indies, the North Equatorial current sieves through the narrow channels of the Windward and Leeward Islands and into the Caribbean, sometimes running in excess of 3 knots and creating a major navigational problem for craft as limited in speed as a kayak.

In the Mediterranean, a current of quite different origin exists. Rapid evaporation of surface water increases salinity, and the denser solution sinks, setting up a deep flow into the Atlantic through the Strait of Gibraltar. The inflow from rivers is not sufficient to compensate for this outflow, and as a result, a steady *surface* flow of Atlantic water runs *eastward* over the top of the deep westward outflow, sweeping the coasts of North Africa and Southern Europe. The entire Mediterranean is said to be flushed through in this manner every seventy-five years.

7

Hazards

Books like this usually seem to be full of dire warnings of doom. So as not to disappoint you, here is a whole section of doom; but remember, such hazards are only a small part of this game, albeit crucial ones, without which sea kayaking would probably interest a very different sort of person. Sitting at home reading lurid descriptions of freak seas can be intimidating, but it somewhat resembles the panic one feels upon waking suddenly in a car which has braked heavily before a corner: you are confronted by the hazard without the reassurance of the approach. Most sea kayaking is plain paddling, sprinkled with more than its share of euphoric moments.

SURF

Surf is probably the most serious hazard for sea kayakers, who must frequently land and launch on exposed coasts. Surf kayaking can be great fun and is good for building confidence, but it is usually the aim of a cruising kayaker to spend as little time in surf as possible, since the boat is often loaded with expensive equipment and not really suited for riding breakers. True surf kayaking is a different sport, with different boats, different rules and often different people, but some of its tricks are very useful to the sea kayaker. The most important thing the surfies can teach the sea kayaker is how to judge a wave from seaward—a skill that would otherwise have to be learned through painful, expensive trial and error.

The three main types of surf are discussed in the preceding chapter. Dumpers or plunging breakers are worst and should be avoided where possible, since they can smash your boat to pieces against the sand. If you cannot avoid surf, spilling breakers are your best bet, particularly if there is no explosive quality to the wave as it first breaks. The ideal wave has a crest that collapses well out from the beach, gradually spilling its energy on its way to the land.

Beware of areas where the dissipation of the soup is abruptly completed before the wave reaches land. This smooth area may indicate the presence of a rock or coral shelf with a very shallow layer of water over it. If you come surfing merrily in, you may rip the bottom out of your boat.

Surf seldom breaks evenly on a beach. There will usually be a quieter spot at one or both of the ends of a crescent-shaped bay due to the refraction of waves hitting the beach obliquely. If there is kelp or a reef off the beach, the waves will be broken in the lee of this and you can probably sneak in behind it.

Out Through It

Assessing surf from shore is relatively easy. If you decide the waves are marginal for the experience of your group, you can improve your chances by timing them and counting the sets of big ones. There may be three big then two small followed by five medium—or some similar pattern that will enable you to judge your break for open sea—though I confess to having poor success at predicting slack periods accurately. You may be able to take advantage of a rip current —discussed in more detail a few pages on—to get a fast ride out through the danger zone. Any relative novices in your group should follow the example of a more experienced paddler, but leave a veteran ashore until last to help them out if things go wrong in the danger zone. If you only have two boats, send the less experienced boat first so that these people will have assistance getting off the beach and someone ashore to rescue them if necessary.

Presume you are travelling in a group and your kayak is chosen to go first. Make yourself snug and secure the spray skirt while someone from another boat holds your bow into the incoming soup. When the timing is judged to be right, the person holding the bow pulls your boat past himself/herself, giving it a mighty push into the breakers while, at the same time, you begin to paddle as hard as you can, gaining sufficient momentum to punch through the wave. Continue to paddle with a strong, steady rhythm until you are well beyond the line of surf. From there you can watch the performance on shore and wait for the party to regroup.

If you are travelling solo or when yours is the last boat, the manoeuvre is a little trickier. Place the kayak at the edge of the surf where it can be reached by the larger waves which sweep up the beach. If you have a double, No. 2 holds the bow while No. 1 (the forward paddler) gets seated and zipped up. No. 2 then quickly slips into the boat and, if time allows, makes the spray skirt fast. If the receding wave is already carrying the boat out to sea, the arrangement is necessarily a hasty one since both of you must immediately paddle hard directly into the surf. More often than not you will find yourself sitting in your boat on the wet sand and feeling a little foolish with the sea still 20 feet away. It is just as well. Stay put and arrange your spray skirt snugly. When the next wave reaches you, push off with the paddles or bare hands (not easy with a loaded boat!). Watch where you put your hands since cuts can be bad news. It is also easy to break a paddle when launching in this manner.

In Through It

Forward is usually the easiest way to come in through surf, but not necessarily the safest when you have a heavily loaded kayak. It involves considerable commitment—perhaps, in view of the difficulty assessing an unfamiliar beach from seaward, a reckless commitment. The great virtue of this method is that it is quick, thus minimizing the time spent in the danger zone. It is a method for heavy surf where you want to get through fast and the beach is clear of obstructions. Let me quote Paul Caffyn (whose first major challenge was the formidable west coast of New Zealand) on how he gets a Nordkapp through.

> When waves are over 4 feet, I wait offshore and count the sets of big ones going in (usually 3). I wait till a big set is on its way then hammer in behind the last one—casting occasional glances over my shoulder to watch the next set building. This usually gets me past where they are breaking because I'm doing sprint speed of 6 knots or more. When I hear and see the leading breaker of the following set, I let it get within 20 yards, then I do a right rudder and go into a broach position parallel to the breakers, then lift my paddle into a high brace and lean into the breaker as it hits. It carries the kayak in front, sometimes high up the face, but more often on the smooth water immediately in front of the breaker. . . . On two occasions, I got in through 15-foot surf using this method. By going in at 90 degrees to the beach on steep waves, the bow digs in just as the wave caps, and the boat executes a graceful loop.

When entering sideways through surf, it is essential to lean seaward. Leaning into the land inevitably results in capsize.

Method number two is to go in backwards. This technique is useful for unknown or marginal beaches since you are

pointed the right way to get out of it fast if you have to. I
don't recommend it for crests in excess of 6 feet or for dump-
ing breakers. Once you have chosen an apparently clear path
of entry, turn the bow to the oncoming waves. Cock the rudder or skeg clear of the water, then paddle in backwards.
When the cresting wave approaches, revert to a normal
stroke and paddle hard *into* the wave so that the boat gathers
enough momentum to prevent its being swept backwards at
great speed. As soon as the wave passes, back-paddle quickly
again until the next wave is almost upon you, then repeat. Although this method offers greater control over your entry, it
leaves you longer in the danger zone and you can take quite a
hammering. As you are going in, you should look over your
shoulder frequently to judge distance to obstacles and the
beach. In a double, the No. 2 paddler should take this job
while No. 1 watches the waves. If you do see a hazard astern,
you can usually manoeuvre sideways within the line of surf
by ferry-gliding across the flow of the soup.

Method number three: swimming. This is a last-ditch technique, for when you must get through exceptionally heavy
surf with your equipment dry and intact. It entails getting out
of the kayak seaward from the surf then swimming it ashore
through the breakers. It is only suitable for beaches which are
definitely clear of obstructions, and for strong swimmers.
Put on either your life jacket and helmet or mask and fins, according to preference, then go over the side. Collapse the
paddles and stow them inside the boat along with rudder and
cables, if applicable, then seal the cockpit by tying off the
entrance to the spray skirt. Even if the boat capsizes, it will
take in little water. In a double, swim the boat stern-first towards the beach with one person pushing the bow and the
other holding a loop at the end of the bow painter. (Do not
put the loop around your wrist in case a wave carries the boat
away with you tied to it.) If you keep her going stern first,

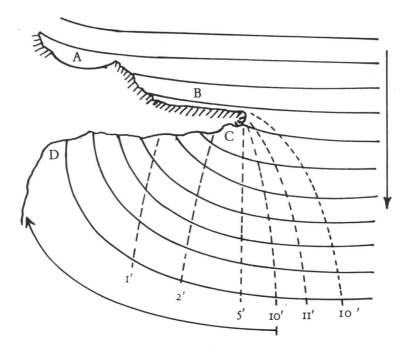

You can often predict a safe landing site from your chart once wave direction is known. Site A has 10-foot surf on the beach and should be avoided. At site B, steep cliffs make landing impossible and will cause chaotic waves offshore. Site C would offer adequate protection for most parties, with waves usually 3 feet or less. At site D, wave strength would be dissipated still further.

she should hold into the waves, thus minimizing the drag on the anchor person. A good swimmer will find it an advantage to reduce buoyancy in the life jacket during this operation, so as to duck below most of the turbulence. The person steadying the boat should take care never to get "downhill" of the kayak, which can be lethal in the grip of a big wave. If you are a solo paddler and find yourself swimming in surf, simply push the boat ahead as you swim for shore.

The way to land in heavy surf on a rocky shore is, don't. Stay at least two wavelengths away from the breakline as a precautionary measure while you hunt for a spot where the waves are truly benign or the land less forbiddingly constructed. Derek Hutchinson has suggested a daring technique for surf-landing on rock, which he calls "seal landing." It involves riding up onto the shore on a breaker (assuming that you have managed to stay at the front of the wave), holding your position as far up the rock as possible then scrambling out quickly and dragging the boat clear of the next wave. This may work for an unloaded boat under surge conditions on smooth rock shelves, but it should not tempt a well-loaded kayaker confronted by real surf and a jagged landscape.

A method I have used for landing on sheer, rocky shores is to search the coast for a protected location. (If you can't find such a place, don't land! You can anchor or paddle on all night if you have to.) Preferably, the shore should be vertical, with a shelf you can reach and no underwater ledges which could catch the approaching kayak and topple it as the wave recedes. Once alongside the shelf, before you can lift the kayak up onto it, you have to get rid of most of the weight. In doubles, one way is for No. 1 to squat in the cockpit while No. 2 edges the kayak close enough to the rocks to scramble ashore. (Check to make sure you can pitch your tent there above high tide before unloading all your worldly belongings.) No. 2 then takes out the bags and balances them on the deck or sits them just inside the forward cockpit then returns with the boat, riding in on a surge to where No. 1 can snatch the bags. The boat is eased clear again as the wave recedes. When the boat is light enough to be handled (it must of course be thoroughly bailed), No. 2 scrambles out on a surge and, with a paddle, holds the boat off the rock while at the same time keeping a hold on the bow painter. The boat can then be brought in on the next suitable surge and pulled higher as the wave recedes. This method is quite out of the question unless the direct force of the waves is already spent. It will also be much trickier with a single. And don't forget: after a very long crossing, your legs may have trouble supporting your body weight. They're unlikely to enable you to leap nimbly over the rocks with your boat.

If you are paddling near beds of bull kelp, you have the makings for a fine natural anchor should night catch you on an inhospitable shore. Kelp tends to take the sting out of breaking waves, and if you get in behind a dense mat of it, you will find the waters subdued. Drag the kelp into bunches and lash it firmly with the painter. Sit the boat back on the line and then haul more long fronds over the decks so that the boat is held fast.

RIP CURRENTS, TIDE RIPS, WIND RIPS & WHIRLPOOLS

As surf piles up on the beach, countercurrents form to return the excess water to the sea. If, as sometimes happens, the breakers have built a beachfront sandbar, these counterflows may take the form of rip currents or beach rips—often called riptides, though since they have nothing to do with tides, this seems a poor name for them. The neck of the rip current is a narrow outflow from the beach, gouging through the sandbar, splitting the breakers and dissipating into the sea beyond them. Its velocity will rarely exceed 2 or 3 knots. Water is supplied to the neck by shallow feeder currents running *across* the beach and into the neck. In a big surf, the feeder currents can be forceful enough to complicate the task of exiting onto

*Where water flows between masses of land, eddies and backflows form
complex patterns which may assist as well as hinder a kayaker, who must
be able to read and anticipate their flow.*

unsteady legs from a kayak. The neck of the current, being
deeper and stronger, can provide a quick route out to sea
from the beach—as unwary swimmers have so often discovered.

Tidal currents and tide rips can pose other, greater problems. As suggested in the previous chapter, swift tidal currents and tide races can so alter the game that, in dealing with
them, river experience may be more valuable to you than
knowledge of the open sea. Remember to lean your boat
away from the current as you enter it, and always brace on the
down-current side. A bracing stroke to the up-current side
will only capsize you into it. Large tide rips are best dealt
with by staying in the middle of the main flow of water if you
are going with them or *very* close to shore if you are obliged
to fight them. If you have to cross a major tide rip area, wait

for slack water. For the smaller ones, it is simply a matter of muddling through, watching your balance and, again, leaning your boat away from each new band of current you come across. Wind rips, caused by the wind running counter to the current, at least have the advantage that the current is more or less uniform, though the chop can become very steep and unpleasant, readily forming overfalls.

Converging and diverging tidal currents create other hazards as well—eddies, or, in their larger, more frightening form, whirlpools. These may be encountered off points and behind islands even where the surrounding sea appears quite calm, but the small ones are unlikely to do you any harm, and of the large ones you are likely to have forewarning. Big whirls will probably appear on your chart and be mentioned in your coast pilot. They are also likely to be a part of local folklore, usually in an exaggerated form. It is often worth examining island channels from a cliff top before paddling them or, as the case may be, paddling around them.

CORAL

Coral thrives in the warm clean waters between 30 degrees north latitude and 30 degrees south latitude. It forms as long fringe reefs on exposed lee shores and as scattered outcrops on the more sheltered coasts. Each reef is a mass of spiky, jagged calcium formations, often quite close to the surface. It is hard to imagine a more deadly snare for kayaks. Atolls are coral reefs that have formed in shallow water, usually in a circle with calm water in their centre.

Coral reefs can sometimes be crossed by a kayak at high tide when almost no other craft could make it, but this is a dangerous game to play. More often, lines of breakers crash

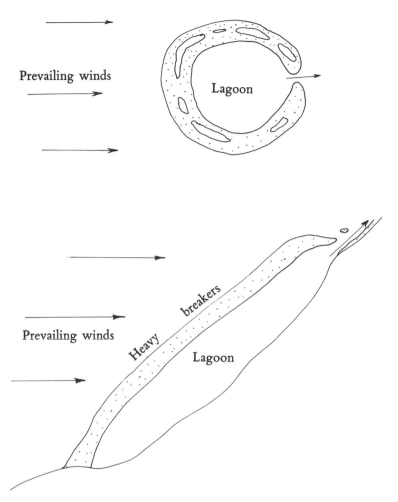

What goes onto a coral reef must come off. There will be a run-off channel somewhere—usually on the side opposite the prevailing winds. The rip current in this channel may be strong, but it is far better to buck the current than to try to surf over the coral.

onto the shallows and cream in over the coral pools to the lagoon, making landing out of the question. Never attempt to run heavy surf on coral. The water that breaks over a coral reef must come off, and a run-off channel can usually be found away from the direct force of the prevailing winds. Scattered offshore reefs frequently offer a sheltered lee, and finding the entrance may be just a matter of reading your chart carefully, if it has been recently surveyed, or simply taking advantage of openings as they appear. Try to get the very latest charts available.

RIVER ENTRANCES

When large rivers pour into rough seas, very dangerous wave conditions may form. There is frequently a shallow bar off the entrance where plunging breakers dump hard. This danger zone can usually be avoided by either closely following the coast or, if you are crossing rather than entering the mouth, by staying well out from shore. Which you choose might depend on the weather and how far offshore the waves are breaking. If you intend to enter the river, it is usually best to sneak in via the shallow water on each side of the entrance. Unless the wind is blowing straight upstream, there will be a side of the mouth that receives some shelter from the killing effect the strong current has upon waves. Use this wave shadow if the water is clear of obstructions.

Rivers in flood carry trees and other debris down to the sea. These obstructions are often deposited in the muddy shallows near the mouth and may lie just below the surface. Keep a careful lookout. It can be most embarrassing if the top of a snag appears through the bottom of your kayak when you are half a mile offshore.

LIVE HAZARDS

Whales, Dolphins & Porpoises

Whale watching from kayaks has become quite the rage in North America over the past few years, and a dozen or more tour companies offer the opportunity for a close look at gray and humpback whales. Novices can also be assured of a heart-pounding encounter—frequently at very close quarters—with killer whales in the Robson Bight region of Johnstone Strait in British Columbia.

Because of a kayak's stealth, it is probable that these boats unnerve dozing whales more than power boats. There have been several reports of whale-watching kayakers being attacked by Pacific grays breeding in the lagoons of Magdalena Bay, Baja, Mexico. Kayaks have been upset and smashed by great flukes, and it is fortunate indeed that nobody has been killed.

Gray whales were known among the old whalers as devil-fish because they sometimes retaliated by smashing boats and drowning their crews. On the recent occasions when kayakers were attacked, the whales had been harassed on previous days by motorboat loads of tourists, and a couple of times a kayaker had ventured very close to a calf, causing the mother to take action.

Once in the Caribbean our kayaks were shadowed for two hours by a shy, apparently amorous humpback. Our first indication of its presence was a piercing, pinging squeak much like that of a misbehaving rudder but which seemed to be coming from everywhere at once. Only when the great tail rose in the air several hundred yards ahead were our suspicions confirmed. It is very exciting to be sharing the sea with such creatures; still, their great size demands caution.

Porpoises will often come to investigate a kayak. They are

fine company and will not normally harm or upset you, though when playing they may come close enough to clip your hull with their fins. I have personally experienced the delight of being escorted into harbour by porpoises after one particularly arduous night crossing in the Caribbean. Lindemann, however, reports being almost capsized by large porpoises in mid-Atlantic, and would no doubt advocate giving them a wide berth.

Sharks

It is said that where you have porpoises, you won't get sharks, but don't count on it. Once, off the coast of New Zealand only a couple of hundred yards from a school of porpoises, I surfed down a wave almost onto the back of a very surprised 12-foot hammerhead.

Sharks do not normally bother a kayaker, but they are a bit like people; there are good ones and bad ones. A kayak is an unfamiliar object to them, and it is rare indeed for one to attack without checking you out pretty carefully first. This checking-out process at worst involves a dummy-run bump with the snout, at best a casual glide by. Your instinct will probably be to clout the shark with your paddle, and that is no doubt the best thing you can do under most circumstances. Aim for its snout or eye. But don't splash excessively with your paddle, since this may be interpreted as distress and have an effect opposite to that intended. The only reliable exception to this comfortable rule is the great white, who, so the story goes, checks you out with a bite. I believe I have had one encounter with one of these. It came at us without warning in the Tongue of the Ocean, a deep-water trench in the Great Bahama Bank, and it was pure chance that my paddle entered the water forcefully just as its snout was speeding towards the middle of our kayak. It seems that the unexpected blow with the paddle put the shark off its aim enough to miss the first pass; then the commotion we kicked up as I fumbled for the shells for our bang stick checked its confidence and cast doubts on our edibility. The shark turned off at the last moment in making the next few passes, clipping the rubberized hull with its dorsal fin while circling beneath us.

Wade Doak, well-known New Zealand diver and researcher, found that sharks would not come near a diver wearing a zebra-striped suit. As soon as the striped diver left the water, the sharks were back again. Maybe there is an idea there for the hulls of sea kayaks. An interesting conclusion of U.S. Navy research into sharks is that the most effective protection for a swimmer to use is a black survival bag. Their experiments with the sharks' reaction to colour revealed that the beasts were liable to attack bright colours such as orange or yellow life jackets. Indeed, one shade of yellow popular with life jacket manufacturers was dubbed by the researchers "yum-yum yellow" because sharks attacked it so readily.

Discourage sharks by being quietly aggressive with them whenever they come within reach. The greatest risk occurs during a capsize when one is obliged to remain swimming beside the kayak while a difficult pump and re-entry job is performed. In these circumstances have a diving mask, snorkel and fins close at hand—and carry a bang stick or shark stick (a 4-foot stick with a nail in the end) at all times while paddling tropical waters. It is of course important that the person entrusted with fending off sharks in this manner be a competent free diver, and if this is not the case, one may be better off pumping the boat dry from the protection of a black survival bag.

Seals, Sea Lions, Walruses &
Renegade Sea Otters

Seals and sea lions can usually be relied on not to attack unless provoked, though deciding what constitutes provocation is something open to their interpretation, especially that of the larger bulls. Large bulls get particularly annoyed with paddlers venturing too close to their colonies, so bring binoculars if you wish to observe the mammals undisturbed. If you are on a wilderness expedition that requires hunting seals or sea lions for food, avoid shooting them from the kayak. A wounded seal or sea lion will attack, and one that is shot dead sinks like stone, which is of course why eastern Arctic and Greenland kayak hunters relied on harpoons connected to air bladders as floats.

Encounters with walruses must be avoided strenuously as these animals do have a reputation for apparently unprovoked attack, and their size makes them doubly threatening. A smaller mammal not normally associated with sea kayaking hazards is the sea otter, which finds it way into this paragraph merely because one very deliberately nipped me on the elbow and threatened to claw its way into my cockpit as I paddled the waters of British Columbia's Bunsby Islands some years ago. The 90-pound critter, it turned out, had befriended the crew of a marine research vessel used during the 1969 transplant of Alaskan sea otters to the depleted B.C. coast. Amazingly, my playful attacker followed me ashore and curled up on my seat as soon as I vacated it.

Sea Snakes

Sea snakes may be encountered in the South China Sea, Java Sea and Indian Ocean, sometimes far out of sight of land. They are usually yellowish brown, seldom more than 4 feet in length, and can be seen lolling lazily on the surface. The main risk for a kayaker is accidentally picking one up on the paddle so that it falls aboard, or having one washed onto the boat by a breaking sea. Sea snakes are non-aggressive creatures but very venomous. Their bite is fatal in 25 per cent of cases and is unusual in that the effects are not felt for as long as two hours after the bite, when paralysis and spasms finally occur. Survivors reportedly recover completely, with no aftereffects.

Portuguese Man-of-War

The man-of-war is a variety of jellyfish found throughout tropical and temperate zones. It possesses a blue flotation bladder supporting a mass of stinging tentacles which can extend 40 to 60 feet down or, during windy days, may lie along the surface of the sea. The sting is painful and is dangerous to some people, especially if it covers a large area. Normally you will only be caught by the occasional filament swept over the arms and face by breaking waves. The effect does not appear to be more serious than that of stinging nettle. Some relief can be gained with a topical application of an antihistamine cream or a weak solution of ammonia (or, simply, urine, which is universally available). Should the stinging be extensive and in a dangerous place, such as the throat, the best treatment is with antihistamine tablets, which should be carried in a handy place for just such an emergency. In badly infested waters, it is advisable to wear a long-sleeved, high neck shirt and gloves and tie a bandanna over your nose as a preventive measure. Australian lifeguards, who are exposed to regular encounters with stinging jellyfish, use a protective suit made of stretch nylon stocking material.

Sea Urchins

There are many varieties of sea urchins around the world's shorelines. All of them should be treated with respect by the lightly shod paddler. Sea urchins affect primarily those obliged to wade ashore across reefs or to launch in shallows. The tropical varieties with long slender spines and remarkable powers of penetration are especially unpleasant. They are found on all sorts of shores except soft mud and are particularly common on coral reefs. Some tropical varieties contain toxin in the shorter spines.

If you are unfortunate enough to get sea urchin spines in your feet or legs, you will doubtless be flooded with earnest advice about dripping candle wax, lemon juice, chicken entrails and goat semen as curatives. Speak politely to all free advisors, then leave the spines alone for a couple of days, disinfect the foot, and coax the blighters out one by one with a needle. Very deep spines will work their way towards the surface over a period of a couple of weeks. A few years ago my paddling partner and I acquired 128 spines in our feet after a capsize on a coral reef. Some spines went right through our feet. None infected, however, and the deepest emerged almost a month after the accident.

Note: You must not attempt to remove the spines with tweezers, as the pressure from the metal jaws will only crush the end of the brittle spine shaft.

Stingrays

Stingrays and stone fish can be a problem for tropical paddlers wading in the shallows. These creatures often lie half covered with sand, and will slash or spike the unwary foot that lands on their backs. If you must wade the shallows, prod the ground ahead with a paddle to warn them of your approach. Sturdy shoes will be your best protection. Always wear shoes around coral shores.

Jumping & Flying Fish

It is not uncommon to be assailed by dozens of herring or mullet as you paddle through a school of them, usually in shallow water. The shape of the passing kayak panics them into bouncing all over you, and the air is heavy with the smell of fish.

Flying fish aboard are a rarer occurrence, though my wife

has had the dubious privilege of being slapped in the face by one during a night crossing. As a rule they will fly away from the kayak but, like garfish, they can fly away from one boat and into the next, or away from a hungry dorado and into you. Flying fish weigh as much as 2 pounds, so they can give you a nasty surprise. Garfish have substantial swords on their snouts, and there are occasional reports of a venturesome mariner having his cheek pierced by one.

SHIPS AND OTHER MONSTERS

Don't expect to be seen by ships as you sit in your kayak on the sea. You won't even show up on radar unless you have a radar reflector aloft. It is you who must move.

When a ship appears to be coming straight for you, you may find it difficult to decide which side to move to get out of her way. It is worth a few seconds' pause to get it right. Resist the common reaction to scuttle across in front of her; instead, watch the line-up of the bow and the mast closely to see if she is likely to pass in front of you or astern. Then paddle away from the line of her course, taking care to watch the vessel until she is past—just in case she alters course. Don't use flares unless it appears that you truly cannot avoid her course. If you do put a flare up in front of her, she won't alter course, but at least her crew will likely check to see that you are not wrapped around her bows. You don't usually need to worry about the wake of a big ship capsizing a kayak. A supertanker at full speed just sends out something like an ocean swell which hardly affects existing wave patterns. Tugboats are more of a menace but seldom so bad as to seriously threaten a competent kayaker. Naval vessels under power are a different matter: their wakes can be *very* steep.

Powerboats

These are the bane of the poetic paddler's life. Near marinas they can be as thick as hornets, and many is the time I have wished my Schermuly flare gun was a bazooka. Some powerboat operators seem to think that if an object is lower than their bows, they will bounce over it if they are going fast enough. Unlike those moving monoliths the merchant ships, small powerboats have the nasty habit of zigzagging and bouncing about so that it is almost impossible to anticipate their course if they are heading your way. You never know if they have seen you or not, and there persists to the last instant the fear that the operator will suddenly see one kayak and swerve into another.

Flares are not the answer. Leaving a major port on a weekend may produce close encounters with a score or more powerboats, and you can't go firing off flares every time a boat points your way. Instead, carry a big black or orange garbage bag. Keep it handy and when you see the frothing upraised bows headed your way, stuff the bag over your paddle and wave it in the air as high as you can reach. At the same time, turn on your rudder so your boat faces the menace. If it is determined to hit you, at least it will be a glancing blow which will tend to push you aside rather than ride over you. Should a broadside collision be unavoidable, don't hesitate, roll the kayak away from the speedboat and push with your feet against the inside of the kayak so you are projected well below those propellers (not so easy if you are wearing a life jacket). Don't surface until the crashing stops. In some parts of the world (such as Miami), powerboats are the greatest single hazard to sea kayakers. As we approached Miami Beach at the end of a twenty-hour crossing of the Gulf Stream, there were speedboats everywhere, and our two kayaks were almost run down by what looked like a brace of giant fibreglass shoes thundering along at 70 mph: We had unwittingly entered the unmarked lanes of an ocean power-boat race. With boats screaming by within 50 yards of us, one of our group fired parachute flares over them, but without effect. We did the only thing we could, which was to paddle on through, consoling ourselves with the thought that at 70 mph any race pilot not looking out for obstacles would be courting suicide.

Encounters in Fog

When vision is drastically reduced by fog, you must rely on your compass and ears. When you hear shipping in the fog, paddle gently towards the sound so that you have steerage, following the engine noise until it passes. Then resume your course. By keeping your bow towards the source of the sound, you reduce the chances of a dangerous collision. If the source of the sound moves in relation to your compass setting, you are probably safe. If it stays in the same position and is getting louder, you are not. Sounding a whistle is not likely to help you much unless the boat has a very silent engine and an alert watch, though I suppose a fog horn or trumpet might do the trick. Your best defence against shipping in fog is to raise a radar reflector on a fishing pole or some other similar makeshift mast.

One nasty little story on this subject is told by Hilary Collins, who was in a cross-channel party which was almost run down in heavy fog by the Dover to Calais hovercraft.

ICEBERGS, BERGY BITS & GROWLERS

Most of the ice encountered on a summer or autumn trip outside the extreme polar latitudes will be of glacial origin. Icebergs are calved into the sea by hundreds of tidewater glaciers in Greenland, Alaska, Baffin Island, the Svalbard Ar-

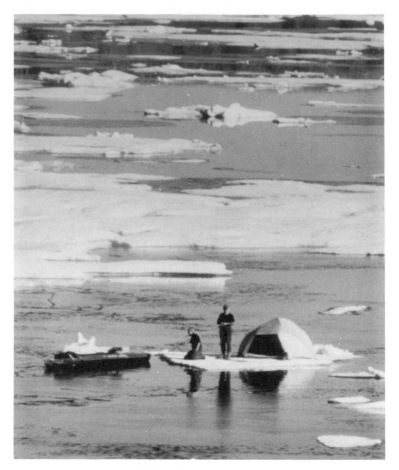

Going with the floe on an Ecosummer tour

chipelago and elsewhere in the Arctic, and by several such glaciers in Patagonian Chile. These bergs split and melt into smaller pieces affectionately known as bergy bits (on the order of 500 to 1000 tons), which split and melt into yet smaller pieces called growlers. Since 80 to 90 per cent of an iceberg is normally below waterline, a bergy bit which looks to be the size of a house may in reality be the size of an apartment block, and a growler which really *is* the size of a house may be awash in moderate seas.

For a kayaker, the principal danger inherent in icebergs and bergy bits is that they may calve unexpectedly from a glacier, producing enormous swells, or that anywhere, anytime, they may roll. Icebergs are sometimes beautiful and compelling pieces of sculpture, but anyone who has spent a few days among them must have seen the unpredictable somersaults they perform.

In 1932 the kayak belonging to the talented young British adventurer Gino Watkins was found bobbing in the waves off the coast of Greenland. Watkins himself was not found. It is assumed that he boarded an appealing iceberg just before it rolled.

A domed iceberg has probably rolled already, and you should expect it to roll again at any time. A berg with two distinct horns—a so-called "drydock iceberg"—probably has *not* rolled. It may still be stable, but there is no guarantee. Tabular icebergs, which are calved from shelf ice rather than glaciers, are far less likely to roll than the randomly shaped glacial bergs, but tabular bergs are rarely encountered outside the Antarctic Ocean. Floebergs—floes disengaged from the pack ice and drifting along—are also quite stable as a rule, but they are still not to be trusted, because they may calve growlers or floebits (baby floebergs) at any time.

The truly small pieces of ice rubble sometimes found around the faces of tidewater glaciers (or in leads through pack ice) are called brash. Remember when paddling among brash ice that, just as with bergs, there is five to ten times as much ice below the surface as there is above it. The pieces are larger than they look, and if you jostle them with your paddle they may jostle you heavily in return.

SEA ICE

In winter and spring, you may well encounter another form of ice: sea ice. During a normal winter, the sea freezes as far south as the coasts of Nova Scotia and Hokkaido, while other waters at far higher latitudes, irrigated by warmer ocean currents, remain ice-free. During very cold winters, ice may form in the North Sea and even in the Adriatic.

The freezing point of seawater depends on its salinity, but as a rule it will be in the vicinity of 28°F (-2°C). When this temperature is reached and sustained on the ocean's surface, sea ice forms in the following stages:

1 *Frazil:* minute crystals which give the sea an oily sheen.
2 *Grease ice:* a thin layer of coagulating frazil, more viscous and with a dull or matte surface.
3 *Shuga:* small, woolly, white lumps in the grease ice.
4 *Nilas:* an elastic crust several inches thick. It flexes with the waves but has a definite calming effect on the sea. Thin nilas is dark like the water beneath it, but as it thickens it becomes a light grey and looks something like a mixture of ground glass and paper pulp.
5 *Ice rind:* a thin but brittle crust. As the rind begins to form, it enforces an angular shape on the waves. Under certain conditions, ice rind may form directly from grease ice and shuga, without the intermediary nilas stage.

The first four of these stages are varieties of soft ice. Frazil, grease ice, shuga and dark nilas can all be paddled through—though they will definitely slow you down. A kayaker who continues under these conditions, however, may well find himself beset in ice that is too stiff to paddle through but far too weak to walk on. New sea ice is notoriously weak in comparison with freshwater ice, because it is honeycombed with brine. A thick ice rind may well prevent passage of your kayak *across* the surface and yet do nothing much to prevent your falling *through* the surface. New sea ice as much as a foot thick may be quite inadequate to bear the weight of a man.

As sea ice ages and thickens, the salt gravitates out of it and the ice becomes considerably stronger. Early in this strengthening process, the crust is often broken by wave action into relatively small slabs which rub each other round like two-dimensional pebbles. The result is called pancake ice. The discs thus formed freeze back together with renewed vigour, and in a few weeks the ice may be sturdy enough to bear enormous loads.

Once sea ice passes the dark nilas stage, it is navigable by kayak only through leads and polynyas. (A polynya is an area of open water in the midst of the icepack.) During the colder months, leads and polynyas may begin to freeze over soon after they are formed, so that grease ice, shuga and nilas may be encountered deep in the pack ice in mid-winter or early spring. A kayaker travelling in such conditions should be extremely well prepared—not only for sudden immersion in icy waters but also for camping out on the ice and for an extended walk across rough ice, pulling the kayak as a sled. The most insidious danger, however, is that leads can close just as suddenly as they open. Particularly during the spring or summer break-up, small leads may grind shut as icefloes or broken bergs are shifted by current or tide.

If you are serious about kayaking in areas subject to sea ice, you may want to equip your kayak with a sled such as those once used by the King Islanders in the Bering Sea, and by Fridtjof Nansen during his 1893 attempt to reach the north pole. A light sled can be carried on the afterdeck while the boat is in the water, and strapped beneath the hull for travel across the pack or shelf ice.

SEA KAYAKING SOLO

To say that a kayaker should not go to sea alone is a bit like saying that someone should not walk in the mountains alone: it is prudent advice, but the reality of sea kayaking is that many of its most dedicated adherents prefer going out alone. The risk is increased, but so, arguably, are the rewards. Indeed, I believe that the appreciation and level of awareness of one's environment is diminished by a factor of the number of people in one's party. It is in the nature of some people to take their own risks and gamble their skill against the sea with their lives as the chips, depending on no one to assist them. Travelling solo is the most direct sea kayaking experience, and, because of the greater risk, there is considerable social resistance to it—a resistance not dissimilar to that at first afforded to solo yachtsmen and alpine climbers. I do not wish through this book to discourage anyone from taking to the sea alone, nor to encourage them either. Those who truly have the solo kayaking inclination will not be stopped by anything I could say, and do not stand in need of my blessing. I do want to point out the dangers, suggest some precautions and techniques, and make it quite clear that the danger *is* greater. The sea will more readily kill you for your mistakes if you are alone. Above all, a solo paddler must be capable of quick and efficient self-rescue if (s)he is to survive.

Solo kayaking demands the commitment and serious intent of a high wire walker or solo rock climber. Once you are out there, you are very definitely on your own. As a young single man, I always prepared for my solo trips by telling nobody I was going—so that nobody expected me back and no one would think to bother the coast guard. Irresponsible in a social (and personal) sense, perhaps, but in another sense of the word, totally responsible.

Here are some special tips to help improve your odds. Think safety. Run through "what if?" scenarios so as to be prepared for all possible mishaps. Have the right equipment ready to use and know how to use it.

1 Choose a kayak with good stability for solo paddling. You may need that extra margin of safety if you become incapacitated on the water.
2 Maximize your buoyancy and back-up buoyancy systems.
3 Check the condition and effectiveness of your spray skirt and keep a spare handy.
4 Develop your skills, particularly your bracing, roll and paddle turns in wind and waves.
5 Match your level of fitness with the type of trip.
6 Develop one or more solid back-up self-rescue systems that leave you in a more stable position after the capsize than you were before it.
7 Dress for the occasion; in cold water, dress for immersion.
8 Carry a wide range of attention getters: flares, EPIRB, VHF radio, strobe light, flashlight, etc.
9 Carry a waterproof shore survival kit.
10 Avoid taking any unnecessary risk.

Running before a squall. Note that the paddles are unfeathered to prevent the wind from spinning them, the boat is running between 30° and 45° off the direction of the wind, and the paddlers are ready to brace on the windward side if required.

8

Storm & Other Emergency Procedures

It makes sense to think about what could go wrong at sea and what you are going to do if it does.

Storms may be the most common fear of sea kayakers—particularly those attempting difficult passages with many miles of open sea. What do you do if you are caught in a storm? The answers will depend largely on where you are in relation to land and what kind of boat you are using, since the best tactic is usually to get ashore. If the land is within your grasp, you may be able to run with the wind to a safe harbour; if the wind is blowing athwart, your best course would be to ferry-glide across the storm.

In a severe storm, fighting upwind is out of the question as a means for reaching land. You should avoid wasting energy fighting it unless the storm is expected to be a small one and battling it is seen only as a holding action until the wind drops enough for you to make headway. In such a situation, you simply maintain your course as best you can.

Sometimes you will not be able to make land either because the land to leeward is too dangerous or because the only available landfall lies into the wind. If you have been caught by a major blow and the wind is too strong for you to lift your paddle, or if there is a complicating factor such as a current which will hinder your return to shore, you will have to ride it out. The decision to do so is a critical one and should be acted upon as soon as it becomes clear that this is your best choice, since the object of passively riding out a storm is conservation of strength. The moment you realize you cannot escape a storm, check that:

1 All bags and equipment are secure inside the boat;
2 Foot, hand or electric pump are working;
3 The drogue is rigged and ready to go;
4 Food is handy; also, in the tropics, mask, fins and snorkel;
5 Your emergency locator beacon, if you have one, is at hand.

Then do the following:

6 Tie your paddle to the bow line or paddle leash. In a double, tie off both paddles, one to the bow line, the other to the stern.
7 Take in all sail and unstep the mast if you were sailing.
8 Put on any protective clothing you are not already wearing.
9 Secure your life jacket.
10 Eat a meal of energy food, drink a little water from each bottle (so they won't sink), relieve yourself, then put a little food in your anorak pocket, together with your flares and a flashlight.
11 Prepare some warps ready for trailing. A 150-foot climbing rope will do nicely, if you happen to be carrying one. Your anchor warp, chain included, would also serve well enough; alternatively, use a shorter length of line with something (like clothing) tied to it to increase the drag.

When you decide to ride out the storm on the open sea, you are again faced with a choice: you can run before the wind or you can lie to a drogue. Your choice will depend on what lies to leeward, how strong the wind is, how large the waves are and what your plan is when the storm is over. It will also depend on what sort of boat you are in, and on your previous experience with the different methods.

RUNNING BEFORE A STORM

This is a method suitable for situations where you have a great distance available to leeward or you are running with the wind to a safe harbour. In this circumstance you will appreciate using an unfeathered paddle and having a rudder. Turn the boat and steer a course about 45 degrees off the direction of wind and waves. Vary this angle according to your relative comfort or lack of it with the size of the waves. Try to avoid surfing directly down the wave face. You may decide to trail your prepared warps at this stage. Have your paddle ready to brace into any heavily breaking crests. Normally, the paddle should be held across the coaming, with the blades tilted forward so that the wind pressure holds it down, but you may prefer to trail it on the windward side, thus reducing windage and placing you in a position of constant support.

As the wind increases, lean forward or snuggle lower in the boat to reduce windage and lower your centre of gravity. In the event that you do capsize, your paddle will be attached to the kayak; you need only hold on to one to be assured of still having the other.

LYING TO A DROGUE

Lying to a drogue is useful in the open sea, or when you plan to return to windward after the storm, or where it is important to reduce wind drift because of a dangerous lee shore. There is considerable disagreement amongst bar-stool sailors

A drogue off the bow will hold the bow into the wind and reduce drift. If a sea-chute is used, a float should be attached to prevent the chute from sinking

concerning the use of drogues during a storm. It is generally conceded that they are fine for reducing drift under average conditions, but their use in a severe storm is hotly debated. So be it with kayaks.

In theory, a well-set drogue off the bow of a kayak will hold her head into the weather. This may indeed be the case with a sea-chute, but with a standard sea anchor of traditional dimensions, my experience is that the boat yaws badly in its backward drift unless fitted with a counterforce off the stern. Another kayak is such a force, as we discovered while rigged in series for sleeping one night during a fresh wind. The boat at the end of the series yawed wildly as usual, while the kayak to whose stern she was attached held steady in the waves.

It is important to lift the rudder or skeg clear of the water when you are lying to a standard drogue, since you will still be going backward quite fast. Hold the paddle so it won't be blown out of your hands, or lash it firmly along the deck.

too low. A drogue which allows significant drift will cause the boat to yaw unless a counterforce—such as a second kayak—is tethered astern.

During a gale, far more spray hits a kayaker than would hit a yachtsman. (The yachtsman, no matter how small his vessel, sits higher out of the water.) With the drogue off the bow you will be facing the wind and you run the risk of being blinded by spray. A diving mask will protect your eyes, and you can draw breath inside your parka lip. This arrangement can also be of assistance when you near the limit of paddleable conditions or where an imminent lee shore demands that you claw your way along the coast by ferry-gliding against the wind to a place where you can land. To increase your stability and reduce wind resistance, snuggle low into your boat so only your shoulders, arms and head are above the coaming. Keep the bilges pumped dry. Lindemann, on his Atlantic crossing, trailed his drogue off the stern, wrecked his rudder assembly and capsized twice. He might have done better with a larger drogue off the bow, though it would have put the spray in his face.

213

If you trail warps, they should run from cleats abaft the cockpit and out through a loop near the towing point. Warps often have the bonus value of "tripping" a breaker astern of you rather than having it dump on your rear deck.

RAFTING UP

Rafting up is often taught as a storm procedure, but I do not advise relying on it in really severe conditions. It can, however, be a useful manoeuvre for stabilizing a party when some emergency occurs or if you just want everyone to come together for a snack or a discussion of route during moderate conditions. The two most common ways of doing it are to raft the boats cockpit to cockpit or bow to cockpit like sardines. In both cases it is necessary to hold the boats apart at arm's length in choppy water to stop them crunching together and riding up one on the other. Rafting up can stabilize a capsized kayak during re-entry, and it can provide enough stability for sleeping in slender singles during calm weather. It is dangerous, however, to put too much faith in rafting up for stability in heavy weather. Rafting up tends to be the optimist's answer to any emergency, but it can be very strenuous keeping your raft together in high seas, and it turns into an awful mess when you are swatted by an ocean creamer. There can be broken paddles, crushed fingers and bleeding people wearing kayaks in strange places all over the sea. It is equally dangerous to count on rafting up when you cannot stay awake any longer.

Let me repeat what I have said in discussing self-rescue. I believe that to be safe in a sea kayak, you must be capable of surviving alone. The rhyme "less than three shall never be," though helpful for the lower level of emergency, deceptively lulls the inexperienced into believing that their ultimate safety

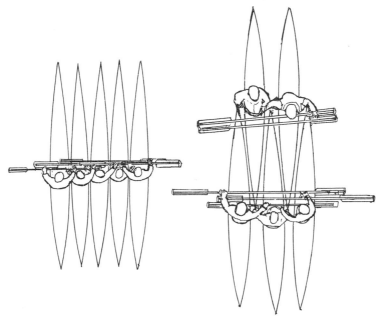

Rafting up cannot be relied upon for security in really rough water; however, under normal cruising conditions, it can provide a secure platform. Of the two methods, bow-to-cockpit is the most secure. Side-by-side rafting is useful for rescue aid or to provide stability for some unusual operation.

relies on clutching onto two companions—but things are just not like that in heavy weather. Then, any boat close enough to touch you is an extreme hazard. A loaded fibreglass kayak carried into you by a breaking wave can cause serious injuries, including concussion and fractured bones. One kayak can be driven right through another—and how do you brace into a breaking wave if there is another kayak on top of yours? By all means paddle with two companions—it is certainly safer—but *don't* base your philosophy of survival on them.

THE ULTIMATE STORMS

Hurricanes—or typhoons, as they are known in Asia and the Pacific—are the ultimate storms: circular monsters anywhere from 60 to 1000 miles across. They, together with their less ferocious cousins the tropical storms, lurk like wolves in the backs of the minds of sailors (and tropical kayakers).

Your first thought must always be to get yourself and your boat to high ground as fast as possible. Chances are you will have plenty of warning of the approach of such storms (see Chapter 5). The danger of low ground is that a hurricane may cause the level of the sea to rise 15 feet or more. Combine this with giant waves, and you have a sea which will sweep right over the lower atolls and coastal plains. Ideally, you want something like a bomb shelter on a mountaintop to weather it out. Certainly you want some form of substantial protection against wind-blown objects.

I am thankful never to have been caught in a full-fledged hurricane, but when in vulnerable areas my plan and priorities have always been carefully thought out. I frequently cast about me when camped at a new island and think, "Where is the best hurricane shelter around here?" Generally I have decided, if no hurricane-proof dwelling was handy, that I would carry the boat inland to some natural protection such as a rocky outcrop or a thicket of small trees and tie it down. (Larger trees might fall on the boat and smash it.) If my boat was of the folding variety, I would dismantle it and bury it on high ground.

As the eye of the storm passes over an area, there will be a lull in the wind and then it will start again from the opposite side. Remember that when you choose your protection it must serve from both sides.

SLEEPING IN A KAYAK

The ability and willingness to sleep in the kayak are indispensable to long journeys. Sleeping in the boat is also a necessity for surviving bouts of illness or incapacitation at sea.

The kayak becomes extraordinarily stable when the centre of gravity is lowered, and the lower you can go the better. George Dyson has built kayaks into which he can retreat fully, closing a watertight perspex dome over the cockpit; but it is possible to wriggle down into any high-volume kayak if there is no forward bulkhead and if the bow is not laden with too much gear. (A beam of at least 25 inches is usually required for an average adult.)

Many a kayaker seeking a better mousetrap has dreamed up a system of inner tubes and paddles to stabilize the craft, but this is not necessarily a solution. A beamy kayak with the weight kept low is extremely stable. It will *slide* when hit by a wave. Lindemann used an inner tube outrigger on his Atlantic crossing and capsized twice *because* of it. His boat would slide until the outrigger dived, at which point the kayak would trip on the outrigger. Ed Gillet was more successful with two inflatable sponsons each side of the cockpit of his double on his transpacific crossing.

I have slept slouched down in a kayak on many occasions, and have ridden through gales in such a posture. This is not the greatest way to spend the night, but neither is it the worst.

SEPARATION AT SEA

Once you have agreed that you are going to travel as a group, no one should leave that group unless everybody knows about it and an arrangement is made to link up again. During bad weather, it is important not to spread the party too thinly. Not only will you be slow to give assistance if needed, but you may lose sight of a member who pauses to make repairs or readjust gear. In a party with three boats or more, leave a strong paddler to take up the rear if there is doubt about any of the members being able to handle the conditions. It is the lead boat's responsibility to see that no one is left behind. This is because a delay up front automatically draws the group together while one astern spreads the party.

Surprisingly, it is often fine, calm weather that causes separations at sea. Everyone is relaxed and confident that nothing could possibly go wrong on such a fine day—"So let's not wait for those turkeys in the other boat. We'll go on and wait on the island." Then of course there is a misunderstanding about which island, or the following boat gets into some sort of unforeseeable trouble and is delayed or obliged to alter course. Once our kayak, which was travelling second on an 8-mile crossing of the Strait of Magellan under miraculously calm conditions, was attacked by a wounded sea lion. The animal bit through the rubberized hull in eleven places, and we scurried for a rock a couple of miles distant while the other boat continued, its occupants never suspecting that anything could possibly have gone wrong. It was two weeks before we were again able to make contact. There was, naturally, a misunderstanding as to the rendezvous point, and it is no simple matter to locate a solitary kayak in the midst of a peppering of wilderness islands with no radio contact.

Separations at sea can usually be avoided by following these guidelines:

1 Make it clearly the responsibility of the lead boat to see that everyone stays within communicating distance. (It is easier for someone to wait than for the others to catch up.)

2 Everyone in the group must hold the same course as the lead boat and nobody is to strike off alone. If you disagree with the course set by the lead boat, discuss it. If you can't agree, establish a rendezvous point.

3 Establish a rendezvous point each day. Normally this will be your lunch stop or the spot where you expect to camp that night. As an extra safeguard, you might agree also on a more distant, back-up rendezvous point, or on the emergency principle of a return to the last camp at which you were all together. The first option is preferable since it won't involve backtracking.

It can be very difficult to hunt for a kayak on a rough sea, even from a cliff top with binoculars. If you are carrying VHF radios, then your chances of prolonged separation are greatly reduced—but only if you have an agreed-upon listening time. This might be, for instance, five minutes each side of the hour.

TOWING

In an emergency, such as illness, exhaustion, accident or hypothermia, the best solution may be to tow the incapacitated boat. Towing is also an emergency measure to keep together two boats in which one individual or a crew is paddling more weakly than another.

The towing point of most singles is about a foot astern the cockpit; that of a double kayak is immediately abaft the rear cockpit. A bridle attached to cleats each side of the cockpit, or looped around the lip of the coaming if you have a fibreglass boat with a small cockpit, will provide secure attachment.

In doubles, a simple system is to pass the rigged drogue

from the boat about to be towed across to the towing boat. It is delivered to the No. 2 paddler, who ties it off to the cleats each side of the coaming and tucks the canopy away under the deck rigging. This will often place the drogue swivel neatly over the towing point. It is handy to have a resilient support such as a short whip aerial just above the rudder to prevent fouling of the rudder assembly. Just put a clove hitch in the towline and drop it over the aerial.

Unfortunately, kayaks don't usually tow very well. They tend to yaw badly and must be steered carefully in the wake of the towing boat. This can prove a problem in a single if the kayaker is incapacitated. If the victim is in one of the less stable boats, a third kayak will be needed to prop him/her up, so the formula is complicated even more—your one strong boat will be towing two kayaks.

A stronger system is to lay the injured or hypothermic paddler as low as possible in the kayak then link up the two remaining paddlers in series (or a double) to pull the crippled boat. Ideally, you should have at least one double kayak in every party so that you can transfer a sick person into its forward cockpit. The Outward Bound school in British Columbia uses three-seater kayaks with the centre cockpit blanked off. This gives the option of using the middle space to carry an inert passenger or even a third paddler for extra towing power. A strong paddler can paddle a double alone and still average two knots under neutral conditions. Once when I was injured, my petite wife paddled a fully loaded two seater 10 miles in four hours with me as an inert lump in the passenger seat.

9

Camping & Food Gathering

Some folks carry all sorts of imaginative gadgetry to make camping easier, but the wilderness has a healthy knack of trimming these extras so that by the end of the second or third week, you will be reduced to the most basic equipment. Chances are that by the end of a long trip, if the weather has been tolerable, you won't have used your primus for ages, having realized that you could light a fire almost as quickly and that the fire was a lot more friendly. Your pressure cooker will become an ordinary cooking pot, since you won't have to worry about fuel shortages once you begin to use firewood. (Obviously, where wood is becoming scarce it is better to use the stove.) And as for cooking time, what does fifteen minutes matter away from the hustle of city life? Your knife, fork, spoon, cup and plates will probably be reduced to a spoon, a bowl and a jackknife. The dinky little hatchet you started out with will have been traded for a three-pound, long-handled axe. Who knows, you might abandon the tent altogether and carry only a waterproof fly and groundsheet like native hunters.

CAMPING IN THE LAND OF STORMS

Selecting the best campsite from the sea is an important first step. (In British Columbia or Patagonia you know you are

doing it right when you start finding the remains of old Indian camps as you clear the ground for your tent.) Your chart
will often give a good indication of the most favourable sort
of place for a landing. According to preference, you might
select a sheltered cove or fjord close to the jumping-off point
for the next day or go in behind a headland which offers a
better view of the seas outside. The head of a larger bay will
usually have a stream, better shelter and easier landing.
Streams large enough to appear on your chart may well offer
a protected path to shore, and of course a supply of clean
fresh water. If you plan to camp for a day or two at the one
site, choose a location with plenty of firewood. In Patagonia,
this means looking for stands of tepu or cypress. Tepu, a
feathery leafed tree common along the shores, is such good
firewood that it will burn green. Cypress too is excellent. On
one occasion I pulled a pole of cypress from a bog where it
may well have lain for fifty years. Once it was split it burned
fiercely. In Alaska or British Columbia look for a windfall
cedar or a beach piled high with driftwood.

If you are travelling by double or in a group, you will develop a routine. Try to make it a good one. For instance, as
soon as you land, one person can take the tent, primus (if you
are still using primuses) and pot to the selected site and put on
water for a brew, then pitch the tent and loft the sleeping bags
while another person unloads and cares for the boats.
Whether you use a fire or a primus, it pays to get it going
without loss of time since if someone is cold, the warm drink
is cheering and the activity of making a fire and a meal is
good for morale. The first fifteen minutes after you clamber
out of the kayak on a miserable day is the easiest time to catch
yourself an incapacitating chill.

If firewood is plentiful, build a good-sized fire. The initial
blaze will boil the water quickly and the resulting coals can be
used to cook the main meal, with a pile of driftwood and

dead timber collected ready to throw on as soon as the meal is done. During bad weather, a lightweight canvas fly erected well above the fire protects it from rain. Nylon is no good for this purpose since sparks quickly ventilate it.

Starting a fire in the rain has probably occupied more pages of Boy Scout manuals than anything else. My own solution is to carry an old rubber inner tube. A few square inches of this can easily be lit and set in the midst of small twigs—gathered from the underside of some fallen tree or split from the centre of a dry log. The flaming molten rubber quickly establishes the heart of the fire if you have selected a site sheltered from the wind.

Contrary to popular belief, a kayaker *can* usually find a sheltered campsite on stormy coasts. Although you can expect to need a storm tent (and occasionally you will be glad of it), you can get by with a waterproof 10-foot by 12-foot tarpaulin pitched well into the trees and a sheet of plastic on the ground. Nylon or PVC is good for the fly, but make sure it is set well away from the fire.

Mice and rats are frequently a problem. Sometimes islands are overrun with them, and if you camp in old dwellings you are bound to meet the resident rodents and raccoons. In Chile I once had fifteen holes eaten in the buoyancy tubing of my boat; it seems the rats there fancied plastic, and from then on my equipment included a sturdy rat trap.

In British Columbia and Alaska, bears, especially grizzlies, can also pose a problem for camping kayakers. Camping at river mouths in August when the salmon are running is a particularly reliable way of getting into trouble. Woe betide the hapless kayaker who pitches his tent by a happy bear's exclusive fishing hole or beaches his boat on the bear's buried food supply. Climb a tree if you must. Grizzlies, unlike blacks, are restricted to the ground—though some are reported to be ignoring this rule.

If you are venturing into bear country, it pays to give serious thought to some special equipment. For a start you have to decide if you are going to go armed and if so what sort of weaponry you would choose. Personally I would certainly carry an effective rifle (not lighter than a 30.06) or shotgun; to me, having the option to use or not to use it makes more sense than going unarmed and then needing to protect myself or my companions without having the means to do so. If I were travelling with children I would not consider going unarmed.

For those who have no confidence in their ability to use a firearm effectively, or who disagree in principle with the idea of intruding into a bear's territory then killing it because it challenges your presence (a principle which I agree with but am not prepared to die for!), there is now a magnum aerosol cayenne pepper dispenser that has proven extremely effective at repelling bear attacks, including charges by both grizzly and polar bears. As for me, I would happily try the cayenne, but I'd have a shotgun in the other hand just in case.

Apparently there have been no reports of grizzly attacks on groups of six or more people. Ken Leghorn, who runs commercial kayak tours in Alaskan bear country, is convinced that small groups are more prone to bear encounters than larger, noisier groups and that solo campers place themselves at a significantly higher risk. Indeed, the only two fatal bear encounters in Glacier National Park in recent years have involved solo campers.

A great deal of risk can also be eliminated by the careful choice and care of a campsite. A good site is a fairly open and unrestricted area at least a hundred yards from a stream so that a curious bear, or one on its regular path to a favourite stream, is not obliged to walk close to your camp. Another problem with streams is that they mask the sounds of man and beast, making both vulnerable to surprise encounters. When you get ashore, look for the wide, flattened bear paths and make sure you don't camp close to one of these. Give the bear plenty of room to circle you at an unthreatening distance.

Part of the strategy for avoiding bear trouble is to take meticulous care to keep the camp clear of food smells and scraps from plates. Fish in particular should be cleaned well away from camp. Greasy plates should be washed thoroughly and stored a hundred yards or more from the tents, preferably in a tree, or wrapped and cached clear of all bear trails. Human waste is best disposed of below the high tide level and the toilet paper burned.

Hungry bears are more difficult to avoid than full ones. Members of the Washington Kayak Club had their camp raided by black bears on a 1980 summer expedition. They found the bears were far better at climbing trees than they themselves, and that the trees were too close together to rig a safe food cache. Eventually they anchored a kayak offshore with their food supply in it and drove the bears off with much yelling and stone-throwing. (The same trick tried by inland kayakers on B.C.'s Bowron Lakes a few years ago was less successful. The bears swam out to the boats, wrecking kayaks, cameras and other gear as they helped themselves to the tastier items in the cache.)

Jim Allan, a Canadian tour guide, uses a different technique. He carries a piece of ripe pepperoni sausage and ties it tantalizingly out of reach of the bears, well away from camp. "They'll fart around that all night," he says. On his tours to the North, however, Jim takes a gun.

To avoid surprising a bear—or worse, surprising a mother with her cubs—travel with a noisemaker: a clanking sierra cup or a chatterbox companion. If you do meet a bear, back off carefully; don't run. If you *are* attacked, your last resort is to curl up in a tight ball to protect your face and belly. Play dead and hope the fantasy doesn't come true.

CAMPING IN THE SUN

Life is easier in the tropics, but camping has its own special problems. Shade is a priority, and you have to consider insects (especially if you are near a swamp), breeze and water supply. Tropical rivers are more contaminated than those in cold climates, and you must regard pools of water with great suspicion. All but rainwater should be boiled or treated with purifying tablets. (More on this in Chapter 11.)

Coconut plantations make great campsites, but watch out for falling coconuts—and that is no joke: a 10-pound coconut falling 20 or 30 feet is quite capable of killing you. Your cooking fire and tent should be well clear of delicately poised coconuts and loosely hanging fronds. If you must camp beneath a coconut palm, first pull off all dead fronds and knock down threatening coconuts. Of course, you may have some trouble convincing the plantation owner that the coconut threatened you first, so it is well to befriend him beforehand.

Coconut plantations also provide an abundance of old dried coconuts for campfires, and the dried flowerstalks and fronds burn very well. If the plantation has been frequently worked, there may be piles of discarded dry husks left by the copra gatherers. These make excellent fuel. The young coconuts yield an abundance of sweet water compared to the mature nuts prized for their white flesh. Sharing your swaying garden of palms you may find a population of large, edible crabs, either the tree-climbing variety or the burrowing land crabs. Unfortunately, coconut plantations are also host to mosquitoes and a variety of sandflies which may breed in the old coconut husks and down the burrows of land crabs. A tent with a fine-meshed netted entrance is well worth carrying, as is, of course, insect repellant. Warning: Land crabs are notorious for stealing things. We once retrieved a fine fountain pen from one of their burrows, along with an impressive collection of cups, forks and spoons from our own stock.

The problem with camping in a mangrove swamp is that the tide usually floods your campsite twice a day. Assuming there is no high ground, this leaves you two choices: sleep in the trees or sleep in the boat.

The best way to sleep in the trees is with a hammock. A good one is the U.S. military jungle hammock with sewn-in roof and mosquito netting. Take care to sleep on a layer of blanket as well as covering yourself, since mosquitoes are quite capable of biting into your back through the tight fabric.

If the mangroves are too tight or small for a hammock, you will have to turn your boat into a bed, and your comfort is going to depend to a large extent on the type of craft you have. If you come in to the swamp at high tide, be sure that you have not moored your kayak above a stake or submerged branch. Hang your gear in the upper branches to give you space, then inflate your air mattress and rig a mosquito net from the thinnest nearby branches. (These will flex when the tide drops.) Mosquitoes can be particularly bad in mangrove swamps near river or stream entrances.

SECURITY

When camping in populated areas where you fear malicious behaviour or theft from the locals, you must give some thought to security. The following points should be considered for protection against sneak thieves:

1 Pitch the tents within easy earshot and with the entrances facing each other.
2 Put the boats in the midst of the camp so they are visible from every tent. You might also make the tents fast to a cleat on the coaming.
3 Take valuables into the tents and store them between the occupants or under your pillows. Put the remainder of your gear inside the boats with the spray skirts tied off.
4 If you must, stretch a fishing line tight around camp at a height of four inches. Attach it to a precariously balanced pot of cutlery which will crash down when the line is tripped. (Dogs are especially vulnerable to this trick.)
5 Keep a pack of mini-flares and a powerful flashlight handy. A dazzling light can be most intimidating, as can a flare fired aloft. Mini-flares are dangerous firearms and should not be pointed at prowlers unless life is threatened. (Cayenne pepper spray, on the other hand, incapacitates without causing injury.)
6 Don't leave axes, machetes, spear guns or knives lying around camp at night; slip them under your tent or boat so *you* know where they are.

FOOD

There has been a great deal written about food and diet on expeditions, and a kayak trip is little different from any other strenuous journey. You can expect to burn up a tremendous number of calories. It is most important to maintain this energy supply. No matter what you eat, you will feel great lethargy and weariness during the early days of constant paddling, but an inadequate diet will make things a lot worse. In cold climates, the problem of energy supply becomes even more serious since so many calories are burned up just keeping warm.

The critical point in making the adaptation from the easy life most people lead to that demanded by a kayak trip of some duration is the availability of energy from the food. A body that is accustomed to extracting its energy from a readily available source such as sugar or starch will become starved as it struggles to cope with a protein diet. When it can no longer get its energy from one source, it moves on to the next, but the breaking down of protein into energy is so slow that at first the body cannot keep up.

During the first three weeks of our Patagonian trip, my companions and I developed an insatiable craving for carbohydrate. The hunting was excellent, and we could eat lean steamer ducks to the tune of 5 pounds of meat each day and still feel hungry. It was not until we were able to purchase forty-eight cans of sweetened condensed milk, which we quaffed at the rate of one can per person per day, that we began to recover from this strange form of starvation. Sweets and plenty of sweet drinks are not luxuries; they are necessities for most people under these circumstances. The right food, and time to let your body consume it, are necessary if you are not going to burn yourself up on a long trip. The ideal is to eat as you did at home: three hearty meals a day, and then sleep for eight hours every night, but more likely you will end up paddling twelve hours or more on a handful of raisins and a couple of buns with bully beef. You may do a lot worse than that, gradually drawing ever more heavily on your body's reserves. My suggestion for long wilderness trips is to carry only fats, milk powder, sugar, spices and carbohydrates (rice, flour, etc.) and rely on nature for the protein and greens. You should always, however, carry a small supply of emergency freeze-dried protein.

The best food for paddling is something with little bulk and high energy content. Raisins are good, as are almonds or walnuts. Peanuts and cashews are usually more difficult to digest. Sweetened condensed milk, granola bars and chocolate are great to keep you going until the next round of buns with bully beef, though it should be stated here that strenuous paddling discourages large meals since hardworking stomach muscles just don't cope well with a full belly. Leave your main meals until you get ashore. Interestingly, Lindemann, who is a physician as well as a German, carried one can of beer for each day of his transatlantic crossing.

HUNTING, FISHING & DIVING FROM A KAYAK

The kayak was originally developed by the Eskimos for hunting seal, walrus, caribou and even whales. It is silent, unobtrusive and swift, and you may hunt from it using rifle, shotgun, spear or bow and arrow. In New Zealand the boats have even been used for small-scale commercial hunting. It is, however, difficult to shoot accurately while seated in a kayak if there is any wave action at all, and on the sea, of course, there usually is. One technique is to swing the rifle freely across the target, squeezing the trigger in brief anticipation of lining up. Plenty of practice with an air rifle is desirable before you start shooting for real.

Probably the best all-purpose survival rifle for a kayak expedition is the AR-7 .22 semi-automatic, which folds away inside its own butt, floats, resists corrosion and is quite accurate. You can carry a thousand rounds of ammunition in the same volume as fifty shotgun shells. For paddling in the Arctic, however, a heavier-calibre rifle is desirable because of the risk from polar bear or walrus.

The normal cruising speed of a kayak is just about right for successful trolling, though it may be a little slow for some species of fish. If you use a sturdy hand-line—say about 80-pound-test monofilament with a stainless steel leader of 35-pound-test—you will have a line you can manage, yet one that will let off anything too big for you to handle. In barracuda country, this means losing a lot of lures, but you don't really want to share your kayak with a barracuda capable of breaking a 35-pound leader. A hand reel or a rod can be worked well from a kayak, giving you control of the line without cutting your fingers. A short-handled gaff with a wrist thong may also prove useful to bring your catch aboard if you plan to do a lot of fishing. Keep a cloth sack handy for carrying fish on deck.

A kayak is not the ideal craft from which to dive, but kayaking and diving nevertheless frequently go together. Besides, as we have seen, basic diving equipment can prove very handy during an emergency involving kayaks. Two divers can operate from a double kayak, but it is usually best for only one to be in the water at a time, the other waiting in the boat, ready to receive a fish off the spear or to give assistance. A good free diver can fish comfortably in 40 feet of water and with practice can go twice that deep. If you happen to have access to SCUBA, the tanks can be carried to the dive site on the afterdeck of your two-seater (in a calm sea) and put on either while sitting on the rear of the cockpit or as soon as you are in the water, where they can be held by slings. A diver should of course avoid carrying speared fish in the hand when there may be sharks in the vicinity; instead, thread fish at the end of 12 feet of rope. When diving on the drop-off of a large coral reef, use the kayak to cross the wide, sandy shallows, which can often go a half mile or more. It can then be tied off to a coral head inside the calm while the divers swim out through cuts in the reef to deeper water.

10

First Aid

This chapter, like the chapter on navigation and the section devoted to tides, is intended to supplement knowledge the reader may already have or which he can and should gain from other sources. In this case, I assume that the reader will have some practical knowledge of standard first-aid skills. Basic instructions such as the treatment of wounds, fractures and burns, mouth-to-mouth resuscitation, external cardiac massage and treatment of shock are therefore omitted from the following discussion.

Ideally, you should try to include someone with practical medical experience in your party. Expeditions, however, may require ordinary members to administer treatment beyond the limits of normal first aid, and it is advisable to carry with you an advanced manual of medical emergency practice. A good choice is *Medicine for Mountaineering,* edited by James A. Wilkerson, M.D.

The following is an outline of some special medical problems a kayak expedition is likely to meet.

TENOSYNOVITIS

This is a painful inflammation of the tendons in the wrist and arm. It is most common in the wrist and arm that twist the feathered paddle.

PREVENTION: Use unfeathered paddles. Work up gradually to distance paddling. Do not grasp the paddle shaft too tightly. Keep the wrist in the same plane as the forearm as you paddle. (Do not rotate the wrist.)

TREATMENT: Some relief may be gained from firm bandaging and a course of anti-inflammatory drugs, but the most reliable cure is a few days' rest.

KAYAKER'S ARM (Carpal Tunnel Syndrome)

This may be just a more advanced form of tenosynovitis. It is a creeping numbness which begins in the fingers and sometimes works its way up the hand, wrist and arm to the shoulders. In chronic cases the kayaker will not be able to hold the paddle. It is probably a result of long-term damage from the use of feathered paddles, since only the arm that twists the paddle is affected. The damage appears to be long lasting and may require surgery to relieve pressure on the median nerve.

PREVENTION: As for tenosynovitis.

TREATMENT: Anti-inflammatory medication and splints may prevent the need for surgery if applied in time. For mild cases, cortisone shots may do the trick.

KAYAKER'S ELBOW

This is tennis elbow by another name: a painful swelling which occurs on an elbow strained by too much paddling. It is similar in nature to "water on the knee" and requires a week of rest with the arm out of action. The elbow and nearby tissue become very sensitive, and the healing of wounds or infection in the area is inhibited because of the impaired blood supply through the fluid-bloated tissue. This affliction is painful and demands to be treated as the serious injury that it is.

DISLOCATIONS

Shoulder dislocation is possibly the most common injury to kayakers after backs damaged from incorrect lifting. The problem for kayakers occurs when the arm has pressure applied at a position that is both behind and above the shoulder approximately in the position adopted for throwing a rock. The shoulder is usually dislocated anteriorly. Such a situation frequently occurs in surf or when rolling.

PREVENTION: Begin by gingerly feeling out the zone of vulnerability by rolling your shoulder back with your arm up in the throwing position—then take every step you can to avoid that position while kayaking. Keep the elbows in close to your sides, particularly during a high brace in turbulent water.

TREATMENT: There are a number of nerve endings and blood vessels around the shoulder joint, so a dislocation should be treated as a serious injury (you can be sure the patient will be taking it pretty seriously), especially if this is a first occurrence. If at all possible, professional medical help should be sought to re-locate the arm. If you are on a remote shoreline, however, you may have no choice but to do the job yourself. A modified Hippocratic method is usually preferred, and this should be performed within an hour or so of the dislocation, before muscle spasm complicates treatment.

1 The injured kayaker lies on his back with the injured arm held at 45 degrees from the chest wall by one of the rescuers.
2 A T-shirt is folded and wrapped around the torso to be gently pulled away from the injured arm by one rescuer.
3 While the body is being so held, the arm is pulled from the wrist along its axis by a second rescuer using a gentle, sustained pull. The traction should be very slow with a grad-

ual increase in the amount of force being applied. This process may take several minutes; it must not be hurried.

4 The arm will be felt to slip back into position, at which time it should be laid across the body, supported in a sling and, ideally, taped to the body.

CHAFING & SALT WATER RASHES

Usually a problem of warm weather, rashes mostly occur under the arms and where the body touches the coaming, spray skirt or backrest, or rubs against clothing. Aggravated by salt water, rashes may be very painful and on long crossings may develop to the point of bleeding. When leaving the beach through surf, wave splashes can also sometimes carry sand up your trouser legs. This sand can be badly irritating if you then have to sit on it all day.

PREVENTION: Rub susceptible places with coconut oil before departure. A liberal coat over the whole upper torso provides effective protection for eight hours or so. Wash the sand out of your pants if necessary after launching through surf. Wear comfortable garments.

TREATMENT: Rest ashore with frequent freshwater washes. Avoid sweating or swimming in the sea. Clean tape and bandages will ease discomfort until land is reached.

BLISTERS

These amount to friction burns and are usually worst near the start of the trip. It is better to tape your hands well before setting off than to patch the blisters at mid-day. Paddling in hot humid weather causes more blisters than cold weather kayaking. If a fluid-filled blister develops, avoid breaking the skin if possible. Don't attempt to pop blisters with a needle.

BOILS, CARBUNCLES & PRESSURE SORES

Lindemann was badly affected by these during his Atlantic crossing of 1956, and the problem has afflicted many sea kayakers with whom I have corresponded or paddled. Some people react to the salt, the chafing, the pressure of continuous sitting and the drastic change of bodily routine that expeditions demand by developing these painful skin infections on arms, backs, buttocks and thighs.

TREATMENT: Boils can be treated either individually as they occur with a sulfur-based powder after being brought to a head with a poultice or, as a last resort when the infection looks as if it is becoming dangerous, with antibiotics either by injection or in tablet form. Antibiotic cream can be very effective once the wound has been cleansed. Should the boil fail to respond to treatment and the infection become angrier, get the victim to a doctor quickly. More serious infection can readily set in, particularly in the tropics.

INFECTIONS

Sea kayaking journeys may force great changes on the body: new and strenuous exercises, irregular sleep routines, strange foods, different temperatures and a whole new variety of bacteria against which your body will have to develop fresh immunity. Add to this the stress factor from anxiety or interpersonal emotional stress, and it is not surprising that on expeditions the body appears to have less resistance to infection than normal. This is particularly so in the tropics, where your expedition medic can expect plenty of infected wounds, sores, bites, ears, eyes, etc. Many will be manageable with ointments and creams, but you should be well stocked with a wide range of antibiotics in both tablet and injection form.

Kidney infections in particular are regrettably common on long-distance kayak trips. Doctors to whom I have spoken about this tend to agree that prolonged periods seated in a kayak combined with diminished water intake can retard the functioning of the kidneys and increase the likelihood of serious renal infection. Symptoms include pain and difficult urination, discharge in urine and fever. Should these symptoms occur when you are unable to reach a hospital, you should treat the condition with the appropriate course of antibiotic, and take plenty of fluids.

Note: Antibiotics in your medical kit must match individual needs and tolerances.

SEASICKNESS

I have several times been badly seasick in a kayak and, as anyone who has suffered the problem knows, it is a grim experience. In a kayak, especially a solo kayak, there is little you can do except grit your teeth and keep paddling. Although no reliable treatment exists for the condition, there are several ways of preventing it.

PREVENTION: The U.S. Coast Guard, having conducted exhaustive tests to find the best anti-seasickness remedy, has concluded that a combination of two prescription drugs, promethazine hydrochloride (an antihistamine with the trade name Phenergan) and the decongestant ephedrine sulphate is by far the most effective preventative available.

More recently an ancient drug, scopalamine, has acquired new respectability when used with a high-tech applicator known as the Transderm Scop. This is a small band-aid placed behind the user's ear. It releases a steady quantity of the drug through the skin and into the blood stream over a seventy-two-hour period. Four hours lead time is needed to ensure effectiveness. Another scopalamine product, Trip-tone, can be taken orally with an even more impressive rate of effectiveness.

Anti-emetic suppositories can be used to prevent otherwise uncontrollable dry-retching, though treatment after the fact is seldom successful. If possible, a period of rest should be taken, since the action of paddling aggravates an upset stomach. Try to eat bland, non-acidic foods and build up your water intake gradually. A bad case of seasickness must be treated seriously in the tropics where dehydration and the resulting hyperthermia (overheating) endanger life.

SUNBURN

The potential for injury by this means on the open sea in a kayak is catastrophic because of the difficulty a kayaker has removing himself from the source of the problem.

PREVENTION: In tropical regions, especially, begin with careful exposure to the hot sun. A wide-brimmed hat and long-sleeved cotton shirt can be removed occasionally to allow a gradual tanning which will give you a degree of natural protection against sunburn. Many doctors may disagree with tanning on the grounds of an increased risk of skin cancer, but the tan can prove a survival asset in an emergency, and certainly makes living ashore in the tropics a good deal easier. For fair-skinned people, the protection required beyond the hat and shirt may include a bandit's mask to cover nose and lips, protective flaps or bandages for the backs of hands and wrists, and a zinc cream or waterproof sunblock for any areas that must be left exposed. If you have a choice between looking like an Egyptian mummy or a boiled lobster, take the mummy. Severe sunburn can occur even on overcast days in temperate climates.

TREATMENT: If serious sunburning does occur, the skin may blister and the victim dehydrate. Take the person to hospital if the burning is that extensive, but if this is not possible, you will have to camp and treat the burns yourself:

1 Be sure the victim drinks plenty of water.
2 Don't break any blisters, since they will be prone to infection.
3 Cool the patient with sponge baths of clean seawater.
4 Avoid the use of burn creams on open skin. An analgesic spray may provide relief.
5 Keep the patient well clear of the sun for several days after the burn has begun to recover.

PHOTOTOXICITY

Sudden overdoses of unaccustomed sunshine can cause distressing skin irritation often associated with sunburn. Symptoms include itching, a red flush and minute fluid-filled blisters. In some cases the situation may be triggered or exacerbated by some soaps or sunburn creams or from eating some types of food.

PREVENTION: I know of no treatment other than keeping out of the sun until the symptoms abate, so prevention is the key. Cover the area with a dry light cotton garment. Avoid soaps, creams and unusual foods.

DEHYDRATION

The risk of dehydration is acute in the tropics, and water must be carried in quantity. Further, I suggest that any group that may face water supply problems during a long journey carry both a hand-operated desalination unit and the means to distill seawater from a fire on shore. Some people require considerably more water than others, and though one obviously must conserve water where it is scarce, it is important that everyone drinks the amount he or she needs. Survival manuals usually suggest one pint per person per day as an absolute minimum, though this amount may be what some paddlers require every hour in hot conditions. A symptom of dehydration is abnormally dark urine, and here it should be noted that the subjective sense of thirst may not be enough to warn of a serious dehydration problem. A dehydrated person is more vulnerable to both hypothermia and hyperthermia.

EXHAUSTION & HALLUCINATIONS

Hallucinating as a result of fatigue and long hours of wakefulness is quite normal and should not be a cause for panic. You are not going mad; all you need is some sleep. Hallucinations occur more readily at night, sometimes after as little as twenty hours awake. They are just like dreams which intrude on your consciousness. Once you are visited by them, you can safely afford to continue paddling for only a limited time, assuming you can still distinguish what is real from what isn't. If you begin hallucinating at 4:00 A.M., you will probably be able to continue paddling until dawn, when daylight greatly reduces the symptoms, but if you begin your fantastic visions early in the night, you will usually have to get some sleep before you next see the sun. Strong coffee or caffeine tablets will help counter the effects. Common conscious dreams include out-of-body experiences and visions of land, trees, lights, farm implements and the like. Obviously, maintaining an accurate course becomes a hopeless task once you find numbers of these floating obstacles in your way. For the record, however, your exhaustion may eventually give way to the paddling equivalent of a runner's high.

HYPERTHERMIA

Hyperthermia is the overheating of the body usually as a result of insufficient fluid intake combined with hot, still conditions. It can also be the result of a high fever or being overdressed and overworked in hot climates. Symptoms beyond an excessively high body temperature and an inability to cool off are: breathlessness, dry mouth, dizzy spells, affected vision, headaches and poor concentration, which may eventually lead to delirium, unconsciousness and death.

PREVENTION: Avoid paddling during the heat of day if it is reasonable to do so.

TREATMENT: Give the victim plenty of water. Keep clothing wet and give frequent cool sponge baths, particularly to the head, neck and wrists. At sea, wet the victim's hat often to cool the head, and have him/her wear a wet neck bandanna. Trail the victim's hands in the water frequently and, if the temperature won't come down, put him/her over the side for a swim.

HYPOTHERMIA

Hypothermia, or exposure, is probably responsible, directly or indirectly, for more accidental kayaking deaths than all other factors combined. Although death by drowning may be the coroner's verdict, the cause of drowning is frequently hypothermia. Because it is the number one killer, it is vital that it be thoroughly understood and that appropriate precautions be taken when paddling in cold water.

Hypothermia is a drop in the body's core temperature below the critical level of 90°F (32°C to 33°C). Once body temperature reaches this level, unconsciousness usually supervenes. When the temperature reaches 85°F (30°C), a victim who has not already drowned through unconsciousness or loss of dexterity will die by means of heart failure.

Susceptibility to hypothermia depends not only on the conditions of exposure but also on body size. Children are considerably more susceptible than large adults, and thin people more susceptible than the fat. The warning signs of hypothermia, in approximate sequence of severity, are:

1 Erratic paddling and an inability to maintain course;
2 Blurred vision and lack of co-ordination;
3 Uncontrollable shivering and an apparent inability to warm up;
4 Despondency;
5 Ashen face and hands;
6 Muscle rigidity, replacing previous shivering;
7 Incoherence and collapse.

Sometimes a person on the verge of hypothermia will recognize in himself such early signs as uncontrollable shivering and blurred vision. If you find yourself in such a fix, you should immediately seek warmth and warn your companions of your condition. It is not safe, however, for members of a party to count on recognizing the onset of hypothermia in themselves. In cold conditions, always keep watch for the symptoms in other members as well as in yourself. Remember too that there is an established link between despair and hypothermia. People without hope are more prone to hypothermia, and those whose morale has sagged should be watched carefully for additional warning signs.

PREVENTION: If you are making a crossing involving wind and rain, wear your full protective regalia. Don't wait until you are already shuddering to put on your windproofs. Try to *maintain* your warmth, rather than lose and regain it. Eat well before setting out on a cold crossing. After a day of hungry paddling, eat well and eat soon—especially if you are in for a cold, miserable night. Wear a hat in the cold. Guard against the possibility of an icy swim by wearing a drysuit with a hood or a wetsuit with a hood.

If you *do* find yourself in cold water without the protection of an immersion garment or your boat, the outlook is grim. Thrashing around will bring your temperature down fast. Treading water will cool you into unconsciousness almost twice as fast as holding still. Swimming will only kill you unless the land is *very* close. Depending on the temperature of the water, you might be able to swim ten yards or you might get half a mile. If help is to be had, you can increase your chances by waiting for it quietly. If you have on your life jacket, inflate it and hang in the fetal position. If you don't have a life jacket, treading water is better than keeping your head in the drink. The so-called "drownproofing" technique, which involves hanging with your head underwater between breaths, may be fine in a warm swimming pool, but in a cold sea it is suicide. It may be stating the obvious, but get out of the water and into the boat again as fast as you can!

TREATMENT: If someone in your party develops advanced symptoms of hypothermia, deal with the problem at once. The victim must always be treated as a stretcher case. That means that (s)he does no more paddling. The victim should be dressed as warmly as possible and should ride as a passenger in a double.

Carry the victim as gently as possible (preferably in the kayak) to shelter, and remove wet clothing so that heat— from whatever source is available—can reach the body more easily. The normal field procedure is for one or two other members of the party to strip and join the victim in a dry sleeping bag to provide immediate warmth. In the meantime, water should be heated. The latest recommendation from the U.S. Coast Guard, based on recent research at the University of Victoria and elsewhere, is that pieces of clothing soaked in warm water should then be applied to the victim's head, neck, sides, chest and groin (or use chemical heat pads if you have them), and these warm compresses should be changed as often as required for continuing gentle warming.

Note: Stimulation of any kind—through physical exercise, jostling, rubbing the limbs, or the administration of alcohol or hot drinks—should be avoided. Do *not* give the victim a warm drink until his/her body temperature has returned to near normal. A hot drink can apparently stimulate warm blood away from the vital organs where it is most needed, and physical activity can bring cold, stagnant blood from the extremities to the body core, killing a victim who has already begun to recover.

Remember that it is useless to wrap a victim of hypothermia in a cold blanket or sleeping bag. Once the core temperature has dropped below the critical level, the person is no longer generating sufficient body heat to get warm of his/her own accord. Insulation alone will do no good; insulation and a gentle source of heat are required.

An improvised fire still

I I

Survival Situations

The key to survival at sea is to think survival long before the event. Like the Boy Scout, *be prepared*. If you become a castaway, thinking survival means wasting nothing; potentially useful equipment must always be kept since it may contain a wire or a nail which will save your life. Thinking survival means always carrying essential articles in the pockets of your life jacket or anorak—waterproof matches, a knife, a space blanket, fishing line, hooks and a signalling mirror—so that if you make it to shore without your boat, you will have the means to improve your chances of survival. Thinking survival means taking precautions such as tying up your boat on windy days even if it is pulled clear of the water. I once watched a gust of wind pick up my partially loaded kayak and smash it down a hundred yards away. Such a wind could as well have carried it out to sea—with disastrous results if I had been on a wilderness island. Thinking survival means not throwing away your gumboots if you have to swim to shore; if you must take them off (your life jacket should keep you afloat), clutch them under your armpits. Filled with air they will provide buoyancy for your swim, and you will have boots to protect your feet from the rocks when you arrive. Cold weather survival preparation means having the right thermal equipment, but it also involves getting your body ready for hardship by deliberately underdressing while in camp and swimming frequently in cold water. This may sound masochistic, but it will increase your resistance to cold.

The Ona Indians of Tierra del Fuego wore almost no clothes even under snowy conditions. They were apparently no different from us physiologically, but they had developed extraordinary resistance to cold. Once upon a time they caught a zealous missionary and decided he was worth converting. The first stage demanded relieving him of his smelly clothes and plucking all his unsightly bodily hair. For six months that missionary lived naked on Tierra del Fuego before being rescued by a passing ship, and at the time of his rescue he was in excellent health. It is a good story to remember when you start to think cold weather survival. The missionary would have had shelter, a fire and food—all of which no doubt contributed significantly to his survival—but most important, his body adapted to life in the cold.

You don't have to be on some mighty expedition to get yourself into a sea-survival crisis (though it certainly helps). You are in one of these crises as soon as you are in the water unable to get back into your boat. The main difference between being in the harbour or being in the middle of the ocean is your chance of getting outside help.

SURVIVAL AT SEA WITH NO BOAT

Your survival in the water is going to depend on how much warning you have of the emergency, and on what survival equipment is available to you.

If you have no special clothing to protect you, your chances of surviving in temperatures below 30°F for longer than an hour are slim indeed. Your best chance is to wear a drysuit or immersion suit with warm underclothing. Second best is a wetsuit (the more complete the better); third best is an exposure jacket (floater coat) with a Sea Seat to keep you out of the water, and fourth best is rain gear with all the clothing you can get on, topped by a life jacket. The clothing will hold a considerable amount of body-warmed water. You should have a neoprene hood or woollen hat to cover your head and neck, since this is the region from which the body loses heat most rapidly. The armpits and crotch are other areas of rapid heat loss. If you have only a life jacket, hunch your body into a tight ball and hang in the water, moving as little as possible. If there are several of you, form a huddle to share your warmth. (This can double the time you survive.)

SURVIVAL WITH A BOAT

Touring kayakers will normally have with them all they need to survive. The main danger is that they will squander equipment, strength and energy, abandoning mental resourcefulness through panicky behaviour. As soon as you realize you are lost or unable to reach the land you desire, do the following:

1 Get out the chart and examine every possibility and factor affecting you, then decide on the best course of action and keep to it. Consider it a maxim in these situations that the group must always stay together.
2 Since this course may involve days of travelling on open sea before you reach land, ration water and food immediately and see that everyone in the group understands your predicament fully.
3 In the tropics, paddle by night and conserve your strength during the heat of the day when you can use a solar still or desalination pump to collect fresh water. Build a rainwater catchment system ready for instant use and keep it clear of sea salt. Rig a sail (tent fly) if this is consistent with your direction of travel. Do whatever you can to save effort.

4 If you require assistance, turn on your emergency locator beacon and watch for aircraft and ships. One person should always remain on watch when the group is sleeping, just in case a ship should appear.

5 If you are in cold conditions, dress warmly.

6 Start gathering seafood. A fishing line should be trolled and a spear kept at hand. In the tropics you may catch dorado, jacks, tuna or any of many varieties of school fish. In temperate climates, very small sharks may be caught or speared from the boat, but don't spear anything too big. Fish floats and other flotsam may yield up edible barnacles, crabs and even small fish. The only bird a kayaker could hope to catch for food is probably the ever-curious booby, which is naive enough to think people are harmless. These will often come close to you, even attempting to land on the tips of paddles and attractive hats.

Dougal Robertson, author of *Survive the Savage Sea,* and of an excellent manual called *Sea Survival*, which should be mandatory reading for all sea kayakers, describes the capture and use of turtles for survival. Their blood can be drunk to quench thirst and their meat eaten dried, cooked (if you have a primus) or raw.

"Survival-think" requires intense concentration on the problems involved with gathering water, food, protecting the group and keeping together. You must be prepared to spend the longest likely time on the sea and not develop a rescue-dependent mentality which will only lead to despair when ships or land fail to appear. The morale of the group is most important during such a crisis. Those who fully understand the position should explain it clearly to those who are doubting the course of action. A group whose morale is low, be it through navigational uncertainty or because they have given up hope of ever seeing land again, is a group that is more susceptible to mental collapse and consequent ailments such as hypothermia.

DRINKING WATER

After air, fresh water is your most valuable commodity. Prevention of water loss and collection of fresh supplies therefore should become a priority as soon as it is obvious that you are lost at sea or due for a prolonged crossing. As we have seen, the continuation of bodily functions demands a minimum of one pint of water per person per day, but some people need more than this.

To prevent water loss, especially in the tropics:

1 Rest during the heat of the day.
2 Wear a hat, and cool yourself off by splashing seawater on your clothing frequently.
3 Treat illnesses such as seasickness and diarrhea as soon as they appear; they waste valuable body fluids and hasten the onset of both hyperthermia and hypothermia.
4 Avoid filling water bottles completely. Always try to leave enough air in the container so it will float should you drop it overboard.

The methods of water collection at sea, in order of technological sophistication, are these:

1 Rain storms can fill your water containers quickly. A tent fly spread wide on two paddles can do the trick. If wind accompanies the rain, however, you may have to devise a smaller catchment. Take care not to mix salt-contaminated water into existing freshwater supplies.

2 A survival still is ideal for carrying in a kayak during tropical trips. Depending on the size of the still and the strength
of the sun, this little gadget may produce as much as a pint
of fresh water an hour. It is fragile, however, and will re-
pay rough handling with brackish water. Its greatest drawback may be that it requires the kayak to be stationary.

3 A reverse-osmosis hand-desalination pump will cost you
almost as much as your kayak, but it could be equally important in keeping you alive. Recovery Engineering make
an excellent model, about the size of a large grease gun,
which will produce fresh water at the rate of a gallon an
hour. (Ed Gillet carried two desalination pumps on his
Hawaiian crossing and found them extremely useful, as
have some paddlers on the Baja coast.)

MAROONED

Stranded on an uninhabited island may sound like a junior ac-
countant's dream, but it is not so far-fetched a possibility,
given the sea kayaker's curiosity about the uninhabited and,
of course, the means of getting there. You have only to mis-
judge the surf and break your boat in two, or leave your
kayak within reach of the incoming tide, and you are marooned. A lot depends on your circumstances, of course. You
may just be in for an uncomfortable night before you are
missed and a search is mounted, or you may be on an Arctic
or tropical island where any mistakes could be fatal. Your
chances will also depend on what you were able to salvage
from your boat, on what protection you have from the elements, and on the availability of fresh water.

Tropical Survival Ashore

On finding yourself marooned in the tropics, your
priorities might be these:

1 See that your partner and other members are safely clear of the sea.
2 Treat any injuries that demand urgent attention.
3 Salvage the boats and any equipment that can be safely reached.
4 Find shelter, and make an assessment of the damage, loss and prospects. Display a large SOS on the beach.
5 See to your water needs. Start rationing water till you know you can get more.

You can survive for weeks without food, but in the tropics few people can survive three days without water. Ashore, as at sea, you must take care to prevent water loss by avoiding strenuous exercise during the heat of the day, by doing what you can to cool yourself off, and by treating conditions such as fever, vomiting and diarrhea without delay.

If you are on an island large enough to have streams, your water problems are solved. Swamps too can provide a regular source. Good water can be collected by digging a hole amongst the matted roots of plants near the edge of the swamp. Bail the hole continuously with a cup so inflowing water is filtered through the ground. It is very important that water gained in this way, or from tropical streams, be boiled thoroughly. Failing that, purifying tablets may do the trick.

On sandy atolls where there is greenery, you will be able to get fresh water by digging to sea level inside the vegetation zone. The water you will find has fallen on the island as rain and been segregated from the seawater by the sand. If the water is brackish, try further inland. One cheeky method is to use the burrows of large land crabs, which frequently reach fresh water. Lower a rubber hose with a cloth filter on the end, link the hose to your boat pump and suck out the water. You may have such a hose in the form of a spare elastic for your spear gun.

Included in your regular survival equipment should be the makings for a fire still. You need: the camp pressure cooker, 6 feet of rubber tubing (your spare spear gun rubber), one aluminum tent pole, an 8-foot coil of ⅛-inch copper tubing, some clear plastic surgical tubing, a large bucket (a rock pool will do) and plenty of water containers. The spear gun rubber should fit snugly over the safety vent on top of the pressure cooker as well as over the end of the copper tubing. It should also fit inside the tent pole. The whole unit is assembled as shown in the photograph on page 246. You can use a water-proof bag or pool as a cooling tank. It will have to be constantly refilled with cool water from the sea, because the condenser heats it up quickly. Make sure you maintain the sea-water level in the pressure cooker and scour the inside every four or five hours; otherwise, you may find some pretty acrid tastes contaminating your new water supply. This is a very reliable method for getting fresh water and, though it demands constant surveillance, it will produce a gallon of good water every two hours.

Once your supply of water is assured and you have shelter from sun, rain and wind, you will probably spend all your energy gathering and preparing food as well as perfecting your efforts to attract the attention of would-be-rescuers.

The sea is a vast larder for the wilderness paddler or the castaway. At low tide, shellfish can be gathered from rocks or coral reefs and an amazing variety of pool fish caught with a stick. Crayfish and crabs can often be nabbed in quite shallow water, and the pools may contain small octopus as well as shrimp, sea cucumbers and sea urchins. You may, however, encounter naturally contaminated sea creatures in many tropical areas, and world-wide there can be occasional danger from red-tide poisoning. If in doubt, in the tropics it seems safest to stick to filter feeders (scallops, oysters, mussels and the like) and to small species of carnivorous fish; in temperate regions, where there is danger of red tide, it is best to avoid precisely these species.

Bottom fishing with a hand line is efficient if you can reach deep water without having to throw your line out over sharp rocks or coral. Fishing off steep rocks works well, or if you can get beyond the reef on a raft or a kayak, you can usually catch fish just beyond the drop-off. For bait you can use small, crushed sand crabs or shrimps which you'll find in the coral pools.

If you have a good free-diver in the group, and a mask, snorkel and fins, you will be eating well indeed. A spear gun is a great survival tool, but even without it the diver can collect crayfish and shellfish (such as conch) not available on the reef. Let me repeat here that divers in tropical waters run the risk of attracting sharks by carrying bleeding fish on their spear gun or Hawaiian sling. To be safe, keep speared fish on a long string and get them ashore or into a boat as quickly as you can.

When the tide is out, you can hunt crabs, eels and snakes in the mud of tropical mangrove swamps. Great fun! As the tide comes in, varieties of herring and mullet can be caught either by stunning them with a paddle or beating them with a spiked stick as they gulp on the surface. You can also fish using a light line baited with a bit of crushed crab. Oysters grow on the trunks of mangroves in some parts of the tropics and are easily knocked off with a diving knife. Many birds nest in the swamp too, and you may find a nest with eggs or young. Keep an eye out for larger creatures as well. Sharks often swim right into the mangroves to feed, sometimes in as little as 2 or 3 feet of water. If you fancy shark steak, it may even be possible to lure one into an enclosed piece of the swamp with carrion or fish heads, then close its only exit and wait for it to die when the tide recedes.

Remote islands are often the nesting grounds of sea birds

whose eggs can be eaten raw. So can birds themselves if the castaway is hungry and stealthy enough. Day-feeding birds may be caught sleeping on their nests at night. Night feeders, often living in burrows, may be grabbed with a gloved hand and a long arm during the day. Land crabs, lizards, snakes and wild goats are widely distributed on remote tropical islands. Turtles too may provide an excellent omelet if you can locate a new nest—identifiable from the scratchings in the sand above the high-tide mark.

If you have coconuts on your island, you have a source of food and drink, as well as material for roofing a shelter and a source of fuel. Getting any variety of food from the jungle, however, requires specific knowledge of plants and trees. The roots of ferns, wild taro and yams, the young centres of palms, succulent shoots of creepers and grasses, fruit and nuts, may all be found by those who know what they are looking for. If in doubt, use great caution and to any plant which you believe may be edible apply the following tests:

1 Are other animals (birds, pigs, insects) eating it?
2 Break it in your fingers then sniff the juice. Be suspicious of pungent juices such as are found in many lilies.
3 If the juice is not too repugnant to the nose, put a little on the tip of your tongue and leave it there for some minutes, testing it for a tingling or excessively bitter warning taste.
4 Should the plant appear safe, chew a small portion, then spit it out and wait to determine the effect it has on your mouth lining.
5 Should an abundant food supply prove unpalatable raw, boil it with salt then repeat procedure 4. Many vegetable toxins are destroyed by heat.
6 No matter how tasty it seems, eat only small quantities of strange food at first.

This test is by no means infallible. Leeks, onion or garlic would probably fail, and it is possible that deadly nightshade would slip through. The best thing is obviously to know your jungle plants. Second best is to carry a manual on jungle survival to help you identify the plants you see.

Cold Weather Survival Ashore
In the event of an accident, your priorities upon reaching shore are:

1 See to the needs of anyone suffering exposure or serious injury.
2 Salvage the boat and all the equipment you can safely reach.
3 Find shelter from the elements.
4 Make a fire and dry your clothing.

If you managed to get your boat and equipment ashore, you will have the means to survive almost indefinitely provided you don't squander your resources.

First, build a permanent camp well protected from the wind.

Second, prepare a signal for attracting the attention of any passing vessel. A cairn with an orange survival bag over it may suit the terrain, or an SOS written in orange plastic on the rocks or snow so that it can be read by aircraft. Lay a smoke fire, ready to be ignited at the sight of a vessel, and keep it dry with a sheet of plastic.

Third, all around you is food. Wilderness survival techniques can become a way of life when kayaking in the cool temperate or subarctic regions of the world, where it is usually both unnecessary and undesirable to carry masses of unpalatable freeze-dried mush. All varieties of seaweed are edible. There are hundreds of edible ground plants. In season, there are wild berries rich in vitamins. There will be fish, duck, goat, bear, deer. Water is seldom a problem in these latitudes, even on the most barren islands, since pools abound and rain is frequent.

Seals, common to most cold latitudes, can provide the castaway with meat, oil and skins. When a colony has been located, a hunter armed only with a club can be quite successful if he approaches carefully from downwind. (You will be in no doubt as to which is downwind of one of these colonies!) The quicker you regain your hunter's instinct the better when it comes to wilderness survival, in hot or cold climates.

12

Planning an Expedition

The information in this chapter will help you plan a major kayak expedition either abroad or at home.

THE SCHEDULE

Most expedition schedules are governed by such considerations as the length of the favourable season and the date at which you have to be back in the city for work, but it may happen, if you take sea kayaking seriously enough, that you leave your job and put your savings into paddling some distant sea which has always fascinated you. At least I hope that is not too improbable a suggestion.

Even with no time limit at all, you still need an idea of how long your journey is going to take. You will still have to estimate costs, choose equipment, plan provisions. To do this you must estimate both the total and the average daily distance. When you divide one into the other to estimate trip time, add 20 per cent for the unexpected. Most sea kayakers can easily do 20 miles a day on a short trip in good weather. Many can do 30 miles a day under such conditions, and some, like Paul Caffyn, comfortably cover 40 miles a day, every day, so long as the sea is agreeable and the weather holds fair. On a long trip, however, you will not likely put water behind you at such speed. As a general rule, I think in terms of a 10- to 15-mile-a-day average. Ten miles would seem about right for a long wilderness trip, if you are surviving off the land. (If

you are exposed to continual storm, as in the Aleutian Islands, your progress could be slower still.) Fifteen miles
would likely constitute a comfortable pace for trips of less
than 350 miles.

On an expedition, you should expect to paddle 30 or even
40 miles a day on some days, but if you plan to keep going for
weeks or months, such efforts will have to be interspersed
with rest days. After a 40-mile crossing, you may need three
days of rest and good eating so you can maintain your
strength over the long term. During a six-month trip in
Chile, we evolved a routine of two days on and one day off,
then two days on and two days off. This gave us one day for
resting and two days for food gathering, hunting and preparing food for the four days of travel. This was a good arrangement, but it is only possible for straightforward coastal cruising; where you have open sea, such regular schedules have
little meaning because you can't stop paddling until you reach
land.

Some kayakers, eager to travel at a fast clip, organize land-
based support teams. This requires a carload of friends willing and able to follow your progress along the coast and meet
you most nights, as Paul Caffyn was able to arrange on his remarkable circumnavigations. Under these conditions, you
should be able to make considerably better than 10 miles per
day, since you will be able to travel more lightly. You may
also eat better and will no doubt save precious hours by not
having to pitch a camp and prepare your own food. Paul av-
eraged 21 miles a day over the two summers required for his
New Zealand voyage, 26 miles a day on his well-supported
voyage around the U.K. in the summer of 1980, the same
mileage for his Australian circumnavigation (a year-long,
10,000-mile epic) and some 35 miles a day for Japan.

Often, one of the most difficult tasks of the whole expedition is selecting who is to go, and it is a job that has to be

done right. The safest thing, one would think, is to go with old friends—but you might in actuality be better off choosing competent strangers. Old friends taken out of the environment in which the friendship developed have a tendency to *become* strangers, and everyone seems to drag along unspoken preconditions and unrealistic expectations which fester badly on a long or dangerous trip. In published accounts of kayak expeditions, conflict is often played down, but if you read carefully you will soon realize that conflict is the rule, not the exception. Aside from the insecurities of being away from home, and the element of danger, the effect of polarization between the leader and the led tends to invite trouble. In fact, my advice—given with sadness, not cynicism—is, if you really value your friendship with someone, *don't* take him or her on a long sea kayaking expedition unless the friendship was forged on a similar trip in the first place.

You should no doubt avoid taking moody and depressive people, who can affect group morale and may become a great liability under stress. People rigid in their ways or reluctant to chip in are no help either. (Have I just eliminated someone you know?) Be willing to judge and to trust your judgement. You will probably select the right balance of companions intuitively and do a better job than if you psychoanalyzed everyone. All too often, though, the final decision boils down to who has the funds and the time. If you really get stuck, a carefully worded advertisement in a newspaper can produce an amusing variety of applicants from which you may well be able to select a good companion.

Before everyone makes a commitment to the trip, get your heads together and sort out what you all expect from it. This is a very important step no matter what your trip involves. Even if yours is just a bunch of friends paddling up the coast for a week, you should clarify your hopes and expectations in advance. A casual chat over a beer in the local pub may be sufficient in such a case, but if your trip has a $50,000 budget from a scientific foundation, forget the beer. You will have to work out in advance as much detail as you possibly can and get it down on paper—and you may also need a lawyer if the stakes are that high.

For most expeditions, however, a home-made written agreement is in order. What is needed is a statement of intent by people of good will so that in times of stress—and there are always plenty of them—the group can refer back to established common goals. The exercise of writing this statement down will serve to make quite sure that you all have compatible aims and priorities, and it can help in clarifying the division of workload, responsibilities and privileges as well as the financial status of the enterprise. It is usually obvious who is the expedition leader (assuming there is to be one since agreeing on a leader will eliminate some needless indecision and jockeying for position), so it is sometimes a good idea to put this in writing.

Roles such as medic, treasurer, route researcher, secretary, photographer, transportation organizer, equipment and insurance organizer, fund raiser and press liaison should be assigned at this stage. If your expedition is this elaborate, the agreement should be also; and remember that it must be fair to everyone. Inequities will only fester until a more inconvenient time—such as the middle of the trip.

The agreement may cover details of finance, liabilities, distribution of profits from photograph or article sales, and ownership of equipment, and it may lay down procedures for resolving disputes. It should establish a policy for such occurrences as walkouts, accidents, illness and death. It can define an attitude to publicity, the acceptance of outside assistance, use of sails, hotels or tents. You should agree on a rate of travel and the relative priorities of science, filming, photography or other activities. Finally, the agreement should include a clause that spells out amendment procedures.

The Caribbean expedition I participated in in 1977–78 was structured so that all four members had a single vote, with an additional tie-breaking vote available to the leader (myself). Since there was considerable discrepancy of experience, I was given an absolute veto on sea decisions. This, we hoped, might save us the pains of the democratic process in emergencies. I am pleased to say that at no time did I need to use either the tie-breaking vote or the veto, though we had our share of differences.

Disputes will arise. The very nature of the exercise seems to attract people with well-established personalities and strong wills. The agreement and the will to stick to it can help to resolve many of the differences. If you can preserve the willingness to discuss problems, you will be able to handle most policy and personality disputes.

PRE-DEPARTURE WORK

As D-Day draws nigh, the organizing acquires a frantic quality. Equipment piles higher and higher in various living rooms, and mountains of letters are shuffled in and out. The garbage is full of crumpled envelopes while the paperweight can hardly maintain its position on top of the ever-growing pile of exotic cancelled stamps. There is hardly a clear space to put down a cup of coffee while you answer the telephone. People are visited by gut-flutters and second thoughts as they begin to realize what they have let themselves in for. Training is well under way, muscles ache, and there is a sore spot in the place where your back rubs the backrest. The medical kit is in order, and you have a memo to pick up the prohibited drugs at the airport. You have found an airline that is prepared to bend the rules and give you a discount on your air ticket and

263

free freight in exchange for some sort of public acknowledgement if you succeed. Nobody has agreed to back your movie,
but you are still working on that.

Amid this excitement, insurance may sound a strange priority—especially from someone who has pontificated on the
virtues of self-reliance—but once you have decided to travel
as a group, you are obliged to take extra precautions. If you
have a sponsor, you have an additional duty to keep the odds
in favour of success as great as possible. Most kayak trips are
run on budgets so tight that having a member hospitalized
overseas could spell financial disaster for the project. It is for
this reason that you need adequate insurance. I would suggest
at least $20,000 in medical insurance per person. Since your
kayak is carrying valuable equipment, the loss of which you
may not be able to absorb, you may need insurance on the
goods as well. When you talk to the adjuster, it may be wise
to designate your trip as simply "travel" rather than trying to
explain your mode of travel more explicitly since few insurance adjusters can distinguish between sea and whitewater
kayaking.

By this time, the area you are visiting will be taking shape
in your mind. You will all have read up on local history, geography and politics. You'll already have had to put plastic
over your charts, not to protect them from the water, but to
keep them from wearing out as you paw and ponder their
mysteries. Everyone on the expedition should be familiar
with the charts and see the full route mapped out on them; the
leader should have them virtually memorized. Coast Pilots
and yachtsmen's guides should be studied carefully and
marked where relevant. Escape routes should be marked for
difficult passages. Where your course follows a dangerous lee
shore, estimated times to safe harbour should be jotted on the
chart with chinagraph pencil. Check the history of past
weather from as many sources as possible and be quite sure

you understand how weather will affect your course. Don't hesitate to alter your plans radically as you learn more about the area you are visiting. Know what to expect from currents and winds, how frequently you can restock with food and what nature can do to supply you en route.

You won't find room on the charts to make notations about local history and geography. Put this information into a notebook instead, where you can review it day by day as your voyage proceeds. Even if your expedition is not obligated to bring back salable photographs or publishable accounts of the wonders you encounter, you'll want for your own sake to remember to paddle up that fjord where the big glacier is hiding, or to look into that cove to see what's left of the nineteenth-century whaling station. Preparatory historical research will not only give your expedition an added dimension of enjoyment, but it will also put your effort in perspective.

If your journey takes you through the Caribbean, along Central America or even along some of the coasts of Europe, you may face a new country and a new set of laws every few days. Again and again you may be confronted by a platoon of officials whose job is to check you out and see that your papers are in order. They may request such wonders of the past as deratting certificates, ship's doctor's report, quadruplicate lists of crew and cargo, as well as port clearance from the country you have just left.

Most authorities don't know how to handle the arrival of a kayak, and your presence will probably be the cause of great hilarity. This can be to your advantage. While they are laughing they are unlikely to make things too difficult for you—but don't count on it.

Part of your pre-expedition work should be to contact every customs authority along your route, providing an approximate arrival date and a list of the equipment which may be of interest to them. The letter should be addressed to the Chief Inspector of Customs and if possible should be written in the language of the country involved. Authorities will feel better disposed towards you if you ask in advance about restricted items such as fruit and firearms. Another letter to the local diplomatic representative of each country to be visited will clear up any conflicting rumours about the various visas needed. Check to see if there are any restrictions on coastal landings or the use of cinematic equipment.

The rules vary widely. For example, if you are going to the Dominican Republic you may need a special cruising permit even to approach the shore. In 1978, in order to cruise the remote north coast by kayak, we needed a letter from the Vice Admiral himself. (We really did need it, too. Without it we would have been explaining our position from behind bars on a number of occasions.) Often a letter from the minister of tourism will be useful as well, but in troubled areas nothing may help. Charles Miller, an American kayaker who has paddled extensively in the Aegean and Greek Islands, tells of intensive interrogations by both Greek and Turkish authorities, and reports that both Bulgarian and Rumanian shore patrols fired shots at him.

In more volatile countries, your embassy should be given your schedule and contacted as regularly as they advise. If you present your passport to them on your day of arrival, you may have an easier time replacing it should it be lost. Where political unrest is extreme, notify all local authorities whenever you arrive in a town. (You may be required to do this anyway.) Remember that after a few days' paddling, a kayaker can look as wild and woolly as any guerrilla or desperado, and jumpy authorities may need a little reassurance. A good trick is to contact the local press as soon as you get to the country where you plan to paddle. You can give them a photograph and an outline of the trip, then keep several copies of the published article. When you are later faced with a suspicious police officer or a gibbering seventeen-year-old soldier with a machine gun, you can wave your press clipping at him; it is an impressive example of the power of the printed word.

My first Patagonian kayak trip began only three months after the overthrow of Allende, at a time when the military were still pulling communists out from under the beds. Near the end of the six-month trip, the police picked me up while I was taking photographs in the poor part of the town of Castro, on the island of Chiloe. I did look suspicious (though I was not under my bed). I was wearing a bushy beard and beret, and I had a military-looking pack full of fancy cameras. I had loose ammunition in my pockets and my visa had expired, yet none of this mattered once I produced the newspaper clippings with the story of our expedition. To my considerable relief, I was immediately treated as a bosom friend, and a special letter was provided to cover the expired visa which could only be renewed in Santiago.

There is, of course, another way to do things if your party is really small and you make absolutely no contact with the press—and *if* the countries you visit are safe and peaceful. During my first paddle through the Caribbean, in 1967, I was so ignorant of procedure that I entered and left half a dozen countries without bothering to disturb the authorities at all. Nobody complained. I just paddled up to a white sandy beach, made my camp, caught my fish, bought my stores in the local town and moved on. People who saw me thought I had come from one of the cruise yachts or from the next town. Nobody suspected that I had paddled in from the faded blue island on the horizon. I do not seriously advocate this procedure, however, since it *could* get you into trouble and spoil your trip. There is usually little to be gained from it anyway, since most authorities are friendly to kayakers.

One of your most important pre-departure contacts is the coast guard. Write and tell them your plan before you get where you're going. Once you arrive, contact them personally and discuss with them, in as much detail as they can bear, the finer points of your journey through their jurisdiction. Give them an outline of your schedule—but with a reasonable delay factor, in case you are holed up on a beach during bad weather. You can do without the embarrassment of an unnecessary rescue. Let the coast guard know your storm procedure so they can anticipate your thinking in case there *is* a need to search.

It can save time if you carry a printed list of expedition information useful to coast guard and other local authorities. As well as your route, it should contain a description of your boats and the names, addresses and next of kin of all members. List the safety equipment you carry, as well as your expected supply of water and food. If you carry a radar reflector, tell them that.

The attitudes of coast guards vary more from station to station than nation to nation. Generally, though, you will find them friendly, helpful and prone to underestimate kayaks. One blustery Easter day when we contacted the British coast guard at Dover to tell them we were paddling to Calais, they not only gave us detailed advice on currents and weather but also actually drove us about in search of some last-minute safety equipment we had been unable to pick up in London. The Miami coast guard were just the opposite. When we contacted them from the Bahamas to warn of our attempt at the 62-mile crossing of the Gulf Stream, they did not want to know. "If you aren't in trouble, we don't want to hear from you," their operator said curtly, and then hung up. They did not even record the frequency of our radio transmitter—a simple enough precaution which could have saved them a lot of effort in the event of a search, not to mention our lives.

(Miami is a busy shipping area, of course, but Dover Strait is busier.) Fortunately, the Miami experience is not typical. The U.S. Coast Guard in Puerto Rico was extremely helpful on that trip, and we were able to return the favour by assisting in the prosecution of an oil tanker we photographed pumping its bilges between the islands.

SPONSORS

Most sea kayaking expeditions are financed entirely by the members, but lengthy ones in foreign waters can be too expensive for ordinary folk. You somehow have to find enough money for boats, equipment, food, transport, freight, medical and equipment insurance, cameras, film, spending money and a 20 per cent contingency fund. When costs are high, finding a sponsor may be your only hope.

The important thing to remember when seeking sponsors is that they too will want something out of the deal. Begging letters only cause irritation and waste postage. Instead, think carefully about which manufacturer could use your trip to promote its product, then write the company a letter outlining the trip and the ways you would be prepared to assist with promotions in return for assistance. You should include a detailed outline of your track record—previous expeditions and any satisfied sponsors you may have had in the past—and a profile of each crew member. If your list does not look very impressive, you will have to produce a very good idea for the actual kayak trip and promote your cause personally. It can be a disheartening business. Even when you are sure a company could benefit from your trip, you may have no joy convincing their advertising manager and will probably have the greatest difficulty just getting in to make your pitch. Make your plans at least a year in advance to avoid being told that "this year's advertising budget has been fully allocated."

Lay hands on all the newspapers of the area into which you plan to paddle (the country's embassy will have them) and read the advertisements. Find out who is spending money on newspaper advertising and what angle they are using, then tailor your proposal accordingly. But be warned: few advertising managers have the imagination or nerve to risk a break with tradition. You might point out to your potential backer—and to yourself—that Columbus, Magellan, Vasco da Gama and Marco Polo were all sponsored by commercial interests. Still, it is likely to be an uphill job, perhaps the toughest part of your journey.

If yours is a noteworthy adventure, you can get assistance from newspapers and magazines themselves, but make sure you don't give away more than they are paying for. Here you will need a very knowledgeable friend ashore, or a professional agent. But take care. Publicity, far more than commercial sponsorship and promotion, can seriously warp the adventure itself, and may lead you to continuing beyond reasonable limits of safety.

PHYSICAL PREPARATION

Sea kayaking depends on stamina and efficiency more than strength, and stamina, apart from being a mental attitude, depends on training and being fit. Set your body a training schedule including regular sessions in the boats and general fitness activities such as running, swimming and exercises for the back and arms.

An excellent specialized exercise, which can be done before going to bed each night, requires an 18-inch stick and a good hefty climbing boot. Tie the boot to the centre of the stick with a 5-foot bootlace. Hold the arms out horizontally and rotate the stick until the boot reaches it then wind it steadily down again. Start with five of these exercises, then increase by one every night until you are doing thirty. This fine exercise for arms and shoulders will give you the chance to explore the subtle distinction between stoicism and masochism without even having to get wet. As for the kayaking side of the training, get out there and train hard in the boats at every opportunity. Most kayaking discomfort results from sitting in one position for long periods of time, and from chafing. There seems to be no way to improve one's tolerance to these evils, but do take the trouble to rig yourself a comfortable seat. The only training for endurance is to endure—and that, I am afraid, is what sitting on your butt for twelve hours is all about.

If your expedition takes you to a new climatic zone, you will need to allow a period for adjustment to the new conditions. Two weeks at least will be needed when travelling to the tropics from a temperate climate. Ease up your training program a little when you get there and take care to drink plenty of water. Moving to colder climates, you will have to make a conscious effort to underdress. Where possible, cold swims will help with this adjustment.

Note: An alternative regime is to not train at all but simply to begin paddling gently each day starting with five miles the first day and increasing this distance by a mile every day.

Participants in an Alaska Discovery guided trip.

13

Tours, Lessons, Clubs & Rentals

For beginner paddlers, kayak tours, lessons, clubs and kayak rentals provide the opportunity to try paddling without significant financial commitment and with the presumed advantage of getting guidance from someone knowledgeable.

TOURS

Tour companies specializing in sea kayaking are springing up all over the North American continent. They offer a wide range of trips from local day cruises to exotic expeditions exploring Belize, Baja, Baffin Island and even Antarctica. Most tour companies are excellent and provide a sociable, safe introduction to kayaking. Some, however, may be less than adequate with client-to-staff ratios that are far too high, poor equipment and/or poorly trained staff. As far as possible, check out the company you are considering. If you can't get a first-hand account of the sort of trip the company runs, be sure to ask the right questions before you sign up for a tour. Such questions would include:

How long has the company been in business?
What is the client-to-staff ratio? (5:1 is acceptable.)
What is the focus and philosophy of the company? Of the trip?

Who is leading the trip you are considering? How many
times have they led that particular trip before? What are
their qualifications?

How far will trip participants be expected to paddle in a day?

Does the company carry liability insurance?

What does the price of the tour include? (When comparing
prices, be sure you are comparing like products. For example, are the trips of equal duration, and do they offer
comparable menus or services?)

What type of boats and other equipment does the company
use? How much safety equipment will be available to the
group?

Does the company run trips that adhere to the safety
guidelines set out by their trade association?

To locate sea kayak tour operators, check the advertisements in the specialty kayak and outdoor magazines; in
North America you can phone TASK (the Trade Association
of Sea Kayaking). Or contact a specialty store and ask for a
list of tour operators. As kayaking becomes a mainstream activity, more tour operators are registering with regular travel
agencies, and you can be sure that such companies at least
carry insurance.

If you are dissatisfied—or especially satisfied—with your
trip, write and tell the operator; copies of your letter can be
sent to relevant parties such as an appropriate consumer or
trade magazine, TASK or other trade association, and the
place where you learned of the trip. You should register satis-
faction or dissatisfaction regarding commercial courses or
kayak outfitters as well.

Novice Tours with Teens—A Note for Organizers
Many community centres and schools have fine introductory
ocean kayaking programs. These are frequently open to juve-

niles, and when this is the case, an entirely different approach is needed from the one I have stressed thus far in this book. Where I have preached self-reliance and acceptance of responsibility for one's actions, the organizer of a trip of juvenile novices must be a defensive thinker— defensive to the point of extreme caution.

For individuals in the 13 to 16 age group (a younger novice will likely be in a double with an experienced adult), you will need to take special precautions against hypothermia. Since children succumb to hypothermia much more quickly than adults, wetsuits should be worn and warm, windproof clothing kept on hand when paddling in colder climates. Be prepared for the unexpected such as a capsize in totally calm waters. Boats with good stability are an obvious advantage.

The organizer of juvenile groups should see to it *personally* that every boat has the required safety equipment and that everyone—including instructors—wears a life jacket.

If you decide to send young beginners to sea in kayaks, you are, in my view, obligated to provide massive supervision by experienced adults. Avoid novice parties that are too large. Open-sea kayak excursions for juveniles with an experienced-to-inexperienced ratio of greater than 1:2 should include a safety boat. The question to ask yourself is, could you as leader handle an emergency if all the novices were in trouble at the same time? *You cannot afford to run novice trips of juveniles if the answer to that question is no.*

In the early seventies, I accompanied a group of Outward Bound boys on an ill-advised sea trip in New Zealand's Marlborough Sounds. Fourteen boys, 16 to 19 years old in slalom singles, were making a 2-mile crossing of a bay during rather rough weather. A sudden squall capsized nine of the boats in one blast. It immediately became so rough that any form of group rescue using the techniques the boys had been taught was out of the question, even though they were in unloaded kayaks. There were two instructors with the group as well as myself and another instructor shadowing them in a 24-foot jet rescue boat, watching through binoculars from a distance of half a mile. In less than twenty minutes we had picked up all nine paddlers and their boats. Without the rescue boat, we would have needed a 1:1 staff-to-pupil ratio to handle the emergency, and even then, the result would have been in doubt. My advice to anyone running an exposed novice trip, particularly involving children, is to take a safety boat whenever you have any doubts, and provide the youngsters with appropriate training beforehand.

LESSONS

Kayaking courses are often available through kayak retailers, kayak clubs, schools and community centres. They can range from a two-hour introduction to paddling techniques to comprehensive six-day paddling courses that include class-room and pool sessions and, in the field, current and surf experience. In addition, there are specialized courses in rolling, bracing, surfing, navigation and weather. The first government-sponsored training program in North America for guides and outfitters was held at Powell River, British Columbia, in 1987.

Neophytes may have trouble sorting out the good courses from the not-so-good ones. As with tours, it helps to go on the recommendations of friends who have already taken the course, since it is difficult for a teacher to conduct a hands-on class without revealing the limits of his or her knowledge.

What is sometimes not so clear is the value of the course itself. The instructor may have dazzling boat-handling skills but the course content may be unbalanced. Request a course outline and look critically at its balance before you sign up. In many cases, the teacher may be willing to add specific topics or techniques at your request.

Also of relevance is the type of kayak being used in the course. Can you bring your own? Pool time is of value for refining technique and introductory rescue practice but there should be time allowed for paddling on the sea as well. As a rule of thumb, look for a weekend course in which classroom instruction, pool sessions and on-the-sea paddling are given equal amounts of emphasis.

CLUB COURSES

The many North American kayak clubs now in existence have appeared in response to a vacuum in the supply of sea kayaking information and as well are creating an excellent source of paddling companionship. Club-sponsored trips that run on a regular basis provide a nurturing environment for beginners—and a testing ground for aspiring leaders.

Club involvement is often an economical way to acquire basic skills, and you can later get open water experience with the attendant support of other paddlers. But keep in mind that the instruction of club volunteers is often more enthusiastic than professional, and that you'll be the one responsible for the overall balance of your learning experience.

RENTALS

Today both double and single sea kayaks can be rented from dozens of outfitters throughout North America and a small but increasing number of overseas locations. The singles are generally either one of the plastic single models or representative fibreglass designs intended to familiarize the renter with the lines sold by a particular retailer. No regulation of the trade exists other than standard coast guard requirements, but a set of guidelines issued by TASK currently sets out reasonable safety guidelines for its members.

Renting a kayak is definitely a case of renter beware; the ultimate responsibility for seeing that the equipment is sound and appropriate is placed firmly with the customer by means of a waiver. If you decide to rent, check the condition of the equipment and be sure it is suited to the area in which it will be used. Most outfitters rent stable, medium- to high-volume kayaks by the hour, day, or week. The rental price will usually include: paddle(s), spare paddle, spray cover, pump, buoyancy, life-jacket(s) and flares if needed. Wetsuits, drysuits and emergency radio beacons are often available separately.

Don't be surprised by the type of questions the outfitter will want you to answer. You will be asked precisely where you intend to go and when you plan to be back. Very likely you will be asked for a description of your vehicle and where you intend to park it. There are good reasons for all this. Should you be overdue, the coast guard will first call the local police to see if the vehicle is still parked at the put-in point. If it is, a water search will be initiated. If not, the authorities will assume that the kayakers are safely off the water. A conscientious outfitter will call the telephone numbers supplied by the customer within an hour of his or her failure to return from an hourly rental; if the renter has not been heard from, the outfitter will assume the worst and notify the authorities. It is obviously in everyone's interest to let the outfitter know of any changes or delays in your schedule.

At least one kayak rental company in California requires anyone renting a kayak to first complete their course on basic kayaking. This laudably responsible attitude is not universally followed because some legal counsel suggests that it could imply an endorsement of the paddler's competence, which could then be held against the outfitter in the event of a mishap. So today most rental kayaks come on the same basis as skis: you pay your money and are responsible for what you do with the equipment.

Appendix A:
Transoceanic Solos

*On the morning of 1 August 1928, Capt. Franz Romer was dis-
covered fast asleep in his kayak in the harbour of St. Thomas, Virgin Islands. Romer had paddled and sailed nearly 4000 miles from
Lisbon, Portugal, via Las Palmas in the Canary Islands. He had
encountered two hurricanes—one between Lisbon and Las Palmas and another between Las Palmas and St. Thomas—and on the
last leg of his journey had been continuously at sea for two months.
Between April and August the* New York Times *carried several
brief articles on Romer's voyage. A more extensive report appeared
in the issue for Sunday, 23 September 1928—ten days after it was
written. Here are some excerpts.*

SAN JUAN, PUERTO RICO, Sept. 13— . . . Captain Romer's
visit here was unheralded. He put into port from St. Thomas
after about twenty hours' sailing time. At St. Thomas he had
had a rest of six weeks after 58 days of calm and storm from
Las Palmas, Canary Islands, to the Virgin Islands. His experiences during that time can best be imagined, for he spoke
little of them. He knew though, he said, that he was going to
get all the way across the Atlantic, and he still had the greatest
confidence in reaching the United States safely when he left
here. From Florida he plans to make his way up the coast to
New York City. If possible he will fly back to Germany.
Neither the air nor the sea nor things above or beneath seem
to have any terrors for him.

Other men have crossed the Atlantic alone in various kinds

of boats, have gone around the world, in fact. But Captain Romer's craft is certainly the first of its kind to venture on such a journey and probably the tiniest.

The *Deutscher Sport* is a wooden frame craft of the sailing canoe type, covered with rubber and canvas. It is 21 feet long with [2.5] feet of beam, and a depth from canvas covered deck to rubber bottom of 18 inches. Frame and covering may be dismounted and rolled in a bundle a man might haul under his arm. It carries an 8-foot mast. The deck is not more than 6 inches above the water line. At most times it is awash. So close is Romer to the water all the time that he may drop his hands over the sides and dabble in the ocean. Water is kept out of the cockpit by means of rubber sheets which he fastens to a framework about the cockpit and then about himself. At night he may cover himself over completely with a combination helmet and cape of rubber which he fastens to the deck. He then breathes through a tube, gas-mask fashion. He puts this on instead of pajamas when he goes to bed—and going to bed is just the same as sitting up. His navigating instruments include a small compass, barometer, sextant and glasses. At St. Thomas, Captain Romer mounted a small out-board motor that was sent out from Germany. He said the motor might come in handy in the case he ran into hurricane weather. His fuel supply—five gallons—was lashed on deck just aft of the tiny cockpit.

The craft is Captain Romer's own design and he set sail in it from Lisbon, Portugal, on the last day of March. . . .

What happened during those first days of the lonely voyage only Captain Romer and his log know. Some day he may publish his log. He told little here. But he suggested enough to set the imagination to work. For instance, he said that the seas were so high at times that he did not even think whether he would ride them. When he anchored at Las Palmas he said he knew that his trip would be successful, that nothing any worse than the experiences of the first part of his journey could possibly befall him.

In those first days there were periods when he was wholly unconscious, he believes, and other times when he was only partly conscious. He managed to keep his course much of the time with rudder line tied to the boom so that it mattered little whether he was asleep or awake. But there were days and nights when he had no sleep. And during all this time he was steeling himself to the discomfort and soreness that came from the necessity to remain for hours in one position; the exposure to sun and wind and rain and spray; fair days and storm; nights of either stars or clouds. And day or night for companions he had the waves and the uncommunicative inhabitants of the sea. Sometimes he sang to all outdoors, or talked to himself.

Arriving at Las Palmas on April 17, it was not until June 2 that he got underway again. During that time he says he was ill and had a fever. If it was from exhaustion he neither admitted nor suggested it. But during that six weeks he got himself in shape to sail again, only to find that officials were so astounded at his daring that they refused him clearance papers for his ship. He slipped out of port at night.

If it may be said he had a little more room in his canoe after leaving Las Palmas, it is as much figure of speech as fact. At Lisbon he had stored in almost the entire hold of his craft sufficient supplies of food and water to last him across the Atlantic. The more food and water there was, the less room he had to stretch his legs. Gradually he ate himself into his own ship.

. . .

From Las Palmas Captain Romer set out again, little dreaming that it would take him 58 days to travel the 2,730 miles between Las Palmas and St. Thomas. At St. Thomas they gave him an official public reception and a medal. But this was after he had caught a few winks of sleep and visited the barber for the first time in two months and had had a chance to park his canoe in George Levi's store, where thousands viewed it with much awe and exclamation.

Between Las Palmas and St. Thomas there were days of dead calm, days of blistering heat, days and nights of storm. Sun and salt spray tortured Romer's hands and arms, and they were swollen and blistered and stiff. He lost his hat in a wind. Then his head and neck and back got more of the sun. He sat until he could sit no more. He stood until his feet and legs would bear his weight no longer. Then he sat some more. Three sharks took a curious fancy to his craft. They played about the canoe, swimming from side to side, at times darting under the boat and coming so close that he could feel the scrape of the fins through the flexible rubber bottom. Romer, lonely, talked to the sharks. They swam away.

His trip from St. Thomas to San Juan was probably the shortest leg of his whole trip to New York, unless he makes more stops up the coast than he seemed to have in mind here.

Romer is 29 and was born at Constance, in South Germany. . . . During the war he was in submarines, and before that he worked in the Zeppelin plant. After the war, for a time, he took up aviation and later went to sea.

Captain Romer said he did not swim. "What good would it do me?" he asked.

A few days after the foregoing piece was written and before it was published, Romer slipped out of San Juan harbour, missing the hurricane warning which apparently had just been posted. The addition of motor and fuel tank had ruined the trim of his kayak, but given the fierceness of the storm he unwittingly paddled into— surely the worst of the three he met on that voyage—it is hard to believe that he would have survived even in a perfectly balanced craft. As it is, no one ever saw Franz Romer or his boat again.

Fifty-seven years after Romer's solo transatlantic voyage, American Ed Gillet made a successful transpacific crossing, from Monterey in California to Kahului Harbor, Maui, Hawaii, paddling sixty-three days to do so. The following are excerpts from a story which appeared in the Maui News *on August 28, 1987.*

The 35-year-old San Diego man set out from Monterey Bay on the central California coast June 25, hoping to become the first person to make the 2,400-mile transpac crossing in a kayak. He made it, but the voyage took longer than expected, and Gillet's tardiness made national headlines when his family pled with President Reagan to order a Coast Guard search for the overdue paddler. Gillet knew nothing about the furor ashore because he lost his communications system July 7. His last contact was with a Navy convoy. . . .

The 80-pound yellow kayak, which Gillet named "Banana-fish," proved its seaworthiness by carrying its owner and 600 pounds of survival gear across the Eastern Pacific without capsizing or swamping. The only signs that it had made the crossing were clusters of barnacles growing along the rudder.

Gillet had planned to "kite surf" much of the way across by deploying a small colored parafoil that would catch the tradewinds like a sail and pull the kayak along at a smart clip. But light winds restricted the parafoil's use. . . .

Gillet lost 25 pounds on the crossing, much of that in the week before landfall, when his food ran low. At the same time, a northerly current coupled with unexpected Kona winds from the south made his parafoil useless and threatened to drive him past Hawaii altogether. "For the last 10 days or so I really didn't know whether I'd make the islands or not," he said. "One day I wrote out my will.". . .

Gillet ran out of food four days before he reached Maui,

but twin "reverse osmosis" desalinization units provided enough water to keep him alive and paddling, if not altogether coherent. "I was in such a weird state of mind, not expecting to see land after all that time, that when I finally saw it I didn't realize what I'd seen. I was taking a sight and I thought 'Too bad that mountain's there blocking my horizon.' It was the Big Island."

Gillet had hoped to land in Hilo, but the current and Kona winds swept him northward. He . . . finally settled on Kahului Harbor as the safest bet. . . . "I was steering on the Pauwela light all night long," he said. "I had been without food for three days and without sleep for 40 hours, and I was getting a little bit lightheaded. I was looking at these lights (on Maui) and I thought: 'I could be dreaming all of this: I wonder if I am.'"

He finally entered Kahului Harbor just after dawn [August 27], paddled to the beach fronting Maui Beach, and walked for the first time in 63 days. "I just stumbled around the beach like a drunken fool," he laughed. Then he pulled "Bananafish" above the high water mark and wobbled into the hotel to find something to eat.

Appendix B: Sea Kayaking Photography

Good sea kayaking photographs are not easy to get. They usually fall into two categories: impromptu and contrived. Impromptu pictures result from your being ready and willing with your equipment. In a kayak this means having a waterproof camera close at hand, preferably around your neck. On land it entails watching for the magic moment as kayaks cruise by and having the right equipment to record that fleeting shot.

In both cases the lens most likely to be required should be kept on the camera. For shots from a kayak this is usually a wide angle lens between 24mm and 35mm, either of which offers a depth of field allowing you to keep both the kayak and the middle distance in focus.

Some movement is almost always present when you are sitting in a kayak on the sea. Consequently, any use of long focus lenses usually results in fuzzy pictures unless you have a film fast enough (ASA 400 or more) for really fast shutter speeds. I try to avoid a lens with a greater focal length than 135mm if I am shooting from the kayak.

When using a 35mm lens, bear in mind that it is usually important to keep a strong image in the near to middle distance to avoid exaggerating the distances and the long thin line of the horizon. Ashore, I prefer to keep a zoom lens on the camera for ready use.

The set up picture is frequently necessary because of the

elusiveness of that "pure moment" in real life. In its loosest form it requires asking your companion to "paddle close to that rock where the wave is breaking." Or it can mean waiting hours for the right light then contriving a realistic scene in which the paddler is supposed to look natural. The best scenes are those in which the set may be contrived but the action and interaction of the paddlers is real. Someone who has been sitting in one place for half an hour as you tinker with your equipment is likely to be wearing a bored expression and the resulting photograph, though perfectly composed, will look lifeless.

The most dramatic light is found in the early morning and early evening, and it is wise to be in position for the picture ahead of time. Storm clouds building can provide a dynamic set for kayaking pictures. If you are waiting for the right light to get a series of kayaking pictures, remember to get both the shore-based long focus lens shots as well as wide, in-close angles. A very dramatic angle for the latter is from the perspective of a swimmer. Surf shots are particularly well suited to this position, though the swimmer runs the risk of becoming impaled by the speeding kayak. That situation, on the other hand, could lead to its own dramatic series—for those on the beach!

CAMERA CARE

Salt water and cameras don't mix unless the camera happens to be of the waterproof variety, of which there are an increasing number on the market today. Most paddlers, however, use the standard single lens reflex because it gives them access to a wide range of lenses and accessories. This type of camera, however, is vulnerable to the ravages of water. If you drop a single lens reflex into sea water, you may as well leave it there, for it will cost you more to repair than buying a new one and its reliability will be in doubt from then on.

Pelican waterproof boxes are ideal containers for cameras. These polycarbonate plastic cases with their foam inserts provide excellent shock protection and are airtight enough to require a pressure release screw to compensate for changes in altitude. The problem with such boxes is that they are an awkward shape for storage inside a kayak so that getting to them at sea can be cumbersome. They are also expensive.

More pliable, but offering minimal protection against impact, is a series of waterproof bags made of PVC or proofed nylon which have been heat sealed with radio waves. These less expensive options use a fold-down flap to seal against water. If you choose this option, wrap the camera and lenses in some bulky fabric such as a towel which will provide impact resistance as well as absorb any drips that might enter through an imperfectly closed seal.

From Europe comes the EWA camera bag which has a 52mm lens built into one panel, an eye piece on the other panel and a surgical glove built into one side so that a standard SLR camera can be operated from outside the bag.

Keep your camera out of direct sunlight, particularly in the tropics. The heat has been known to melt the cement which holds some lens components in place. Film is another vulnerable item, not so much because of water damage since it comes in waterproof containers, but because of sun. Film can be ruined by leaving it in direct sunlight; the emulsion breaks down into blotchy patterns, and the reds and yellows become bluish. In the tropics, refrigerate your film in small quantities along your route if possible. Otherwise, carry it inside your kayak well wrapped or protected from the heat by a soft cooler or gear bag stuffed with clothes.

Appendix C: Kayak Clubs & Associations

*Advanced Sea Kayak Club
7 Miller Close, Newport
Isle of Wight, England Po30 5PS

*Association of North Atlantic
Kayakers (ANorAK)
14 Heather Drive
Suffern, NY 10901

*Baidarka Historical Society
Box 18, Belcarra Park
R.R. 1
Port Moody, B.C. V3H 3C8

Bay Area Sea Kayakers (BASK)
1248 8th Avenue, #3
San Francisco, CA 94122

Boston Sea Kayak Club
179 Farm St.
Millis, MA 02054

British Canoe Union
Flexel House, 45, High Street
Addlestone, Weybridge
Surrey, U.K. KTIS IJV

California Kayak Friends
Suite A-199, 14252 Culver Dr.
Irvine, CA 92714

CK/mer—Connaissance du
Kayak de Mer
B.P. 67B, 22500
Paimpol, France

Coast Busters
P.O. Box 22723
Carmel, CA 93922

Hui Wa'a Kaukahi
Box 88143
Honolulu, HI 96830

*International Long
River Canoeist Club
238 Birmingham Road
Redditch, Worcs, B97 6EL,
England

Juneau Kayak Club
P.O. Box 021865
Juneau, AK 99802-1865

Kanaka Ikaika Racing Club
Box 438
Kaneohe, HI 96744

New Zealand Canoeing
Association
P.O. Box 3768
Wellington, New Zealand

North Sound Sea Kayaking
Association
P.O. Box 1523
Everett, WA 98206

Ocean Kayak Association of
British Columbia
Box 1574, Victoria, B.C.
V8W 2X7

Oregon Ocean Paddling Society
(OOPS)
P.O. Box 69641
Portland, OR 97201

Puget Sound Paddle Club
P.O. Box 22
Puyallup, WA 98371

★Salzwasser–Union
Reinhauser Landstr. 44
D-3400 Gottingen, Germany

San Diego Sea Kayakers
529 Fern Glen
La Jolla, CA 92037

Sea Kayak Association of British
Columbia
16064 80th Ave.
Surrey, B.C. V3S 2J7

Sebago Canoe Club Sea Kayak
Committee
Paerdegat Basin
Foot of Avenue N
Brooklyn, NY 11236

★Tasmanian Sea Canoeing Club
P.O. Box 599F, Hobart
Tasmania 7001, Australia

Texas Sea/Touring Kayak Club
P.O. Box 27281
Houston, TX 77227

★Trade Association of Sea
Kayaking (TASK)
P.O. Box 84144
Seattle, WA 98124

UMD Kayak Club
(University of Minnesota in
Duluth)
108 Kirby Student Center
10 University Drive
Duluth, MN 55812-2496

Washington Kayak Club
P.O. Box 24264
Seattle, WA 98124

Whatcom Association of Kayak
Enthusiasts (WAKE)
P.O. Box 1952
Bellingham, WA 98227

★A substantial newsletter is available
to members.

Bibliography

This list includes many but by no means all of the existing English-language publications about sea kayaks and sea kayaking, as well as a select few of the basic reference works useful to any expeditionary sea kayaker. Coast pilots, pilot guides and sailing directions for individual areas, though vitally important, are quite numerous and are therefore omitted from the list. Generally speaking, the most useful pilot guides and coast pilots are those published by the National Ocean Survey or the Defense Mapping Agency Hydrographic Center in the United States, and by the British Admiralty in the U.K. For Canadian waters, excellent sailing directions are published by the Canadian Department of Fisheries and Oceans. Several Scandinavian countries publish good pilot guides to their own coasts, and the Danish government also publishes a pilot guide which is particularly useful for Greenland waters.

Admiralty Manual of Navigation. London: H.M. Stationery Office, 1970.

ADNEY, EDWIN, & HOWARD CHAPELLE. *The Bark Canoes and Skin Boats of North America.* Washington, D.C.: Smithsonian Institution, 1964.

ARIMA, EUGENE Y. *Inuit Kayaks in Canada: A Review of Historical Records and Construction.* Ottawa: National Museums of Canada, 1987. [Illustrated monograph, 235 pp.]

BASCOM, WILLARD. *Waves and Beaches.* Garden City, N.Y.: Anchor, 1964.

BRAND, JOHN. *The Little Kayak Book—Museum Kayaks: Five surveys with some details of equipment; History of each as far as it is known*. Colchester, Essex: John Brand, 1984.

BROWER, KENNETH. *The Starship and the Canoe*. New York: Holt, Rinehart, 1973.

BURCH, DAVID. *Fundamentals of Kayak Navigation*. Seattle: Pacific Search Press, 1987.

CAFFYN, PAUL. *Cresting the Restless Waves—North Island Kayak Odyssey*. Wellington, N.Z.: New Zealand Canoeing Association and Paul Caffyn, 1987.

———. *Dark Side of the Wave—Stewart Island Kayak Odyssey*. Wellington, N.Z.: New Zealand Canoeing Association, 1987.

———. *Obscured by Waves—South Island Canoe Odyssey*. Dunedin, N.Z.: John McIndoe, 1979.

CHAPMAN, SPENCER. *Northern Lights*. London: Chatto and Windus, 1932.

———. *Watkins' Last Expedition*. London: Chatto and Windus, 1934.

COURTNEY, G.B., *S.B.S. in World War Two—The Story of the Original Special Boat Section of the Army Commandos*. London: Grafton Books, 1985.

DANIEL, LINDA. *Kayak Cookery—A Handbook of Provisions and Recipes*. Seattle: Pacific Search Press, 1986.

(DUTTON, BENJAMIN) *Dutton's Navigation & Piloting*. 14th rev. ed. by Elbert S. Maloney. Annapolis, MD: Naval Institute Press, 1985.

DYSON, GEORGE. *Baidarka*. Edmonds, WA: Alaska Northwest Publishing Company, 1986.

FENGER, FREDERIC ABILDGAARD. *Alone in the Caribbean*. Belmont, MA: Wellington Books, 1958.

FONS, VALERIE. *Keep It Moving—Baja by Canoe*. Seattle: The Mountaineers, 1986.

HUTCHINSON, DEREK. *Derek C. Hutchinson's Guide to Sea Kayaking*. Seattle: Pacific Search Press, 1985.

———. *Sea Canoeing*. 3rd ed. London: A. & C. Black (Publishers) Ltd., 1984.

INCE, JOHN & HEDI KOTTNER. *Sea Kayaking Canada's West Coast*. Vancouver: Raxas Books, 1982.

LADD, JAMES D. *S.B.S.: The Invisible Raiders—The History of the Special Boat Squadron from World War Two to the Present.* London: Arms and Armour Press, 1983.

LINDEMANN, HANNES. *Alone at Sea.* In *Great Voyages in Small Boats, Solo Trans-Atlantic.* Camden, ME: International Marine Publishing Co., 1982.

MCKIE, RONALD CECIL HAMLYN. *The Heroes.* New York: Harcourt, 1960.

NANSEN, FRIDTJOF. *Eskimo Life.* London: Longmans, Green and Co., 1893.

———. *Farthest North.* Two vols. London: George Newnes, Ltd., 1898.

———. *The First Crossing of Greenland.* London: Longmans, Green and Co., 1892.

Nautical Almanac. Washington, D.C.: U.S. Naval Observatory, & London: H.M. Stationery Office. Issued annually.

PETERSEN, H.C. *Instruction in Kayak Building.* Roskilde, Denmark: Greenland Provincial Museum and Viking Ship Museum, c. 1982.

———. *Skinboats of Greenland.* Roskilde, Denmark: The National Museum of Denmark, The Museum of Greenland & The Viking Ship Museum, 1986.

PHILLIPS, CECIL ERNEST LUCAS. *Cockleshell Heroes.* London: Heinemann, 1957.

RAMWELL, J.J. *Sea Touring.* Huntingdon, Cambs.: John J. Ramwell, 1976.

ROBERTSON, DOUGAL. *Sea Survival.* London: Elek, 1975.

———. *Survive the Savage Sea.* London: Elek, 1973.

TRICKER, R.A.R. *Bores, Breakers, Waves and Wakes.* London: Mills & Boon, 1964.

WASHBURNE, RANDEL. *The Coastal Kayaker: Kayak Camping on the Alaska and B.C. Coast.* Seattle: Pacific Search Press, 1983.

———. *Kayak Trips in Puget Sound and the San Juan Islands.* Seattle: Pacific Search Press, 1986.

WATTS, ALAN. *Weather Forecasting Ashore and Afloat.* London: Adlard Coles, 1968.

——— *Wind Pilot.* Lymington, Hants.: Nautical Publishing, 1975.

WILKERSON JAMES, ed. *Hypothermia, Frostbite and Other Cold Injuries.* Seattle: The Mountaineers, 1986.

———. *Medicine for Mountaineering.* Seattle: The Mountaineers, 1987.

ZIMMERLY, DAVID W. *Hooper Bay Kayak Construction.* Ottawa: National Museums of Canada, 1979. [Illustrated monograph, 118 pp.]

———. *QAJAQ—Kayaks of Siberia and Alaska.* Juneau, AK: Division of State Museums, 1986.

PERIODICALS

Sea Kayaker, 1670 Duranleau St., Vancouver, B.C. V6H 3S4; 6327 Seaview Ave. N.W., Seattle, WA 98107 (Quarterly)

Small Boat Journal, P.O. Box 400, Rte. 9 West, Bennington, VT 05201 (Bimonthly with occasional coverage of sea kayaking subjects)

Canoe, P.O. Box 3146, Kirkland, WA 98083 (Bimonthly with frequent coverage of sea kayaking subjects)

Index